PRAISE FOR *THE CORPORATE VENTURING HANDBOOK*

"*The Corporate Venturing Handbook* masterfully presents a holistic perspective on the professional management of corporate venturing activities in established companies. Instead of simply using corporate venturing as a buzzword, readers learn how it can be successfully implemented in everyday business."
Dr. Andreas Nemeth, CEO UNIQA Ventures

"*The Corporate Venturing Handbook* is a comprehensive and invaluable resource for anyone looking to navigate the complex world of corporate venturing. Its evidence-based framework, real-world insights, and practical tools provide a clear roadmap for success. It's a must-read for any CVC investor seeking to unlock strategic growth and innovation."
Stefan Gabriel, MD and CEO Hitachi Ventures

"When corporates meet ventures, two worlds collide. *The Corporate Venturing Handbook* provides a very helpful and handy guide on how to overcome these challenges."
Young Sohn, Founding Managing Partner, Walden Catalyst Ventures and former Corporate President and Chief Strategy Officer, Samsung Electronics

"Driving innovation in a company is both very rewarding and challenging. *The Corporate Venturing Handbook* shows both experiences at their best."
Annalisa Gigante, Head of Innovation, International Airlines Group (IAG)

The Corporate Venturing Handbook

A step-by-step guide to the value creation process

Dietmar Grichnik, Manuel Hess, Jana Reuther, Alexander Stoeckel and Michael Hilb

KoganPage

First published in Great Britain and the United States in 2023 by Kogan Page Limited

2nd Floor, 45 Gee Street
London
EC1V 3RS
United Kingdom

8 W 38th Street, Suite 902
New York, NY 10018
USA

4737/23 Ansari Road
Daryaganj
New Delhi 110002
India

www.koganpage.com

Kogan Page books are printed on paper from sustainable forests.

ISBNs

Hardback 978 1 3986 1358 4
Paperback 978 1 3986 1357 7
Ebook 978 1 3986 1359 1

British Library Cataloguing-in-Publication Data

A CIP record for this book is available from the British Library.

Library of Congress Cataloging-in-Publication Data

Names: Grichnik, Dietmar, author.
Title: The corporate venturing handbook : a step-by-step guide to the value creation process / Dietmar Grichnik, Manuel Hess, Jana Reuther, Alexander Stoeckel and Michael Hilb.
Description: London ; New York, NY : Kogan Page, 2023. | Includes bibliographical references and index.
Identifiers: LCCN 2023048802 | ISBN 9781398613577 (paperback) | ISBN 9781398613584 (hardback) | ISBN 9781398613591 (ebook)
Subjects: LCSH: Venture capital. | New business enterprises–Finance. | BISAC: BUSINESS & ECONOMICS / Corporate Finance / Venture Capital | BUSINESS & ECONOMICS / Entrepreneurship
Classification: LCC HG4751 .G75 2024 | DDC 658.15/224–dc23/eng/20231018
LC record available at https://lccn.loc.gov/2023048802

Typeset by Integra Software Services, Pondicherry
Print production managed by Jellyfish
Printed and bound by CPI Group (UK) Ltd, Croydon CR0 4YY

CONTENTS

PART FOUR Harvesting

LIST OF FIGURES AND TABLES

Figures

Tables

ABOUT THE AUTHORS

Our author team is built up of five practitioners/academics connecting the expertise of front-line practitioners with the evidence-based insights of academics.

Dietmar Grichnik: Dietmar is 'The Scientist' breathing the motto of University of St. Gallen from insight to impact as Professor for Entrepreneurship and Director of the Institute of Technology Management. He is also elected Vice President Innovation and Quality in the Board of University of St. Gallen.

Manuel Hess: Manuel is 'The Researcher' combining scientific rigor with practical relevance as Associate Professor for Corporate Finance at the Grenoble Ecole de Management and not least as an Entrepreneurial Finance specialist. Both, the masterminds behind the preceding book Startup Navigator.

Alexander Stoeckel: Alex is 'The Corporate Venture Capitalist' – former Investment Director at Philip Morris International, operating on a global scale. Former partner and board member of btov Partners AG (today: b2venture) in Switzerland.

Jana Reuther: Jana is 'The Strategist' as St. Gallen PhD and consultant tackling Corporate Venturing from both perspectives. Driving the book project from South Africa.

Michael Hilb: Michael is 'The Entrepreneur', founder of DBP Group, serves on several boards of directors and is also a professor in Asia and Europe.

Introduction: Getting started

We face a conflict of two worlds: startups want to grow as fast as possible to become established while incumbents strive for rejuvenation to be as entrepreneurial as startups. Corporate Venturing (CV) promises to combine the best of both worlds – the innovation and dynamism of youth with the resource and market power of a mature company. Unrealistic? Yes and no!

Have you been looking for a holistic tool to build, operate and harvest Corporate Venturing with success all at once? And what would it be like to make all value generated by Corporate Venturing, both financial and strategic, tangible for business performance? Well, we can help!

By the end of this guide, you will have an up-to-date understanding of all the rationales to make the most impact from the beginning to the end of your CV programme. But we don't want to lecture you. We want to help you make your CV programme work in practice so that you can achieve your set goals and expectations. By knowing where your pitfalls and potentials are, you will have a set of tools at hand to improve your CV programme.

Today, you as well as most of your peers are challenged more than ever by disruptive technological advances in a very dynamic ecosystem. It is necessary to persistently generate new capabilities and expertise to compete in the marketplace and to continue to grow for sustainable competitive advantage.

Corporate Venturing in this regard is often seen as an organizational vehicle, which is complementary to internal innovation such as Research and Development (R&D) and Mergers and Acquisitions (M&A). In contrast to those internal innovation vehicles, which create incremental innovation, CV allows for disruptive innovation. It is realized as a vehicle to build competencies through external corporation and has proven to be a promising means to foster corporate innovation. CV is the concept of large corporations investing in companies, either monetarily through minority stakes or through non-monetary alliances, to develop innovative products or services. These corporate dinosaurs have recognized the risk of distinction and are using CV to find the next venture unicorn to ensure their own longevity. In other words, companies strive to extend their lifespan and improve their business health in older age (that is their longevity) by creating game-changing innovations or strategies that become incredibly valuable (that is, a 'unicorn', typically defined as a venture worth beyond one billion dollars).

The Corporate Venturing Handbook, developed by The University of St. Gallen, is the first handbook that combines all the steps and elements necessary for successful CV through an iterative and dynamic process design. But it is not just a handbook – it is also an output generator. You will receive several tools to take your CV programme to the next level.

No approach available today considers all relevant aspects in a temporal context to optimally build, operate and harvest CV activities. The CV Navigator should be understood as a continuous, iterative process tool, divided into four phases, which proceed sequentially and are closely interrelated. Those phases cover the development of a CV programme right from the start by defining the CV mandate in the Profiling phase and the according set-up of a CV programme in the Designing phase. Furthermore, the CV Navigator supports you in managing and terminating a CV programme to meet set objectives and expectations in the corresponding Investing and Harvesting phase. Along the navigation process, the CV Cockpit delivers transparency and a clear understanding of relevant performance indicators to validate and drive your CV programme progress.

Observations of the daily operation of existing CV programmes and the difficulties corporates face in setting up new CV programmes motivated us to develop the CV Navigator and *The Corporate Venturing Handbook* at the University of St. Gallen. We are convinced that this impact-driven approach will make a significant contribution to the corporate and venture building community. Why? Simply, because we have seen the need for it – the deficits and corporate problems. Plus, we have validated it! We wrote this book together with different corporate venture capital executives and with the founder of the DBP Group, who is also a professor. In addition, we conducted several case studies to verify and extend the academic expertise and resources with best practices from the field. Beyond this, we bring along over a thousand hours of coaching solo entrepreneurs and entrepreneurial teams, both in corporates and in startup settings, in commercializing research-knowledge by building ventures, and in developing entrepreneurial ideas from scratch.

Who are the partners?

The partners are the Institute of Technology Management, with its Chair of Entrepreneurship at the University of St. Gallen, whose academics are known for their profound knowledge and ability to bridge the gap between science and practice and the university graduates. They are among the most successful entrepreneurs in Europe and are repeatedly TOP10 in Europe`s University Unicorn Ranking.

Then there is the support of the Startup@HSG incubation programme with more than 200 University of St. Gallen spin-offs and the practice partners from various Corporate Venturing programmes, which have proven to have a very positive impact on their parent companies.

The excellence of the methods used is a result of the best practices of the largest and longest running Corporate Venturing programmes in the world. AXA Ventures Capital & Strategic Partnerships, Siemens Healthineers, Shell Ventures and Bertelsmann Investments provide exclusive cases along the four phases of the Corporate Venturing Navigator. The whole range of technological industries is complemented by special insights from Nestlé, Samsung, Straumann, Deutsche Bank, and more. Become part of this Corporate Venturing community at www.stgaller-navigator.com and secure your bonus material and digital tools.

Corporate Venturing: Why now?

The strategic imperative

For as long as companies have existed, they have been driven by an imperative to thrive and survive – the growth imperative. Only companies that grow faster than their competitors can attract capital and the best talent, not to mention raising the funds to invest in developing new products, services and businesses.

It is the latter growth engine, i.e., venturing, that has become a key differentiator between growing and shrinking companies in times of technological, economic, and geopolitical disruption. While the importance of venturing is particularly evident in times of upheaval, when creative destruction drives the economy, it is often forgotten that Corporate Venturing has always played, and will continue to play, a role in the development of successful businesses.

While managing ongoing business often creates the cash needed to sustain the business, very few companies in even fewer industries can rely on these businesses for long-term growth. As a result, corporate decision makers who want to lead their organizations to sustainable, long-term growth are forced to master the art and science of Corporate Venturing.

The challenge of Corporate Venturing

Despite the great strategic importance of Corporate Venturing for the thriving and survival of companies, venturing often does not receive the same attention in boardrooms as other strategic growth levers, such as mergers and acquisitions or corporate transformation.

The reason for this is multi-fold. Firstly, many companies view Corporate Venturing as an add-on activity rather than a strategic necessity. This could be related to the second reason: Corporate Venturing requires a different understanding and assessment of risks and uncertainties. Finally, many corporate decision makers, whether at board or functional level, lack the appropriate entrepreneurial experience and mindset to successfully initiate, manage or monitor Corporate Ventures.

The need for a new approach to Corporate Venturing

To overcome these challenges, a strategic, structured and smart approach to Corporate Venturing is required:

- *Strategic* in the sense that Corporate Venturing must be fully integrated into the corporate strategy. Only when venture capital investments are part of an integrated process of resource allocation will they be elevated to the required level.
- *Structured* to the extent that Corporate Venturing decision-making and execution follows a clear structure and provides the transparency needed to effectively manage and monitor Corporate Venturing activities.
- *Smart* at its core, Corporate Venturing is about convincing customers, employees and investors of its benefits and upside potential. Corporate Venturing can only be successful if it focuses on people and their needs.

The momentum

Back in the infantile stages of CV in the early 1900s, corporations were inspired to act as venture capital institutions. They began to form alliances with ventures by providing capital and advice in return for access to new technologies, products or services and know-how. The original goal of CV was back then purely financial, as is still the case in the CV world today. However, over the years, especially after the financial crisis and the increasing relevance of open innovation, corporates started focusing on the strategic aspects of CV. The power of new competency building and the potential to format strategy started to be perceived as highly beneficial.

Nowadays, CV is understood as a vehicle and toolkit to drive corporate innovation externally through minority investments in startups in order to maintain a window on technology and a competitive advantage in the future. It has built up a positive image of being a useful and more successful complement to internal innovation activities such as R&D and M&A. CV is needed more than ever as corporates in today's twenty-first century face an ever-changing environment that requires them to become more entrepreneurial in their perspectives and processes.

CV has adopted various forms of operations such as alliances, acquisitions, joint ventures, or Corporate Venture Capital (CVC), among others, with corporates often operating several forms at the same time. Accordingly, there are defined goals that a distinct CV programme pursues with a specific structure and operating mode.

Overall, however, CV has been characterized by cyclical ups and downs and has faced various challenges and abrupt terminations to date. In times of crisis, which occur on average every ten years, CV programmes have often been discontinued or the budget blocked. Corporate switch on the savings mode and very often deprioritize innovation initiatives due to limited resources.

But what has history taught us so far? Corporates need to invest in themselves to drive their business forward and maintain their viability. CV has become a very important business tool for both corporations and startups and has received considerable research attention. Numbers clearly show an increase in Corporate Venture Capital over the last decades.

CB Insights reported in their State of CVC Reports (2021 and 2022) a new record of CV-funded transactions in 2021 – an increase of 142 per cent year-on-year. While this trend declined in 2022 by 43 per cent it was still the second-strongest year on record in CVC history. This trend is expected to continue. However, in practice, companies increasingly face the question of how to demonstrate that the investment in CV is worthwhile for the parent company, especially the more strategic-oriented CV programmes. Investing in CV is quite attractive for companies to take their innovation to the next level, but most companies struggle in having the right understanding, capabilities and resources to do so. It is critical to achieve some performance impact, but this requires the appropriate framework and tool to capture value generated for the most successful usage of CV.

When looking to academia for answers, existing research studies are ambiguous and incomplete when it comes to how best to set up, run and exit a CV programme, and fundamental research insights on how to capture and measure the value generated for the parent company are missing. As a result, both academia and practice show shortcomings and a high need for a solution: the Corporate Venturing Navigator.

What is needed is an improved understanding of the CV rationales and underlying mechanisms, and an understanding of how to capture the CV value generated. Management needs to be clear about what it takes to best establish a CV programme, how to run it, and what is expected of it and when. CV has much more potential to offer, which is neither known nor perceived so far. It's time to change that, and with this book you're on the right track!

Top-10 Corporate Venturing myths and misconceptions

Surely you have played the game of truth or dare in the past?! Well, in the context of Corporate Venturing, not everything that is told is true. There are many legendary, handed-down stories without any facts or real explanation. Is that a surprise for you? Are you even carrying some of the stories you have heard further into the world? We want to shed light on some myths in this section for you.

The Corporate Venture Capital (CVC) sector has experienced an amazing renaissance in recent years. More and more corporations have realized that the world has become much more competitive in the wake of digitalization. Startups are quickly conquering industries that were considered 'distributed', i.e., where a few top dogs divide the bulk of the pie among themselves. Let's take Tesla as a prominent example from the automotive industry, which in just over ten years has become the most valuable automotive company in the world. In other words, no one is safe, and every company risks being disrupted or at least attacked by newcomers unless it succeeds in continuously improving and innovating its own products to appear attractive in the eyes of its customers.

Not least the realization outlined above has led to more and more corporations to engage systematically with the startup universe. Corporations finance accelerators to support existing startups in their development and, if necessary, also to attract investment opportunities in the manner of a vacuum cleaner. Corporations fund incubators, which are quasi birthplaces for new business concepts, both for their own employees and for external founder/entrepreneur talent. Corporations invest in existing venture capital funds that take ongoing stakes in startups. And corporations sometimes launch their own venture capital funds to use specialized teams to specifically track down innovative developments in the market, possibly at an early stage of development, in order to ultimately lay the foundations for longer-term competitiveness or superiority through early-stage participation in such companies.

Nevertheless, corporations face various challenges once they have decided to make systematic startup commitments, especially in the context of corporate venture capital units. Here is a brief overview of **the Top-10 common myths and misconceptions**. You will find more insights and details about them throughout the book.

1 Independent vs. strategic focus

Whether the in-house CVC team should focus on strategic investments or whether the independence of the fund and thus financial performance should be the primary concern.

2 The 'sustainability' myth

Investors are often asked whether sustainability considerations are considered in the investment selection or whether there is even a systematic selection process for this.

3 The 'risk reduction' myth

Investing in startups helps to reduce risk, securing corporate profit and therewith growth.

4 'Startup investments make us more innovative'

Corporate Venturing will make a corporate more innovative as it will teach and share knowledge and insights about innovation.

5 'Commitment to startup engagements'

Corporates emphasize the importance of startup engagement and commitment in particular in regard to innovation and transformation.

6 Unbiased professional decisions

Decisions on CVC are fact-based, as they are made based on an agreed mandate.

7 Not-invented-here syndrome

Critical opinions and rejection of external innovations, as they lead to a loss of capabilities and at the same time create dependency.

8 'Acting again like a startup' – the corporate paranoia

Corporates that work with entrepreneurial thinking, structure and system.

9 'Firm-beliefs in data-driven decisions'

The corporate conviction of data and data-driven decision-making.

10 Eye of the beholder

Again, the corporates' belief in establishing and running CV programmes based on data-driven decisions.

Corporate Venturing Navigator

This book is designed to guide you through the implementation of your CV programme from the very beginning. It is literally a manual to 'get things done' and to start executing.

The CV Navigator comprises four phases: Profiling, Designing, Investing, and Harvesting, which in turn consist of nineteen CV components.

Step by step, we will familiarize you with these components and show you which aspects you should pay attention to and which pitfalls you should avoid.

For optimal use of the CV components, we have developed an intuitive and easy-to-use **CV Cockpit**, which is the framework and steering wheel of the CV Navigator. Here you will find one or more outcomes of each CV Navigator phase to make results tangible and applicable in practice. The mechanisms and dynamics behind this have been applied in practice and enriched by research.

Each CV Navigator phase leads to a CV programme memorandum to feed the CV Cockpit with essential information and data. All phase outcomes combined and collected in the CV Cockpit will result in an ideal, self-contained and coherent CV programme concept.

CV navigation is based on the **Profiling phase**, where everything starts with the question of what the CV mandate is to accomplish. The CV Navigator will be at your fingertips to guide you through all the steps to consider. What CV profile are you aiming for? Which stakeholders should be involved and which ones are key players? What budget is available and needed for a particular CV mandate and what business progress is being sought?

This is where the foundation of your CV programme is born – The CV cornerstones are to provide the impetus to move forward in subsequent phases. You will have a clear and distinct understanding about what your objectives are and which expectations you pursue.

In the **Designing phase**, you then navigate through all the elements required to build the CV programme as such, while defining a corresponding rollout plan. The Designing phase defines the underlying structure and governance. You will disclose the organizational and legal structure on which the CV programme is built. These can range from a very independent CV unit, for example in form of a subsidiary, which is self-sufficient in terms of budget and decision-making, to a fully integrated unit under the umbrella of the parent company. Analogue, you lay out the reporting line as well as the committee constellation e.g., Investment Committee or Advisory Committee, being composed by certain promoters. As soon as the structure and governance forms are sorted out, the CVC team with a corresponding background and culture should be set up. You will have to determine the team size, the compensation structure and eventually additional non-monetary incentives to gain a very high personnel quality. At last, the location of the team, which can be close to the mother company or locally separated, is to be decided. Building on the structures established, it is quite important to then install superior communication systems and an appropriate ecosystem. That means that you have to identify which tools are already available or to be used to guarantee best communication and reporting between all promoters involved – transparency and an exchange of information on an always up-to-date status is key. Contributing to this, you should be aware of available networks and ecosystem attributes, which are to be clarified and installed. By the end of the Designing phase, you will know in detail what kind of CV programme you are running at its best, which portfolio approach you follow and which CV programme USP you will hold.

Following this, the **Investing phase** then builds on the established components and decisions from the previous phases. You will receive support in the actual operation of the CV programme. Yes, you read that right. The CV Navigator will facilitate your sourcing and portfolio management. You will be provided with tool components for optimized deal flow management. However, the CV Navigator also supports collaboration with ventures, the parent company including management and the business units, as well as the collaboration with other parties. Not to forget the shared resources and syndication! Through the Navigator, you will receive access to partnerships and supplier/consumer networks, R&D expertise and much more. Resources from and beyond the parent company are to be leveraged for you as best as possible. The ultimate goal of this phase is for you to then learn where and what CV value is generated. That's all you're up to – adding value to drive corporate innovation.

After you have mastered the long phase of value creation, where many ventures will perish but a few will shine, it is time to check for success in the **Harvesting phase**. Are objectives met and stakeholders satisfied with the results achieved? What added value can be realized? Here you have to decide whether to continue or end the CV programme. Do you want to start a next generation CV programme? Do you want to do it on your own? Are some ventures quite promising to you and need follow-up investments?

We can help. These decisions are facilitated by the **CV Cockpit**, which runs throughout the whole CV Navigation and thereby promotes an understanding of relevant performance indicators. Those indicators allow you to assess the validity of the CV impact and thus gives you performance implications for the parent company. Better self-assessment and better management of change and disruption is given.

There is also an exclusive case study for each phase that will allow you to learn from the best CV programmes on an international scale. Take your unique chance and follow the science-based and pragmatic **Deep Dives** along the CV navigation, because often well-known CV stories turn out not to be true. You will be surprised how many companies do not talk about the problems and failures they are facing on a permanent level. Nor do they want to reveal their 'secrets' on how to deal with CV dynamics.

The CV Navigator provides exceptional behind-the-scenes insight and a new, holistic approach to navigating through a CV programme from start to finish by including easy-to-use tools that make the value generated transparent and measurable. Don't miss the chance to start now! (**Check your Navigator Tool Box**).

The Corporate Venturing navigator

Figure 0.1 The Corporate Venturing Navigator

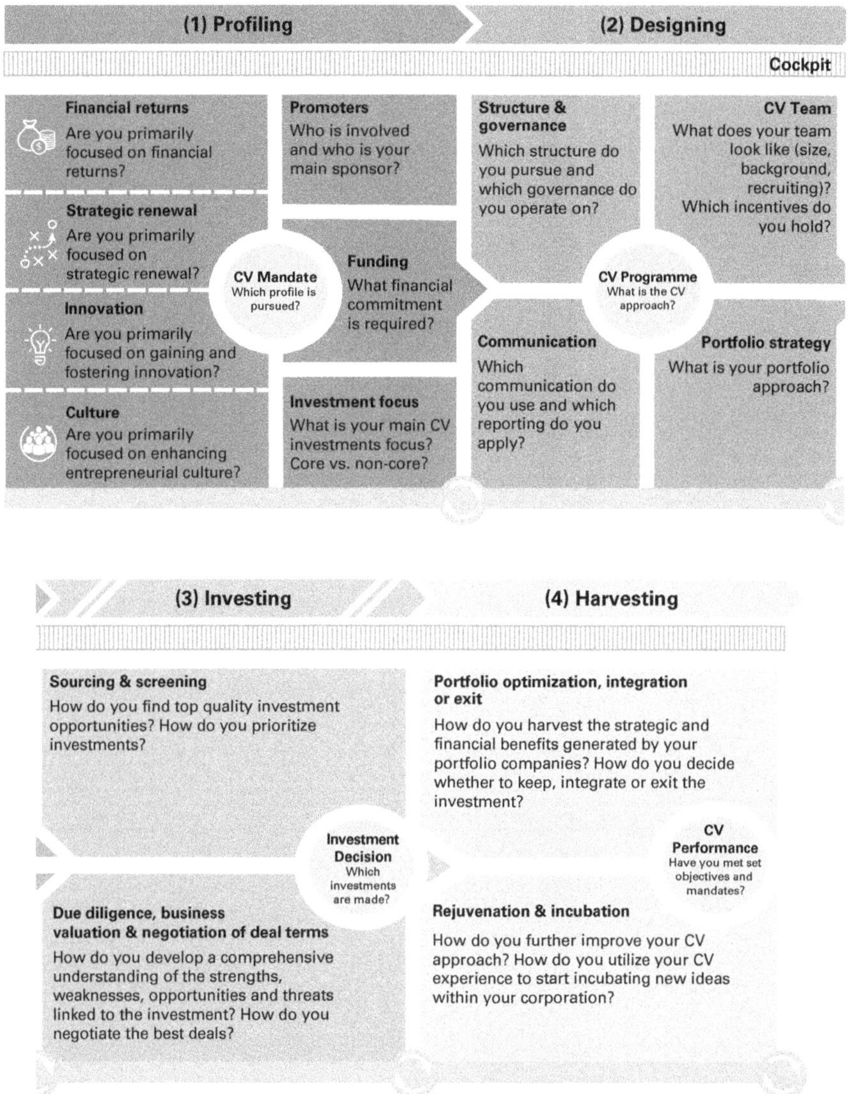

SOURCE Grichnik, Dietmar; Hess, Manuel; Reuther, Jana; Stoeckel, Alexander; Hilb, Michael (2023)

References

CB Insights. State of CVC 2021 Report, (2022) https://www.cbinsights.com/research/report/corporate-venture-capital-trends-2021/ (archived at https://perma.cc/R6Q4-4SHJ)

CB Insights. State of CVC 2022 Report, (2023) https://www.cbinsights.com/research/report/corporate-venture-capital-trends-2022/ (archived at https://perma.cc/ND97-AP2D)

Shibata, H (2020) Tools for Corporate Innovation, Medium, 2 July. https://acv-vc.medium.com/tools-for-corporate-innovation-fdeac077d05f (archived at https://perma.cc/ZDP5-4XUQ)

PART ONE
Profiling

Through profiling, you define your Corporate Venturing mandate: Prioritize financial, strategic, innovative, and cultural goals, identify key stakeholders, and align budget and investment focus.

Your Corporate Venturing profile 01

How do you set up a Corporate Venturing programme? What do you need to consider? And what pitfalls should you be aware of and how can you avoid them? How can you ensure that your investments will pay off financially and return more than just financial value to your parent company?

Most of the answers we came across when doing research and talking to Corporate Venturing teams for this book centred around statements like 'if I had known this' and 'if I had thought about that at the very beginning, I could have saved myself and the programme a lot of stress'.

Starting your CV programme with a proper setup that is tailored to the aspirations (but also capabilities) of your corporation is critical for the future success of your CV team and will likely spare you a few headaches in the future. What this book and the following chapters aim to provide is a business plan structure and conceptual grid that can be used when setting up a CV programme. Moreover, we will share some insider aspects so that you and your corporation do not have to do all the experimenting that other big corporations have already done for you. A CV programme and team are like a company in its own right. Ironically, it's like a startup. It must have a mission, a vision, and a strategy – and then proper execution. More operationally speaking, it will have a team, products and services which the team will make available to its external customers (i.e., targets receiving funding) and internal customers (i.e., the corporation). Furthermore, the unit will have competitors who may search for and invest in similar targets. The team has to position the programme and itself through communication and marketing in a way that is distinct and sharp, possibly unique, and attractive. The unit will address a target market, i.e., certain types of companies, which is often volatile and can change its structure and shape over time. And the unit will need a financing strategy and financial goals. It will also need a governance and a suitable legal setup that can support the execution of the strategy and the achievement of strategic goals.

Let's develop a profile for your CV programme. We believe that organizations that are planning to set up a CV programme will ask themselves the most basic questions first, like:

- What should be the (realistic) overall goal of the programme?
- Why do this?
- Why us?
- Why now?

And whoever introduces the idea to create a CV programme will face the most basic scepticism: 'We are not an investment company, nor venture capitalists or startup specialists. So why do we do this? Why not outsource it, like other corporate activities that are important to us, but that we are less familiar with?'

CV goals – not mutually exclusive

In the market today, we have identified four dominant CV profiles, reflecting what we believe to be the most relevant drivers of CV programmes:

- financial returns
- strategic renewal
- innovation
- culture.

None of these profiles are mutually exclusive. If your CV programme has a strategic renewal profile it can also aim to change the culture of the parent company, and drive innovation efforts with a new spin, for instance. And maybe you decide that your corporation may benefit from two or even three CV programmes or sub-programmes, addressing different topics (maybe in different regions or target markets)?

EXAMPLE

Take the example of insurance giant AXA: Their global organization runs the AXA Venture Partners (AVP) initiative (since 2015, initially launched as AXA Strategic Ventures). The initial scope of AXA Strategic Ventures was focused primarily on Insurtech startups, i.e., young companies disrupting the traditional insurance business model with new technologies and innovative approaches. Over the years, the scope was broadened and the team added enterprise software, digital health and consumer tech startups to their scope (while maintaining fintech and insurtech as focus areas). The AVP team has, as of early 2023, about USD 1.2bn of assets under management, of which roughly USD 800m are dedicated to direct investments, and about USD 400m to investments in other venture capital/private equity funds. Moreover, the team has refined and further sophisticated their approach to address startups at different maturity stages, i.e., AVP Early Stage focuses on investments in early-stage companies, and AVP Capital focuses on investments in growth-stage companies.

Reference

AXA Venture Partners (2023) https://www.axavp.com/ (archived at https://perma.cc/NGY4-29MS)

Financial versus strategic returns 02

In previous scientific articles and books about CV, scientists, experts and consultants (which are not always the same!) advised to position new CV activities distinctively and to go for either a 'purely financial strategy' or a 'purely strategic approach'. They claimed that the initiators of a CV programme should be 100 per cent clear as to the strategic focus of the CV unit. And they argued that hybrids between these goals should be avoided, as they may confuse the team, as well as internal and/or external stakeholders, the investment selection and, ultimately, performance.

Most market participants today, however, pursue multiple goals and strategies at the same time. They believe that hybrid approaches are perfectly normal, and actually better suited to reflect the somewhat mixed agendas of corporates engaging in CV activities. This is because they often follow a number of goals at the same time and not just one single goal. Let's reflect upon this common (mis)conception.

A common (mis)conception: 'Financial vs. strategic focus' – an oversimplification of things

A common misconception around CV is the assumption that most CVC funds are either purely financially or purely strategically driven. Let's have a look and consider what this would mean if you really followed a single focus.

Strategic focus

The CV team would invest exclusively in startups or innovative growth companies whose business concepts or technologies fit the strategic objectives of the CV's parent company. The financial prospects of the target companies, e.g., in terms of return on investment, do not play a role, as the focus would be on the potential strategic impact on the parent company alone.

If a CVC team is formed that pursues a purely strategic focus, then the CFO would still take a closer look at the development of the investments after 3–4 years because after all, the parent company itself also has to justify to its investors and shareholders why capital is continuously being poured into an activity, possibly without any financial returns. Moreover, if a startup (and the technology that it develops) are considered potentially strategic for a big corporation, how is it possible that the financial forecasts for this technology and startup are not somewhat promising? Wouldn't the economic and financial viability of the startup's business concept somehow confirm the strategic value of the startup? Meaning: wouldn't a strategically meaningful startup always have somewhat relevant and attractive financial prospects?

Financial focus

The CV team invests exclusively in startups that in themselves show extraordinary potential for success and growth. Any strategic overlaps of the target companies with the CVC's parent company are ignored. In other words, the financial return from the investments has full priority.

If a CV team pursues a purely financial strategy, then this team is basically no longer a CV team, but becomes a de-facto private VC, with the only special feature that the entire fund/programme is (currently) financed – at least initially – by only one investor, namely the parent company. The parent company may consider whether it really believes that it is better positioned and more successful investing with a newly 'created' team of VC professionals than by investing in an established private VC fund, which may demonstrably achieve good returns on an ongoing basis and where the group saves itself the trouble of creating and maintaining its own team.

Pure forms of either approach are rarely to be found. Hybrids of both approaches are much more common.

The hybrid approach of a financial and strategic profile

For most CVCs, a startup considered for an investment must have a good strategic fit *and* promising financial prospects. Ideally, the startup's plans (e.g., development roadmap) are somewhat aligned with intentions or aspirations of the investing corporation. Nevertheless, the startup has to have good prospects of being financially successful on its own, so if the corporate fails to collaborate with or support the startup effectively, the startup can still prosper independently and the investing corporate will not necessarily lose the investment.

In order to generate strategic returns for the investing corporation, there must be a strategic plan as to how the corporation intends to work with the startup, what non-monetary support it can offer, and in what way it intends to generate benefits for itself.

In its simplest form, such a plan could look as follows:

- We plan to invest €2 million in your company. This should allow you to fund your team and its activities for almost two years.
- During the two years, we believe you can reach milestones (1) and (2). And we plan to make Mrs X and Mr Y from our organization available to you to support you in planning and executing your activities.
- If everything works well, we plan to make another investment in two years allowing you to bring the technology to the market. We may want to take the entire investment or co-invest with other investors.
- Our long-term aspiration is to license the technology from you.

Ideally, the CV team would arrange for conversations between certain units of the corporation (e.g., Research and Development, Manufacturing, Engineering, etc.) and the startup to jointly discuss, refine, and agree upon a form of joint business plan. It is neither expected nor necessary for the corporation to micromanage the startup. But working with the startup is a healthy exercise for the business unit of the corporation. Generally, leaders of business units (BUs) who manage core activities of the corporation act sometimes as 'sponsors' for startup investments. Such supporters of investment should consider some of the following questions:

- What are we as a department (and corporation) trying to get from this investment beyond financial returns, i.e., what is our strategic angle?
- Can we quantify (roughly) what it would mean to our own business (i.e., not for the startup, for our own big corporation) if we actually managed to get this technology from the startup?
- How can we support the startup or are there areas where we cannot support?
- What would be milestones that we would hope the startup to achieve?

Financial performance

Generating financial returns is a paramount objective for all corporations out there. Accordingly, most CV programmes strive to break even or, ideally, even generate (modest) extra profits for their parent companies. Seen from the point of view of the parent company, various ways are available to measure financial performance.

The internal rate of return (**IRR**) is arguably the most common and popular way of measuring the performance of each dollar or euro invested. It helps to determine the (expected) investment return. A target IRR in the venture capital industry could be anywhere between 10–20 per cent per year (measured after 8–10 years). After 8–10 years, you wonder? Remember: it takes time to deliver performance on a venture capital portfolio. Each portfolio company requires years to exit successfully. This is not day trading on the stock exchange. This is growing trees!

Let's look at a small example: If Tetracorn, a fictious CVC arm of an S&P 500 firm, demands 20 per cent IRR and expects to sell their $10 million investment in a tech startup in eight years from the investment date, the exit value of their investment should be 10 million $* (1 + 0.2)^8$ which gives approximately $43 million dollars. In other words, if Tetracorn expects a 20 per cent internal rate of return on their invested capital per year (to compensate for the risks involved in the investment), this necessitates a $43 million payback for a $10 million investment after eight years. While this is an expectation, the true IRRs become apparent in the actual event of an exit. In McKinsey's Private Markets Rally to New Heights Report (2022), the performance of venture capital investments measured as IRR was reviewed and the best 25 per cent of independent funds achieve IRRs up to 37 per cent. In our Tetracorn investment example, this would mean that the $10 million investment returned about $124 million after eight years.

But keep in mind that your CV programme is not a private VC. It is less free in choosing its investment focus and in taking investment decisions, and the people running the programme have different incentive schemes compared to their peers at private/independent VC firms, to name just a few key differences. So do not expect your newly assembled CV team to bring home a performance of IRR 40 per cent or more.

Also, make sure to clarify whether the target IRR that you expect to see from your CV team should be applied to the investments only, or include the entire CV operation (i.e., also reflect personnel costs, travel expenses, setup and maintenance costs, office space, etc.), which means that the overall investment performance must be even stronger.

Multiples (Multiple on Invested Capital (MOIC)), on the other hand, are another financial measure of the total return an investment will generate. The target factor for the CV programme is an average return of 3× the allocated capital. Typically, this is evaluated after the programme's usual duration of 12–15 years. The average may be lower and the time period shorter, depending on the industry and the investment stage of focus. Expressed in figures, this means a capital allocation to a CV unit in the amount of €10 million would generate total exit proceeds (in cash) from all portfolio companies of €30 million after 15 years. And again, you can discuss internally if you want to take the ongoing expenses for the programme into account too, or not. In our fictitious Tetracorn example above, for the top 25 per cent of independent VC funds, the MOIC was 12.4 (with an IRR of 37 per cent).

Other performance metrics that you may want to consider for your unit can be reviewed in the so-called Venture Capital Fund Metrics Cheat Sheet (Diligent Equity 2021) (Figure 2.1a and 2.1b refer to Paid-in Capital, Distributed Capital, Fund Book Value, Investment Cost, Investment Proceeds, Investment Book Value). How these metrics relate to calculations of different kinds of gross and net values for MOICs and IRRs is reproduced here.

Figure 2.1a Venture Capital Fund Metrics Cheat Sheet, based on Diligent Equity (June 2021)

Multiples:		**IRR:**			
MOIC	(Ⓔ+Ⓕ)/Ⓓ	Gross IRR	Outflows	Ⓓ or Ⓐ	*Gross*
Realized MOIC	Ⓔ/Ⓓ		Inflows	Ⓔ & Ⓕ	
Unrealized MOIC	Ⓕ/Ⓓ	Gross Real. IRR	Outflows	Ⓓ or Ⓐ	
Gross TVPI	(Ⓔ+Ⓕ)/Ⓐ		Inflows	Ⓔ	
NET TVPI	(Ⓑ+Ⓒ)/Ⓐ	Net IRR	Outflows	Ⓐ	*Net*
RVPI	Ⓒ/Ⓐ		Inflows	Ⓑ & Ⓒ	
DPI	Ⓑ/Ⓐ	Net Real. IRR	Outflows	Ⓐ	
			Inflows	Ⓑ	

Figure 2.1b Venture Capital Fund Metrics Cheat Sheet, based on Diligent Equity (June 2021)

Metrics:

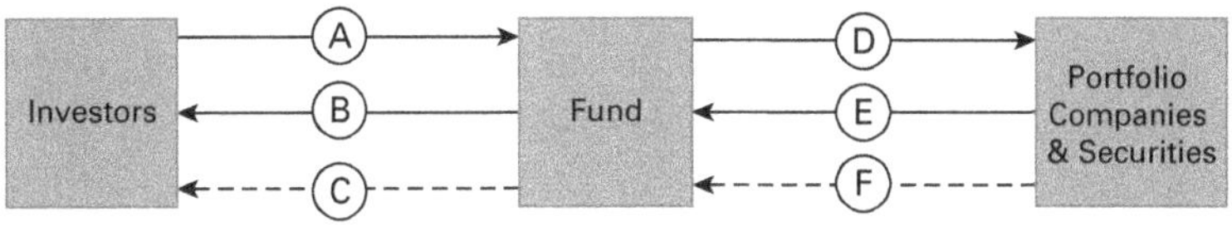

(A) Paid-in Capital (a.k.a. drawn-down capital, contributed capital)

(B) Distributed Capital [net of fees, expenses, carry]

(C) Fund Book Value (a.k.a. NAV) [after provision of fees, expenses, carry]

(D) Investment Cost (a.k.a. basis) [invested capital + deal costs]

(E) Investment Proceeds (a.k.a. returns) [distributions from full or partial liquidation]

(F) Investment Book Value (a.k.a. NAV) [net of fees, expenses, carry]

Unrealistic performance expectations

We have already alluded to the major differences between the managers running your CV programme and their peers in the market managing independent VC funds. And here's another warning to the CFO's team of your corporation: If you measure the CVC's performance during the first 10 years, the results will likely be misleading. Think about it. Unsuccessful startups tend to go 'belly up' first. In other words, years before the successful startups from your portfolio achieve their exit and generate delightful proceeds to their shareholders, your unsuccessful ventures will fail. This is why the performance of most VC funds resembles a so-called J-curve – the fund's performance will be negative for the first 5–8 years, and then pick up momentum as the proceeds from the first successful exits start pouring in.

Your investor reputation

Another thing that goes along with the financial return is the requirement to act like a good and reliable investor, and to build yourself a strong and positive reputation among founders and other investors. As a corporate investor, you are not only expected to support the venture financially, but also with other activities leveraging your assets. Moreover, you are expected to not only invest once, but in multiple rounds of funding. If you build yourself a bad reputation, founders and investors will prefer not to work with you in the future, and your access to good deals will deteriorate over time.

In conclusion, if your goal is to achieve a maximum return on venture capital investments (with everything else seen secondary), then your goal is to build a private VC under the umbrella of your corporation. And if that's the case, you could also consider searching for existing VCs focusing their investments on areas of interest to you, as they might be more likely to deliver that performance, and you can spare yourself a lot of trouble and expenses related to building your own CV programme. However, the learnings and the inspiration for your corporation from such an approach will be tiny.

An example of a rather independent programme is GV, Alphabet's CV programme. GV is run independently as a return-oriented fund. Today, GV manages more than $8 billion, with Alphabet as sole Limited Partner (LP). GV has about 300 active companies in its portfolio, has supported more than 500 ventures, completed 48 IPOs and more than 160 mergers and acquisitions since the first quarter of 2022. Accordingly, GV is one of the most active CV programmes with a highly diversified portfolio focused primarily on the 'next big opportunities' and thus financial returns.

More common is a hybrid financial and strategic approach. If we look at *Samsung's Catalyst Fund* in comparison, we know that the CV programme has a **dual bar**. That is, it considers both the financial and strategic value of a potential investment target. However, the financial return is the top priority, not because it affects Samsung's P&L, but because it is a good 'hygiene factor' as one can only do good things with companies that show quality. Therefore, Samsung's Catalyst Fund takes a shareholder approach of 1+1=3 and ensures that it invests in high-quality companies.

References

Diligent Equity (2023) The Ultimate VC Metrics Cheat Sheet https://www.equityeffect.com/venture-capital-metrics-cheat-sheet/ (archived at https://perma.cc/2WJE-FCP4)

GV (2022) https://www.gv.com/ (archived at https://perma.cc/2VEB-JD3X)

McKinsey & Company (2022) Private markets rally to new heights, McKinsey Global Private Markets Review. https://www.mckinsey.com/~/media/mckinsey/industries/private%20equity%20and%20principal%20investors/our%20insights/mckinseys%20private%20markets%20annual%20review/2022/mckinseys-private-markets-annual-review-private-markets-rally-to-new-heights-vf.pdf (archived at https://perma.cc/TUR8-FEVA)

Strategic renewal 03

As we have already shown, a pure financial focus for a CV unit is a rare thing. In this chapter, we want to take a look at the CV's strategic potential, beyond financial returns.

What we have recognized in academia and practice is that corporates have increasingly outgrown the financial return orientation of the past and are now more aware that CV can contribute to strategic learning and thus strategic realignment.

CV offers the opportunity to gain insight and access to new trends, technologies, processes, and markets. CV also inspires people to start new businesses themselves. It generally follows that CV can be used to initiate a strategic dialogue between multiple parties, both internally and externally.

Internally, a CV programme with a predominant strategic renewal profile has the ability to challenge and thus advance a company's strategy. Take the example of a traditional car manufacturer. Let's say the company is still producing mostly petrol engine cars. Then the CV programme can, for instance, invest in startups that innovate around petrol engines. Or, the management sees a relevant future trend in e-mobility, and then the CV programme can invest in startups that innovate around electric engines and new battery technologies. Alternatively, the management of the corporation believes that the age of petrol engines is over, but they do not believe that e-mobility is the most sustainable technology for the future of the industry, and so they decide to focus the CV program on startups that innovate around other engine concepts, such as fuel cells, photovoltaic concepts, etc. Another scenario is that the management of the car manufacturer can decide to invest in all three directions. Whatever they do, the decision will most likely be based on joint submissions of the several experts from the corporation, such as from R&D, production, customer insights, corporate venture capital, M&A, or corporate strategy. And the discussion between these experts will continue over time, and potentially adjust the investment focus and strategy if necessary. With this in mind, a startup company could be seen as a 'sparring partner', 'development partner' or 'expert challenger', and treated with respect.

As you will learn later, a high degree of openness and understanding of each other's history and culture and ambitions is required, both on the part of the corporate and the venture, to enable a successful collaboration between these completely different animals. Startups often fear loss of control, more bureaucracy, the 'theft' of know-how, or sudden changes in priorities or personnel on the side of the corporate, all of which may change the nature of the collaboration between the big corporate and the small startup dramatically and quickly. The top management of the corporation, on the other hand, is often concerned about wasted investments that do not generate anything for their company, and about reputational or legal/regulatory risks. Moreover, the corporate managers have to withstand the temptation to micromanage and 'optimize' the startup – because this is what will effectively kill the startup.

According to our interview with AXA and its Venture Capital & Strategic Partnerships, their team has a strategic mandate to bring innovation into the company. The mission is not to transform the core business, but to use CV investments for topics with strategic relevance for AXA for example an expansion of the current offering, the creation of more touch points with customers, or the development of sales interfaces and the like. Financial returns are also a goal (apart from being more of a hygiene factor), as stakeholders need to be satisfied and the company's growth needs to remain in focus. But this is exactly what we mean by a hybrid version of strategic and financial focus. What is more in the case of AXA is that there is a top-down management buy-in from which AXA's CV practices benefit a lot. The leadership of AXA knows very well what CV is capable of and how the parent company can use spillover effects to drive innovation while ensuring a competitive advantage and thus long-term survival. Without executive buy-in and supportive employee incentives, changes in key stakeholders, which are not uncommon, can jeopardize the entire programme. Having someone's back is also a mentality that is reflected in working with business units, very often as sponsors. Instead of cannibalizing the current AXA business, CV investments expand prevailing corporate offerings.

Reference

AXA (2022) Interview with Alexander Behr, Principal of AXA DE Venture Capital and Strategic Partnerships

Innovation 04

One of the biggest (and never-ending) challenges for a corporation is to maintain its competitive advantage. Markets are changing with new players coming out of nowhere to disrupt incumbents. Strengthening the innovation capability of a corporation as a whole is therefore imperative. More often than not, major innovations come from external innovators and startups. And smaller, more incremental innovation is created by a company's own R&D department.

But hold on. Here comes another common misperception: 'startup investments make us more innovative'. Some managers may think that investing in startups will magically make their corporation more innovative, and that such investments will 'teach' the bigger company how to innovate, cut corners, be more agile, more creative, more daring, etc. This belief is certainly a bit naïve. But that is not to say that your CV programme will not have any influence on your innovation capabilities and culture, because it will have an impact on both!

Common (mis)perception: 'Startup investments make us more innovative'

This is wishful thinking, right? An 'analogue' company does not become a 'digital' company just because it runs its own website. Neither does a corporation become innovative because it makes investments in startups. Having a proper website is one element of digitization. And engaging with startups is one element of corporate innovation. But there are obviously other elements too. Startup investments don't make you more innovative, but they can encourage and inspire innovation inside of your company and allow you to acquire innovative startups with a discount, if you own some shares of them already.

Also, a corporation should have no illusions about the information it can extract from startup investments. For instance, a Corporate VC making a minority investment in a startup will not be able to obtain particularly favourable business conditions for itself or its parent company. So, if you think you can invest €500,000 and get price discounts for services or products provided by the startup, you are mistaken. And if you believe that you as an investor can get access to customer data of the startup, you are also gravely mistaken. Data and other assets are owned by the startup, and cannot be taken away by investors or shared with their parent companies. Moreover, a startup does not 'teach' a corporation how to innovate or how a particular technology works. No minority investor will get access to or be educated on tech secrets of his or her startup portfolio companies. And even if a startup gives access to such secrets, for example to its board members (representing important shareholders), then these board members are not allowed to share these secrets with their parent companies. Sharing confidential information with outsiders is illegal.

What you need to understand is that your corporate's path to access any secrets or assets of the startup is to pay for that access. Either by acquiring the startup or by some form of license agreement, commercial agreement, etc. The investment is merely a discount on the acquisition price (or provides a kick-back to you as a shareholder, if the startup generates additional profits based on a license agreement). What you also need to understand is that the startup's assets and secrets will be way more valuable to you as an investor if the startup is successful. Your portfolio companies' successes will eventually fuel the success of your parent company. And it will be messier and more time consuming to pick up individual assets as part of a liquidation or bankruptcy process, if you kick such ideas back and forth in your management team meetings. Plus, you may not be able to utilize assets and secrets in full, because you may struggle to retain the team that has developed these assets and secrets. If both sides – the company and the startup – treat each other fairly by acting with open minds and explaining their expectations and aspirations clearly and understandably to the other side, then a good basis is laid for a close collaboration and joint development activities that can be crowned by success for both.

Many corporates use CV to drive their business model innovation. The necessary innovation does not have to come from within your corporation (which often takes years and many resources) but the new approach or technology is developed externally (by a startup or a number of startups), tested in the real world by the founders, and the corporation supports and enables these developments and tests with funding and subject matter expertise.

In AXA's case, corporate strategy will highlight the white spaces, while AXA Venture Capital & Strategic Partnerships will explore what solutions are already on the market and fill that gap through venture investments. They recognize the advantage of gaining access and insight into new knowledge to fill their white spaces, i.e., business areas that are not yet covered but are in demand. For instance, the insurance industry is aware that an extremely small number of their private customers are fond of (let alone interested in) insurance policies. Nobody is interested in that, unless they actually need the insurance. So, insurance companies try to make the service experience for their customers as simple and seamless as possible, e.g., report the damage via your mobile phone, and get quick support from the insurance company in terms of money or other services.

So basically, corporates are using CV as a means of external IP development and testing of new products, services and approaches. R&D and internal organizational innovation processes can be accelerated, which in turn saves not only time but also a lot of resources and money. Even before entering a new business field, the CV (i.e., the portfolio companies) serve as a market-sensing and testing instrument to identify new trends and business potential as well as to avoid wrong decisions. Two birds with one stone.

But, yes, there is a but! What must be considered is the 'digital transformers' dilemma' outlined by Frankenberger et al. (2020). There is this balancing act of (a) maintaining and gradually revitalizing the core business and (b) developing groundbreaking new products and services. Those companies that master the balancing act are the ones that successfully thrive and survive.

Check out the deep dive of a successful two-track strategy called ambidexterity in the box below.

Deep-dive: Double S-Curve and the two-track strategy of investment

What is the mission of a company? Yes, long-term growth and survival in order to obtain ultimately profits, nothing else. This is easier said than done. To achieve consistent profits, a company must invest in its core business to further strengthen its traditional business (as shown on the 1st S-curve in Figure 4.1) as much as possible. The market share is to be improved continuously, as is the market position. However, digitalization and especially globalization have led to disruptive innovations by new players, technologies, economic events, new customer requirements and preferences, and overall, a transformed ecosystem in place.

There are no longer traditional industry or business field boundaries; the boundaries have become somewhat blurry. As a result, companies see themselves innovating in technologies and markets away from their core business to avoid being outperformed by unknown, new competitors all of a sudden (2nd S-curve in Figure 4.1).The key, however, lies in managing a two-track strategy: maintaining and strengthening the necessary skills and know-how in the traditional business, while developing the necessary skills and know-how for transformed, future fields of activity. The two curves in Figure 4.1 provide an overview of the development and steps to take forward. The underlying dynamics and potential approaches have been captured by Frankenberger et al. (2022).

Figure 4.1 Overview of development steps, based on Frankenberger et al. (2020)

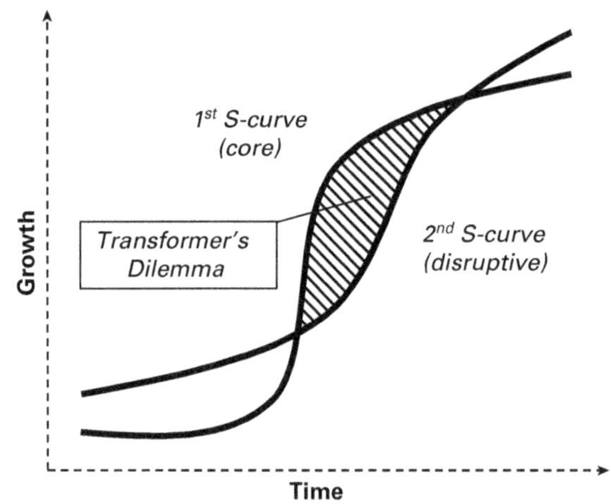

The Swiss FMCG company Nestlé is all about innovation and has managed the balancing act of preserving and nurturing traditional business lines while developing new product concepts and ideas extremely successfully. But not without changing the course from time to time. In the past, Nestlé focused mainly on internal innovation and created trends rather than chasing them, such as Nespresso.

The 'not invented here' syndrome left the company long ago – it had to, for reasons of survival. Today, Nestlé also embraces external innovation through startups and growth companies. Nestlé maintains two CV funds of funds (FoF), both amounting to about CHF 100 million, as well as venture investments through R&D (equity) and an accelerator programme.

External collaborations play a key role in building science and technology capabilities at Nestlé, as brands – the other component of long-term sustainable value creation – are the responsibility of the Strategic Business Units (SBUs). There is a very close interaction between R&D and the SBUs (guardians of the brands). For each category there is a Global Business Strategy (GBS), which defines the medium- and long-term goals for the categories and brands in the categories. A key component of the GBS is what role innovation plays in the context of growth to strengthen the brands. That results in upstream interface with business strategy feeding into innovation and renovation priority and the scope of R&D activities, while the downstream interface lies between operations and market execution.

Corporate Venturing is positioned in the upstream with a mandate to connect externally, and to generate access to innovative technologies and deal flow. Financial returns of this activity play a minor role. The focus is on innovation first as it is the biggest value driver for Nestlé's long-term economic profit.

References

Frankenberger, K, Mayer, H, Reiter, A, and Schmidt, M (2020) *The digital transformer's dilemma: how to energize your core business while building disruptive products and services*, Hoboken, NJ, John Wiley & Sons

Nestle (2023). https://www.nestle.com/investors/overview/venture-capital-funds (archived at https://perma.cc/KV7W-E8YM)

Culture 05

Culture in a CV environment is often underestimated and often stays a bit under the radar. This is surprising because CV is a people business where culture is key. Culture, and therefore people, are the fuel of the entire CV ecosystem.

It is possible to use CV as a marketing tool by not only creating more brand awareness, but also significantly enhancing your reputation as a good corporate citizen and 'preferred employer for talents'. Environmental sustainability has emerged as an important topic, and CV can help you gain more traction in this regard.

In order to reap the benefits that CV can offer, there are a number of key prerequisites. And one of the most important requirements is to actually develop a culture that is necessary and desirable for CV to work, as well as an appropriate mindset for the CV's stakeholders.

Common (mis)conception: 'Let's act like a startup again' – the ability of big corporates to take risks

Is it true that corporations are unable to act as fast and nimble as startups? Or is that a misconception? Corporations are much more in the market limelight than startups or mid-sized private, unlisted companies. The higher the concern of the corporation regarding bad press, the higher the caution regarding risky investments, for example, in startups.

Most large corporations have developed a sophisticated compliance and alarm system to protect themselves. They have assigned groups of internal and external experts ('guardians') advising on the prevention (where possible) legal issues and their solutions, communication issues, liability issues and so on. Such experts do not only deal with problems, they also design and implement processes to protect the corporation from future problems. For good reason, obviously, because corporations bear responsibilities for their actions towards society and governments, their shareholders, as well as towards their employees, suppliers and customers. If a behemoth company goes belly-up, this will impact the lives of thousands of people in a significant way. Think of the Enron disaster or the Lehman Brothers collapse.

Such a protection system only makes sense if it provides *reliable* protection. If individual elements of the protection system fail (e.g., if corporate runs into a big legal problem despite its large and well-paid legal team), then relevant areas are usually rapidly reorganized, often accompanied by changes of personnel. As a consequence, guardians develop (almost automatically) a heightened state of alert (or even paranoia) when it comes to startup investments. From their point of view, it's better to prevent the corporation from taking on any additional risk than to open the door to new risks. In the context of startup investments, this means that from a guardian's perspective, it is better if the group does not invest in a startup, because then no direct risks can arise. At most, there is the risk of missing out on the early stages of a market trend. But who can claim with any certainty today that this trend will be super relevant in the future? And don't forget the following: decision makers will prefer not to contradict the concerns raised by guardians. Or do you, as the CEO of your organization, want to see your name in the minutes of an Investment Committee meeting next to a statement that says 'significant legal and reputational risks where identified by the legal team, but the CEO decided to do the investment anyway...'? Few top managers want to gain a reputation as the company's very own Evel Knievel, right?

In conclusion, large corporates struggle to act like startups. In fact, they actively try to prevent themselves from taking risks. But they also tend to overestimate risks of a minority investment in a startup. We recommend not excluding your guardians from the startup investment process, but educating them!

Now we have established that big corporates are, and will, always be unable to move as quickly as startups. But think about this as an opportunity, rather than a challenge: The corporate's inability to take risks is not news to you, is it? In fact, this provides a super strong argument to justify startup engagements and investments! And all you have to do is to brief your guardians that if you decide to start a CV programme, they have to fight their reflex to say no to all risky investments.

Changing the 'always safe and always successful' culture

Your guardians need to understand that the company needs to try new things and take risks. You cannot act like an entrepreneur and not take risks and always be successful. Certain projects will fail and lead to losses and will not be successful. But your firm is choosing CV as an approach with limited risk to do risky things, i.e., have others (other companies and investors) take on the risk, so that the company does not run into fundamental problems. If you achieve this change of mindset, you have actually changed the culture of your corporation already!

You have somehow managed to empower managers to run certain processes differently, to adjust certain minimum requirements, to (almost) cut a corner. Congratulations! And it does not end with the culture of your corporation below the top management – you will change top management culture, too! Here's why: if your General Counsel joins an Investment Committee meeting and argues against a proposed investment because they see potential legal risks in the future of the company, then they should be reminded that the entire business model is risky. The critical question is: Can the identified (present and future) risks be mitigated (or at least reduced, limited, or controlled), or can they not be overcome at all, because only the latter must be considered a red flag. Your CEO could argue that the most welcomed contribution from the General Counsel is to make viable suggestions on how the startup team could actually reduce their risk. Because that will, in turn, reduce the risk for the corporation, both on the financial side and on the reputation side.

Coming back to the general aspect of culture, CV is a hotspot of multicultural backgrounds and of different personalities working together. CV operates at the intersection of the corporate and the startup world, comprising corporate management, the CV team, employees of your target and portfolio companies, and other investors. The CV unit builds the bridges between these worlds and groups.

AXA's Venture Capital & Strategic Partnerships department has a very good understanding of the company's culture, which is something special and puts it far ahead of most of its industry peers. Why is that? Well, ultimately, it's because of the insurance industry, where employees used to wear ties and suits, were rather formal, or didn't talk to each other much because of the strict hierarchy, especially in cultural contexts like in Germany or

Switzerland. As a result, the insurance industry very often still reflects the opposite of agile and lean.

In AXA's Venture Capital & Strategic Partnerships, there are hardly any hierarchies. The interaction with the AXA Group is informal and very laid-back. This has very positive effects and improves the mutual understanding of cultural differences between a large corporation and a small and agile venture.

Another great example of bridging the gap between a corporate behemoth and the world of startups is Samsung's Catalyst Fund. Here, this task even has a name, 'impedance matching', diverging from physics/electronics. A mutual understanding between the corporate and venture world is enabled by the work of the CV programme, as it helps translate and explain the other side. This applies to the entire life cycle – starting with the term sheet. The key to success for Samsung's CV programme is the so-called 'champions' and 'local teams' that regularly work with the operational units. It is already a big advantage if the CV team is located close to the management of the corporate parent, as it is all about people – staying connected and up to date. Top management, the business units (BUs) and other involved company employees are expected to generally have a culture of welcoming and embracing open innovation. They must be receptive to new or different expertise from the outside, while showing a willingness to take risks and accept failure. But this is often not the case (see 'risk reduction' and 'not-invented here' syndromes).

Above all, middle management faces a dilemma. It often feels stuck in between traditional approaches, attitudes, processes, etc. and the requirement to be innovative and, sometimes, risk-taking. Often, middle management does not even dare to move the needle. Potential failures or risks are perceived as something very negative and not as an opportunity to grow and build up more strength. Therefore, a certain willingness to learn and to challenge and overcome old systems and processes are required to establish the right CV culture, besides trust, mutual support and understanding. From a corporate CV perspective alone, it is a challenge to achieve mutual understanding because there are so many different stakeholders with their own perspectives and expectations. Combining this with an entrepreneurial way of seeing and working requires even more very good communication and expectation management.

As the cultural aspect holds such a key meaning for CV programme success, we want to highlight at this point another best-in-class CV practice, which is Hitachi Ventures. Hitachi Ventures offers entrepreneurial training programmes to work towards a required mindset. This training can take the form of rotational programmes, for example, where employees including leadership are exposed to various CV-related positions. As a result, relevant CV stakeholders gain multiple insights and new perspectives necessary to have the right mindset to promote CV and different perspectives to fulfil a specific mandate.

Having employees in the CV team who understand both the startup world and the corporate world is a prerequisite for optimal collaboration between the corporation and the startup. It is not only about hiring and retaining the right people in the CV unit, but also about finding the right people in the appropriate counterparts of the CV unit, such as the company's strategy department, R&D, business development units as well as other BUs. In this context, you should ensure a healthy balance of people with corporate backgrounds and venture backgrounds. It is then necessary to retain these employees. Appropriate incentives must be put into place. A rewarding compensation often consists of three elements: a fixed salary, a bonus (30–50 per cent of the fixed salary) if the CV programme managed to introduce suitable startups to the corporation and the introductions led to collaborations and/or investments and/or acquisitions, etc. And, last but not least, potentially a carried-interest like incentive that rewards the team for managing the portfolio successfully and achieving a positive overall return on investment. Alternatively, or in addition, teams could also get stock options (vesting over 2–5 years, as to ensure retention of CV team employees). Economically, stock options can be justified because it can be argued that successful CV programmes will eventually improve the performance of the corporation, and, hence, lead to a higher share price.

Financial and non-financial incentives should also be made available to stakeholders working closely with the CV unit, such as BU representatives and executives. Often, corporations assume that BU employees will simply support CV activities – in addition to their 'normal work' – but without proper incentives to support and collaborate, much less initiative is observed.

As with incentives and collaboration, trust is strongly underlined at Hitachi Ventures. Without trust, openness, and mutual support, an appropriate culture is not possible, and measures cannot ensure an appropriate cultural environment. Financial and non-financial incentives are often helpful because they can reinforce and elicit a certain intended behaviour.

But wait. At Hitachi Ventures, entrepreneurial culture is also primarily enabled by the independent structure of the CV programme with its autonomous processes. Well, there is quite a variety of CV setups possible to run a

CV programme, which are explained in the design phase later in the book in more detail. However, to anticipate, what we have seen is that the most promising CV constellations in terms of survival and profitability have turned out to have a rather independent structure with autonomous processes. Why is that?

Agile, lean, fast decision-making is essential for CV activities to be able to operate in a very dynamic environment. A CV team should have the ability to make autonomous decisions to operate and react quickly, taking opportunities. This is one of the key reasons why companies choose somewhat independent CV structures, as they are aware of their own bureaucratic dilemma of not being able to drive innovation internally as effectively.

By now you have taken a good look at the different profile orientations, but what does that mean for you now? You may have a first idea which alignment you will choose as a company and benefit the most from, but we want you to find your ideal match. That's why we've developed the Know Your Profile tool in the CV Cockpit to help you gain clarity on your CV profile, on the core direction you are taking with your CV mandate. The tool shows you a clear tendency of the target direction you are pursuing and is detailed in the CV Cockpit chapter.

References

AXA (2022) Interview with Alexander Behr, Principal of AXA DE Venture Capital and Strategic Partnerships

AXA Venture Partners (2023) https://www.axavp.com/ (archived at https://perma.cc/XY22-DQST)

Samsung Catalyst Fund (2022) https://samsungcatalyst.com/ (archived at https://perma.cc/TK7N-VGQS)

Promoters – who is involved and who is your main sponsor? 06

Now, to apply the chosen CV programme direction, various promoters will become relevant for you. The parties involved are quite diverse: members of the CV team, employees from different business units of the corporation, top management, members of the Investment Committee and members of the Advisory Committee, but also other external stakeholders, such as other investors, as well as the employees and top management of startups in your portfolio or on your target list.

Involved parties

No matter which profile you have identified based on the previous chapter, one thing is clear: Everyone involved must pull together. And that is a big challenge, because the CV promoters are a fairly heterogeneous group with diverse goals and attitudes and agendas.

Top management

Arguably, your most important promoter group is the top management of your parent company: your CEO and other C-level managers. Their mission is to maximize the economic strength and growth of the corporation. And by doing so successfully, they hope to please the shareholders, in order to further advance their personal career.

Top management is often dealing with somewhat contradictory goals, like 'increase revenues and lower costs at the same time' or 'take entrepreneurial risks and progress our agenda, but please make sure the risks are not significant', or 'let's have innovative products and services, but do not spend too much on internal and external innovation, because the success of R&D is not reliable'. Moreover, top managers frequently suffer from a systemic conflict of interest. On the one hand, their own performance will be measured short term, based on the quarterly and annual reports. The better the company's key performance indicators, the better the top management's performance evaluation, bonuses and career prospects. On the other hand, the owners would like top management to think long term, too. Certain investments have to be made today, even if the current management will not benefit from these decisions. Such decisions may enable the company to achieve certain goals in 3–12 years. And startup investments (which often take 3–12 years to mature) would fall under that category of decisions. Therefore, top management is often torn; they are hesitant to approve a startup investment because the results do not directly pay into their own agenda, but also supportive because the investment makes them appear less short-sighted and more strategic.

Business units

Leaders of business units (BUs) manage the core activities of the corporation such as procurement, manufacturing, sales and distribution, and marketing. Sometimes they act as 'sponsors' for startup investments – they validate the investment selection, and they support and steer the collaboration between corporation and startup. Their subject matter expertise enables them to explain to other stakeholders why a certain technology developed by a startup is interesting for the corporation. And they can steer the collaboration between the startup and corporate once the investment is made, because they are in control of the internal teams and budgets relevant for the collaboration.

BU leaders face a conflict of interest similar to that faced by top management. On the one hand, their performance is assessed based on their tangible short-term achievements (for example, monies spent, goals reached, profits generated, etc.). On the other hand, they are expected to work on long-term projects and suggest investments and activities that may be detrimental to their short-term performance, but may also create long-term trends and products, which can become the future pillars of the company.

To illustrate this conflict, let us remember an example that almost every manager working in an old, well-established, but somewhat challenged industry knows well: KODAK. The Eastman Kodak Company (KODAK) was founded in 1892. Throughout the twentieth century, KODAK was a market leader in the photographic film industry. The company began to struggle in the late 1990s, when first competitors such as Fujifilm entered the market.

KODAK became even more challenged when digital cameras became a global trend. Eventually, the former giant and market leader had to file for bankruptcy in 2011, which was, in all fairness not only but still to a certain extent, caused by a poor innovation development and adoption strategy. The arrival of digital cameras and KODAK's inability to embrace digital camera innovation is particularly interesting in the context of innovation. The bitter irony of this case is that it was KODAK engineers who had invented the digital camera in 1975, and it was KODAK who marketed the first-ever digital single-lens reflex camera in 1991.

So, what does this case teach us? Well, it talks to the sometimes-contradictory nature of corporate goal-setting and strategy execution. A corporation grants a budget to a business unit to do R&D around new technologies (potentially working with external partners like startups, too). And the BU develops a brand-new product, which turns out to be potentially disruptive to the corporation's existing line of products. Such a new product or technology will face a lot of headwinds internally. Likely arguments held against the new product include:

- **a** It's too expensive to manufacture and market.
- **b** This innovation is not part of our core expertise. It plays in an industry segment that is slightly different from our traditional core business (e.g., cameras versus film).
- **c** Our traditional core business is actually performing very well. So why defocus the company and invest a lot of money, and risk disruption of our best-performing product line, when nobody forces our hand?
- **d** There is no guarantee for success, i.e., yes this is a new technology, but nobody else is promoting or developing this. So why should we pioneer this?

General business services

Other stakeholders and potential supporters or showstoppers for startup investments are corporate managers from General Business Services such as HR, Finance, Accounting, Legal, Regulatory, etc.

The primary concern of General Business Services is to serve and, more importantly, to protect the corporation. Usually, they are not rewarded for innovation or for more risks taken by the corporation. Quite the contrary – if the corporation gets itself into trouble, for example by working with a startup, and if the General Business Units are believed to have failed in their duty to protect the company, then their current structure and personnel will be scrutinized.

General Business Services can make the life of the CV team – and, indirectly, of portfolio companies of the CV team – much easier or much more complicated. In general, they need to be assured that top management supports the CV programme and they need to understand that the company expects them to support the individual investments, and not shy away from challenges and risks. For instance, the Tax and Accounting team of the company may argue that a potential acquisition of a startup at some point in the future might be challenging because the startup is using a different accounting method and because the acquisition might trigger certain taxes.

A respectful response to the Tax and Accounting team could be that their concerns are certainly valid, but they should also understand that targets are not chosen based on whether or not they are easy to handle from a tax and accounting point of view. And they should also start to not only point to risks, but also think about possible risk mitigations, e.g., maybe the startup could be convinced that another accounting method is more helpful for growth companies, and certain tax risks could be mitigated by putting certain structures in place.

The CVC team

And then there is the CV team itself – the team that actually drives CV activities operationally and sometimes also strategically. The CV team can operate either as a completely independent entity or as an integrated team. Typically, the core consists of 3–5 team members (unless your programme is particularly broad or narrow), covering all roles required to run CV investment processes. In the best case scenario, some team members have a corporate background (they are well-connected in the corporation and able to accelerate processes), some have an entrepreneurial or technical background (enabling the team to understand the innovation and capabilities of the startup as well as possible) and some have venture capital careers to look back to (such as VC experts well-versed in leading negotiations, steering transactions and working with founders, other investors, etc).

Make sure you understand one of the most important underlying motivations of the members of your CV team (that is not necessarily aligned with your agenda as a corporation): the CV team will aim to do as many deals as possible. Why is this?

1. Because it's fun, and if a deal can be executed quickly and successfully this will also have a very positive impact on the individual career prospects of the involved team members.
2. Because each deal adds to the internal and external reputation of the team and each individual team member, whether the investment generates positive ROI or not. For a successful investment career, it is of utmost importance that you have deal experience. If your deals were profitable, even better. But you need to build yourself a deal track record.
3. Because the team members usually do not have skin in the game – i.e., the team members do not suffer personal financial losses or gains if an investment fails or is successful, which makes it easier to take risky decisions.
4. The average team members may stay with the team for between 3–5 years, because promotion and learning opportunities in the team can be somewhat limited, and so they will rarely see the endgame of an early-stage startup investment anyway.

All of the above have caused many corporations to complement their CV investment team with a separate Investment Committee and/or Advisory Committee with veto powers, i.e., the ability to stop deals.

Investment & Advisory Committee

The key responsibility of an Investment Committee (IC) is to approve or reject investment proposals submitted by the CVC team. The IC consists of a select group of individuals, whose main authority is to take the final decisions on most if not all CV activities, like new investments, follow-on investments or exits. The IC is, ideally, a lean team comprising only the most relevant and most qualified decision makers. Note that 'qualified' in this context does not mean 'qualified and experienced venture capital investors', but qualified in a sense that these managers have the shareholders' trust to take long-term investment decisions. Those decision makers can be the CEO, CFO and the head of the CV unit, with the only caveat being that the CEO and CFO may not be experienced enough with startup investments or may end up being conflicted (see above) and inadvertently stop deals from happening.

In addition to the IC, companies sometimes find it useful to have an Advisory Committee (AC), which includes subject matter experts, internal or external, from the field. Normally, ACs meet separately from the IC. An AC can be beneficial as it gives an external view of potential investments. The AC often understands the underlying technologies or innovation better than the IC. In other words, sometimes the IC (top management) uses the AC (subject matter experts) to validate what founders, internal supporters and the CV team present. Generally speaking, the AC tends to have a different and more independent opinion on innovation and development, because it does not carry any personal upside/downside risk related to the final investment or development decision.

Both the IC and the AC can also lead to more bureaucracy, more politics, and longer investment decision cycles. Talking to CVC practitioners in the field, we heard here and there that most love their jobs, but are not too fond of their respective ICs or ACs.

Other investors

Usually, other investors are (or eventually will be) invested and involved in startups considered by your CV team. Other investors might be family-friends-and-fools (FFF), business angels, family offices, private/independent venture capital firms, corporate venture capital organizations, government organizations, as well as other facilitators like universities, incubators and accelerators.

Some of the other investors have already invested in the startup before your CV team considers investing. Others may join the present round of funding. Again, others may already have the startup on their radar, but prefer to join potential future rounds of funding.

Different investors have different goals and follow different strategies. Here's a rough overview:

1 Maximize return on investment (ROI)

Arguably, this is the most popular goal shared by various groups of investors, e.g., Business Angels, family offices, independent VCs, Corporate VCs, even accelerators and incubators. It can be considered the most popular goal, because without financial success of their startup engagements, most startup investors would sooner or later be scrutinized to stop such engagements. Government organizations and universities might be the ones less interested in this, but that does not mean that they do not appreciate the financial success of one of the startups they have supported.

2 Progress certain tech developments in certain fields

Arguably, this is the second most popular goal shared by various groups of investors. One group of investors, potentially the private and independent ones, need their portfolio companies to progress certain technologies to get to a successful exit (i.e., goal 1, to maximize ROI). Another group of investors, for example Corporate VCs, may be more interested in the progress of the technology and less in the financial performance to which it may or may not lead, because the tech development is key for their parent company. And then there might be a third group which wants to see tech progress more than anything, because of philosophical or ethical reasons – for example investors like Business Angels or a family office dedicating some or all of their investments to fight certain problems like climate change or cancer.

3 Attract startups to certain geographies

A third set of goals is not related to the technological scope of startups, but more to startups as future engines of economic growth. Governments and certain other investors may support startups while being agnostic with regard to the magnitude of the financial success or the technology focus. They put emphasis on the startup being established in a certain region or city, and hiring people from that region or city, as a pre-condition for their support. Think of EU incentives (for example, the Horizon funding programme: https://research-and-innovation.ec.europa.eu/funding/funding-opportunities/funding-programmes-and-open-calls/horizon-europe_en), but also country-specific or city- and region-specific investors who offer to invest and support startups as long as the startup complies with the geographic requirements.

4 Other aspects

Last but not least, there are other investors who do not put too much importance on the financial success, the technology focus, or the geographic focus, and still offer to invest in startups and support their growth if the startups adhere to certain principles like diversity in the team, or equal pay and opportunity.

And obviously, you will also meet investors in the market following not only one but a combination of the goals sketched above. It is important for your organization and your CV team to understand the goals and motivations pursued by other investors, because this will indirectly determine the freedom to operate of the startup you plan to invest in, and it may also shape future decisions regarding the startup. We recommend running a basic due diligence process on other (meaningful) investors involved in the startup that you find interesting.

Do not forget: other investors will also scrutinize and challenge your goals as an investor. Many investors are quite sensitive with regards to the investments and involvements of larger corporations. Their prime concerns are often grouped around the fact that the investing corporations have or may eventually have very different goals, requirements and standards than the startup and its private investors. Their other concern is that corporations are, more often than not, significantly less reliable because their strategy, agenda, and personnel may change frequently during the lifetime of a startup, with sometimes dramatic consequences for the startup and its private investors.

The startup team

The single most important external stakeholders dealing with your CV team are the founders and employees of the startups you work with and invest in. Founders and startup employees come in all shapes and forms imaginable (i.e., with diverse backgrounds, maturity levels, personalities, etc.). You are not dealing with a rather homogeneous group of customers; you are dealing with arguably the most diverse group of people.

Founders are often both excited by and cautious of corporate investors (and all other investors, for that matter). On the one hand, they appreciate the capital injection and the strategic support that a big corporate may offer their startup. On the other, they are often wary of risks such as micromanagement by the corporate, cumbersome reporting requirements, strategic interference, brain drain (talents moving to the corporation or 'secret sauce' ingredients of the startup being picked up by the corporation).

The alignment of interest between startup founders and investors is often just a temporary thing, mostly due to changing agendas. An investor claiming to believe in a startup's potential to become a unicorn company in five years (to reach a company valuation of more than €1 billion) may be tempted after only two years to accept an acquisition offer from a buyer with a volume of €100 million, for example because some of the investor's other investments have failed and they want to deliver some positive news to their business partners. A corporate investor partnering successfully with a startup may suddenly change their strategy and discontinue the partnership. For example, a corporate investor partnering with a cannabis startup might be required to discontinue that partnership and sell its shares in the startup if the regulatory environment changes and cannabis products are deemed illegal in the target region of the startup (or the corporation).

A mixed bag

By now, you may have come to understand why we wanted to have a whole section of this book dedicated to stakeholders. As we briefly touched upon at the beginning of this section, 'collaboration among all stakeholders is key with a mutual understanding of the objectives of the CV program being indispensable' (AXA, 2022). As you have seen, each stakeholder involved has different goals, with different timelines and incentives, and therefore will behave differently towards the CV team, the founders, and other investors. Be aware of this.

An interesting example for partnering investors with different agendas is the Helvetia Venture Fund. This corporate venture capital team has a rather unique CV approach as it represents a partnership between a big corporation (Helvetia Insurance Switzerland) and a much smaller private and independent venture capitalist (b2venture AG). The private VC provides the CV management team, as well as access to deal flow and venture capital expertise. The larger corporation controls the activities through an Investment Committee, and it provides the financial resources and inputs to the investment strategy and selection.

The Helvetia Venture Fund has, as of 2022, two full-time VC employees and five Helvetia employees. The VC's employees focus on investment and portfolio management, while the corporate employees focus on the collaboration between the portfolio companies and the big corporation.

The IC is composed of the Head of the CV fund (and member of the VC organization), as well as the Head of Corporate Development, CFO, and CIO of the big corporation, all with one vote per decision. Other relevant stakeholders in the CV programme are counterparts in different business units of the corporation, who can be involved in the sourcing process and in the portfolio management activities. The team managing the fund is supported by other corporate employees from HR, Finance and Compliance, who actively support activities of the fund as needed.

Overall, the Helvetia Venture Fund is an innovative example of the diversity of stakeholders involved in a CV programme, as well as the wide range of different perspectives and agendas that go into a CV programme.

Sponsor

A so-called 'sponsor' of a startup investment in a CV context is usually a representative of a business unit advocating for the investment by pointing out the value to the corporation and proposing to support the startup with their business unit and, hence, with more than just capital after the investment.

In the case of the Helvetia Venture Fund, no business sponsors are required to do an investment. The Fund can invest even if no internal group commits to supporting the investment. This is, however, quite different from many other CV programmes where a sponsor is required. Normally, any (internal) party from the corporation can assume the position of a business sponsor. In general, sponsorship can be viewed from two sides: bottom-up or top-down. A CV programme can be driven either bottom-up, when middle management initiates CV activities, or top-down, when the leadership team has mandated that CV activities are conducted.

You should know that there are success cases where CV investments and activities have been initiated bottom-up, but usually not without C-suite level attention. For instance, within the Swiss Finance institutions, one can see that CV activities have been driven bottom-up, seeking their promoters at the top. Such cases have shown that a CV programme or investment is more likely to succeed if the sponsor is highly ranked. And that is not just because of the funding needed to run a CV deal, but also because of the appropriate understanding of what CV is about to promote it in the corporate ecosystem.

In terms of top-down support, the sponsor is not necessarily someone from top management, such as the CEO, CFO or other C-levels. It can also be the head of a BU who has received the mandate to drive a certain business area further through external innovation. As a final option (and least frequent by far), the sponsor can also be the head of the CV team, especially if the CV team is acting with a high degree of freedom.

So, what can you do to establish a CV programme with solid and sustainable top-down support?

- Involve relevant people from the leadership team at a very early stage and invite input and ideas. The discussions around these inputs will indirectly educate top management on various aspects of CV.
- Create awareness of the benefits of a CV programme for the company. Prepare examples from other corporations (especially but not only from the same industry) who were able to achieve tangible results or progress

based on CV activities. You may also prepare examples like the KODAK case, which shows what happens if innovation and R&D are not embraced by organizations.

- Educate critical stakeholders around CV programmes. Show realistic (instead of sugar-coated) scenarios of what to expect from the programme. For example, talk about failures of certain startups leading to financial losses. Explain potential cultural frictions between startups and teams from the corporation. Point to certain necessary adjustments in terms of attitudes and process requirements on the corporate side, especially with regards to guardians of the corporation, like legal teams, tax/accounting/internal audit teams, etc.
- Consider inviting CV teams from other big corporates to share their views and experiences.
- Explain where the personal support of top management is necessary and helpful, and also explain where top management should not be involved, despite them maybe feeling that they should (e.g., taking investment decisions in companies that may eventually disrupt the existing core business of the corporation).
- Discuss and agree on the profile of your CV team – financial, strategic, cultural, renewal, innovation, etc.

AXA's Venture Capital and Strategic Partnerships department is an excellent example of how to run such a process successfully. The team is supported by both the CEO and several BU sponsors. This means that CV activities are a high priority for the company and thus support is available in the form of resources, but also degrees of freedom and backing. This is important in critical times, as strategically oriented CV programmes, such as that of AXA have a long-term time horizon and only show tangible results later. Without top-down support, such programmes are often the first to be discontinued, without harvesting the fruits from previous years. In the case of AXA often when the venture is selected, a 'sponsor' of a corresponding BU is already determined to better integrate the venture into the corporate business with significance from the very beginning.

References

AXA (2022) Interview with Alexander Behr, Principal of AXA DE Venture Capital and Strategic Partnerships

AXA Venture Partners (2023) https://www.axavp.com/ (archived at https://perma.cc/XY22-DQST)

European Commission. Horizon funding programme, (2022) https://research-and-innovation.ec.europa.eu/funding/funding-opportunities/funding-programmes-and-open-calls/horizon-europe_en (archived at https://perma.cc/EJT2-SVG4)

Helvetia Venture Fund (2023) https://www.helvetia.com/global/venture-fund/en/home.html (archived at https://perma.cc/9VP7-JY9P)

Funding – what financial commitment is required? 07

It's all about the money, isn't it? Well, in our case, it's not. There is far more than just a proper financial budget needed to make CV work, as we just found out with the stakeholders involved. However, the funding volume available for startup investments and the investment period to which the parent company commits the funding are essential. They determine the playing field that your CV programme will have, and they determine how the fund is perceived by startups and competing investors.

Capital injection by the parent company

Before we begin to discuss fund sizes and duration, we should mention the two most common approaches to fund CV investment activities.

Approach 1: All investments are funded through the balance sheet of the corporation. In other words, the cash is taken as needed from the parent company. The CV unit may still position itself externally as if it had a fund. But behind the curtain and legally speaking, a budget is approved (on an annual basis or for each investment separately), and often an overall amount is earmarked for startup investments and reviewed every 3–5 years. The individual investment amounts are then released if and when an investment is approved by the Investment Committee. In a sense, the CV is just a department of the company.

Approach 2: A separate fund and legal entity is created, i.e., the parent company establishes a fully owned subsidiary to which it makes capital available, just like other investors would make capital available to a venture capital fund. Often, such CV units (i.e., with stronger identities and individual legal forms) are more independent from the parent company. Detailed insights are provided in Chapter 2. It is also possible to think of multi-investor CV fund structures.

Multi-investor CV programme

As you have learnt by now, most corporate venture capital (CVC) units are run by, funded by, and focused on the needs of *one* single corporation.

A new idea that has some appeal to both CV managers and the CV-funding corporation is to invite other investors to put money into the CV structure, i.e., alongside the parent company. This would lower the financial burden otherwise carried by the corporation alone, and it could further improve the credibility and financial fire power of the CV unit in the market. Moreover, it can help improve the retention of the fund management team because of presumably lower interference from the parent company, as we will see.

So, let's look at this concept in a bit more detail, because some players, like Swisscom Ventures, have succeeded in successfully building these structures. Here are some things to consider before you start setting up a multi-investor CV programme:

1 Performance

An external investor will only invest in your CV structure if your CV fund performs as well as a private, independent VC fund. In other words, the investment track record of your fund has to be attractive enough, reflecting strong and sustainable financial performance. This is because an external investor is likely more interested in financial returns than anything else. So, if your CV fund is a first-time fund, or the performance is mainly driven by a single outlier investment – a 'lucky punch' – or the fund management team was recently changed, then the fund is not likely to attract investments from external parties.

2 Independence

An external investor who likes the past performance of the fund would also like to ensure that the fund management team can work without interference from the corporation that has launched the fund in the first place. Think about it: for an independent investor it makes no sense to have a successful fund management team consisting of experienced VC professionals waste time on pitches to an Investment Committee composed of corporate managers with little or no real experience in VC. Also, the external investors will likely want the fund management team to focus on investments, and not on never-ending alignments and discussions with other business units of the corporation, let alone adjustments of the fund's investment strategy based on changes of the corporate agenda. Under this structure, the corporation that launched the CVC fund in the first place must become a limited partner in the fund, just like other outside investors, without any special rights related to the fund.

3 Commitment and dedication

Despite the required independence of the fund and its management team from the corporation, investors will always appreciate other investors putting capital into a fund. It would be irritating to external investors if the corporation that had funded the previous investment activities of the CVC does not invest in the new fund structure despite good past performance. Moreover, external investors will also appreciate some level of 'skin in the game' from the fund management team, and proper incentives for team members in place (for example, share of the carried interest). This is very common in the world of private, independent VCs, where 1–5 per cent of the total fund volume is invested by senior members of the fund management team, and where a VC partner can get anything between 1–10 per cent of the overall carried interest (often between 20–30 per cent).

4 Hygiene factors

For obvious reasons, the CVC fund vehicle has to meet certain standards and hygiene factors in order to qualify for an investment from external investors, such as:

a A proper legal structure and governance of the fund that is cost and tax efficient and complies with regulations and market standards.

b Terms and conditions based on the business model of the fund that are similar to or aligned with market standards, such as management fee, hurdle rate, carried interest, and even fund management compensation.

c Suitable corporate structure and capital structure of the fund to meet other management and reporting requirements, for example towards regulators, investors, and employees.

In summary, raising funds from external investors for your CVC fund is extremely challenging but could be financially and strategically rewarding. One could argue that by attracting external funding, the CVC fund does, in fact, become a de-facto private, independent VC fund. Otherwise, it cannot attract investments from other investors. The parent company has to let go of most if not all of its special rights regarding the governance, strategy, structure and management of the fund. This also means that the corporation has to ask itself: Are we better off investing in this particular VC fund (that used to be our own fund), or would we be better off investing in another independent fund following a similar strategy but with better results?

On the other hand, if your fund management team is good enough to attract external investments in a fund that is focused on one of the riskiest asset classes, what choice do you have? Sure, the corporation can act stubbornly and not agree to the 'external fundraising' idea. But then the fund management is likely to resign and start the independent structure without you, which means that you will have to build a new CVC structure from scratch and lose everything that was built between the fund and the corporation so far. You also lose access to what is presumably a good investment. We can only imagine that the Swisscom corporate managers, at some point, understood that it was better for them (and cheaper) to see Swisscom Ventures become more independent, attract external funding, but still carrying the name of Swisscom, still focusing on deep- and low-tech sectors interesting to the company. To our knowledge more and more corporates start to think about a multi-Limited Partners approach for their CV activities, but we also spoke to corporates who reject the idea of independent investors in their CVC funds completely.

Let's take a look at three somewhat 'standard' fund profiles and kick some ideas back and forth as to which profile has the best fit with what you are trying to achieve with your corporation.

Deep-dive: Basic fund profiles

Basically, structure follows strategy, i.e., your investment strategy determines the fund volume.

Table 7.1 Basic fund profiles

	Pre-seed and seed funds	Series A funds	Series B funds and later
Volume	€20–50 million	From €50 million, ideally €100–200 million	€200 million; the bigger the better
Target portfolio size	25–30 portfolio companies (strong emphasis on diversification)	20–25 portfolio companies (less diversified; more focused)	10–20 portfolio companies (very focused)
Capital needs per ticket size per initial round	<€1 million	€1–5 million	>€5 million
Investment risk	High	Medium	Medium to low
Fund size (ticket per deal x #ventures + 2% Mgmt. fee)	~€35 million ~€0.7 million EUR management fee (budget)	~€125 million ~€2.5 million management fee (budget)	>€250 million> €5 million management fee (budget)
Investment period	2–5 years initial investments + 7–9 years follow-on (total ~ 12 years)	2–5 years initial investments + 7–9 years follow-on (total ~12 years)	2–5 years initial investments + 5–10 follow-on (total ~14 years)
Focus	Larger initial portfolio, and then focus on best performers in the portfolio phase (years 4–12) and follow-on	Semi-focused initial portfolio with double-digit shareholdings at first investment; ongoing self-selection leads to focused portfolio of 'stars'	Focused portfolio with significant double-digit shareholdings at initial investment

	Pre-seed and seed funds	Series A funds	Series B funds and later
Region	Primarily regional targets, relatively close to the investor to facilitate hands-on collaboration (e.g., DACH region)	Larger region/continent, e.g., Europe or USA	Continent or global, as the quality of the target (e.g., traction in the market) is decisive
Team size	Budget for the team is about 1–2% of the fund volume, e.g., between €200,000 and €1 million; in the mini version 1 full-time manager and 1 assistant, or in the larger version 2 seniors, 1–2 juniors, 1 assistant	Budget for the team is always about 1–2% of fund volume, e.g., lies between €1–4 million per year; 2–5 partners, 2–5 investment managers (basically fewer investment managers than partners, structure of an inverted pyramid) + 1–2 assistants	Budget for the team is about 1–2% of fund volume, e.g., above €4 million per year, again rather more partners than investment managers and juniors; often also with distinction between senior and junior partner
Examples	Axa Venture Capital and strategic partnerships	Swisscom Ventures; Hitachi Ventures*; Samsung Catalyst fund	Bertelsmann Investments**; Shell Ventures***; Siemens Healthineers**

*Investments also in early stage and Series B / C; **Series B as main investment focus; investments of all size; structure, focus, and setup of each of these funds may change or not be reflected comprehensively

Three basic fund profiles

You should not view Table 7.1 as carved in stone. The three structures are just prototypes, or examples, if you will. All sorts of deviations from each of these models are conceivable and may make sense for individual corporations.

Going through Table 7.1, you will find certain boxes easier to understand and more intuitive than others. So, let's walk through the table together.

1 Total volume

The total volume of your fund is determined by the magnitude of your planned investment activities, in other words, how much money you can and would like to have available to invest in each of your portfolio companies, and how many companies you plan to add to your portfolio. Generally speaking, a pre-seed and seed fund typically has a total volume of €20–50 million. Series A funds often start with €50 million, but ideally should have €100–200 million at its disposal. Series B funds or later stage funds often exceed €200 million. Keep in mind: smaller and larger funds can be found in all three categories. Obviously, we are just trying to give you some ballpark figures here.

2 Target portfolio size

Generally speaking, the earlier – and, hence, riskier – the stage you plan to invest in, the more you may want to diversify the risk. Accordingly, seed fund portfolios, bearing higher risks per company, tend to have more portfolio companies than Series A fund portfolios, which tend to have more portfolio companies than Series B fund portfolios, etc. One important thing to note here is that private and independent funds usually present to their investors the targeted size of their portfolio. In a corporate venture capital programme, we would argue that you do not have to achieve that number. You can inform your stakeholders that you plan to invest in 25 or 20 or 15 companies. But if you invest in fewer companies (or more companies), nobody will likely hold it against you.

3 Ticket size per initial round

Many institutional investors (venture capitalists) strive to gain at least a double-digit (i.e., 10 per cent or more) shareholding in each of their target companies. That means that the average post-money valuation of your target companies (which is dependent on stage, region, industry, etc.) will indirectly determine how much money you will have to earmark and eventually put on the table to get to 10 per cent shareholding (or more) with your initial ticket.

> Let's say your average market post-money is €10 million or lower, then you should reserve about €1 million per target and initial round in order to get to the 10 per cent shareholding.

Accordingly, with higher (average) valuations for your Series A and Series B targets (and funds), you may need to reserve more money per company per initial round to get to 10 per cent.

As a consequence, funds focusing on later stage targets tend to be bigger in volume and smaller in number of portfolio companies, as explained above. Also, do not forget to plan for follow-on investments. They should be as high as the initial investment but will not be made available to every portfolio company, as some companies may not qualify for a follow-on investment and/or fail completely.

4 Duration of capital commitment

If you start to think about a corporate venture capital fund, consider a capital commitment of 10–15 years. Here's why: it will take your team 2–5 years (depending on numerous factors) to do all the initial investments in order to get to the portfolio size that you had in mind when launching the fund.

Once you have built your portfolio, each startup in the portfolio will develop, i.e., grow or struggle or fail. Some will require numerous follow-on funding rounds. Others will go bankrupt after 2–3 years. Others may be acquired after 5–6 years or decide to IPO (Initial Public Offering) after 5–9 years or generate enough profits to grow without additional investments. But all in all, it will take between 10–15 years to build and eventually dissolve an entire startup portfolio of more than 10 companies. Again, take this with a pinch of salt. Super-fast investments as well as super-fast disposals of entire portfolios are possible. You could go on Kickstarter and invest in 10 seed stage companies today. And you could probably announce on LinkedIn that you plan to sell your entire startup portfolio for €10 tomorrow, and you would likely find somebody who is willing to acquire it from you at such a low price. But in general, and on average, it takes more time and effort to carefully select your individual investments, then to support and nurture them through different growth stages, and to eventually sell them again (or acquire them). And so, 10–15 years is a good ballpark figure for the average duration of a CVC portfolio, also corresponding with the average overall investment period of most private and independent VC funds in the market.

5 Team size

A corporation that is about to embark on the journey to launch and maintain a corporate venture capital programme will have questions regarding the operational budget as well as team size and structure to be allocated to maintain and manage the CVC fund.

We are not aware of a golden rule on how to build such structures. Our recommendation is to follow the thinking (and constraints) of private VCs. Private VCs, on average, charge anywhere between 1–2 per cent management fees based on the invested capital or based on the total capital committed to their fund. This means that smaller funds will have a lower budget and will have to be run by smaller teams, while larger funds will have bigger budgets and can afford larger teams.

The required compensation of your team depends on the seniority of the people involved, but also on the background of your team members. Experienced VC managers tend to be more expensive than internally recruited managers from your corporation. In general, the personnel structure (in terms of work experience) in many VC and private equity funds is a reverse pyramid – you tend to have more senior people at the top than junior people supporting them. Other funds, however, are built with structures resembling more normal pyramids with few senior and more junior people.

Ongoing support of the CV programme

A CV activity, like any other corporate activity, is expected to contribute to the corporate's strategy and (financial) results. And it has to make sense on a standalone basis, too.

Like any other corporate activity, the CV structure, activities and team will be reviewed and scrutinized from time to time. Budgets, staffing and setup may change depending on how successfully the CV performs from the perspective of the parent company. It goes without saying that everything may also change depending on how the parent company is doing in other parts of its business, and how the rest of the world is doing, including but not limited to competitors.

Investment focus – What is your main investment focus? 08

Remember the time when you were a child and wanted a lot of attention, but at the same moment you did not want to be controlled by your parents? Well, the problem of ambivalence is a common burden that corporates face today as well. And this is where the dilemma of business advancements comes into play. Do you want to invest in a venture that supports your current core business, or would you rather look far into the future to pick up the next trends with a first-mover advantage? That's what this section is all about: outlining the different options you will face.

CV investment orientation: Core versus non-core

Corporates ask themselves more and more how to effectively run and perpetually further develop or even reinvent their business. On the one hand, a corporate insists on preserving know-how and assets it has built up and developed over many years. On the other hand, there is a growing urge to explore new and future territories in terms of latest technologies, markets, products, services and business models in order to keep a finger on the pulse.

The phenomenon of balancing both exploitation and exploration is a matter of organizational ambidexterity. Hitting this balance is not a trivial matter, as your company must demonstrate the ability to manage both incremental and discontinuous change concurrently to address the growth imperative. The most common approach is the 'onion' approach (Figure 9.4 in Chapter 9), often associated with the Growth Horizon model. Corporates go first to the area of maintaining and strengthening their core business. This allows them to sufficiently address the use of their existing products and services and ensure continuous improvement and the long-term viability of the company.

In a second step, at a later stage in the process, companies can then tackle adjacent and new areas of expansion. This allows them to focus sufficiently on exploring new capabilities to develop innovative solutions that ensure future viability again. And, finally, they penetrate into completely unknown business areas to really create new fields of activity and get to the top of the game. We can understand this a bit better by applying the CV Cockpit to your CV setting (see the next chapter).

CV Cockpit I 09

CV Cockpit overview

The CV Cockpit is by far the most important part of the handbook for you to put into action because this is where your hands get dirty. The CV Cockpit aims to help you keep track of the CV programme performance of your venture portfolio. It supports you in your decision-making, venture monitoring and value-adding activities. The CV cockpit consists of four parts – one cockpit for each CV Navigator phase. Each cockpit part then contains several tool elements. Cockpit III and IV for the Investing and Harvesting phases, are somewhat special, as they cover several levels.

First, there is the individual venture investing level where you regularly enter information to measure progress towards your set objectives as well as the enablers to achieve them. Second, there is the venture portfolio consolidation level, where your venture data is consolidated into a single source of truth to make it comparable and aligned. The progress of the portfolio as a whole can thus be made transparent.

Finally, there is the visual dashboard layer, where portfolio and venture KPIs and performance are provided to stakeholders as a visual representation.

Your CV Navigator toolbox can be accessed here: https://www.stgaller-navigator.com/

CV Cockpit I in general

The basis of your CV Cockpit I tool lies in the specs. The so-called specs are details about the individual elements of the CV Navigator that you enter into an interface – a Google spreadsheet (see Figure 9.1). Specs have several advantages for your CV journey. First and foremost, they help you make relevant decisions by bringing all the required information together in one tool, giving you a good overview of the most important details needed to run a CV programme. They show the available options and clarify interrelationships and dependencies within a phase and beyond.

Figure 9.1 CV Cockpit specifications

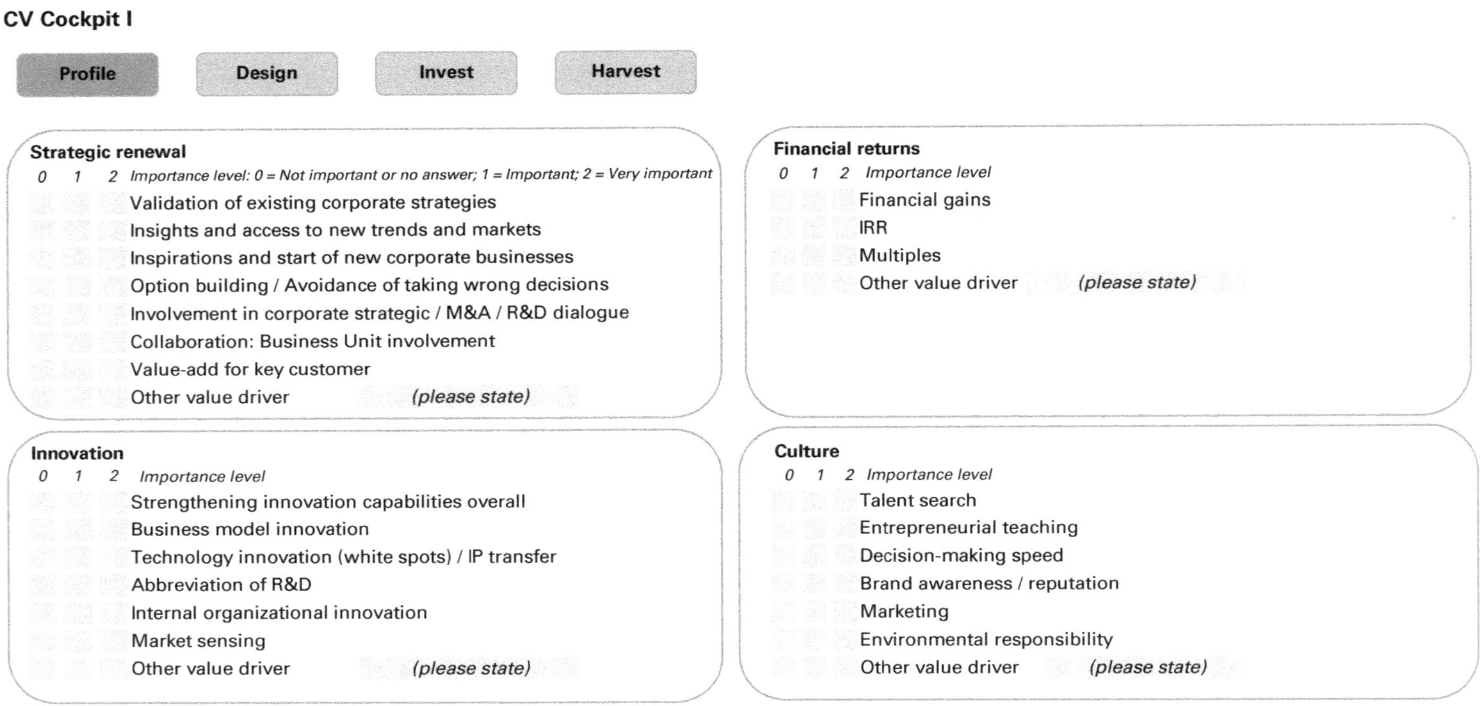

Budget						
Budget amount	*(please state)*			*10k; 100k; 500k, etc.*		
Budget allocation	Balance-sheet	Fund				
Budget time horizon	3–5 yrs	5–10 yrs	Other	All profiles but financial returns are long-term oriented to show expected results		
Budget availability	Lump sum	Annual budget	Other			
Stakeholder						
Involved parties in corporate	CEO	CFO	CIO	Head strategy	Head R&D	
	CTO	COO	CMO	Head corporate dev.	Other	*(please state)*
Number C-level stakeholders involved	*(please state)*			*1;2;>2*		
Main sponsor in corporate	*(please state)*			*CEO; CFO; etc.*		
Other investors	*(please state)*			*Co-investing company*		
Business advancement						
CV investment orientation	Core business	Adjacent business	New business	Other	*(please state)*	

So, what does that look like in Cockpit I? To start with, information is queried on the importance level of the CV programme objectives pursued. Three levels of importance are possible: 0 means that a particular objective is either not known and therefore not important, or simply not important; 1 means that the objective is relevant in some way and has some level of importance; and 2 has clear significance as it is considered very important. In line with this, the objectives of the CV programme, which are consistent with the mandate, are defined, to be communicated and thus made clearly evident for all stakeholders. Accordingly, in Phase I, deciding on the direction of the CV profile is the first action to be taken.

As a next step, budget details must be filled in, starting with the amount, the budget allocation, the time horizon and availability. Then, the stakeholders to be involved must be named, in particular stakeholders from the company's management and, if applicable, a potential sponsor. We have made it easy for you by just requiring you to tick the box and in the case that a certain role is missing, an option to add further roles. Finally, you will be asked in which direction the CV investments are to go, i.e., into the core business, into adjacent business areas, or into new business areas, if not a mixture of these.

In summary, the spec sheet provides a very clear and structured overview of the Phase I elements of a CV programme and, in particular, the preferred CV objectives and orientation targeted. Now you're probably thinking that this is way too easy and maybe even unnecessary, but don't underestimate the power of a CV programme that is set and communicated. Working on a CV programme without having talked about what it is actually about and where it is going to lead is already doomed to failure, and what we want is for it to have an effective impact on business innovation and growth in your company.

Tool A: Know your profile

The first tool of the CV Cockpit I is Know your profile. It holds the intention to gain clarity about your CV profile, the core direction you are taking with your CV programme. The tool highlights a clear trend of objective focus you are following, translating it into a visual illustration. Now, how does that work exactly?

The first step is to find a set of possible objectives for each of the four profile types (see Figure 9.2). These intend to give you food for thought about the extent to which you pursue certain objectives. The objectives

Figure 9.2 CV profile types

provided are not exhaustive, but cover the most important elements of CV programme goals.

Once you have a better understanding of your objectives, your second step will be to use the spider to visually define and outline the focus of your CV profile, marking the importance level.

The spider web (Figure 9.3a and 9.3b) is a fairly simple but powerful tool for working out trends. It consists of a central point, the zero line, followed by a first circle, and then an outer circle. Each circle symbolizes the degree of importance, so you can easily mark the importance of each of the profile directions for your own CV programme. No circle shows no importance (0 points), the inner circle shows some importance (1 point) and the outer circle shows considerable importance (2 points).

This means that there are four possible outcomes, as one of the four profile types must have significant meaning.

It seems like a fairly simple exercise, but you'll be amazed at how profound and effective the result is for your CV programme. Knowing exactly what your profile type is, while keeping the most important goals in mind, will make your life much easier throughout the life of the CV programme. But be careful! You must always refer back to your CV profile and keep it in mind in case you need to make a decision.

Once you realize that you don't really fit your profile type, it's time to rethink the goal of your entire CV programme and the structures, processes, and dynamics involved. It is possible to change the profile type, but not without making corresponding adjustments to all other elements involved. Similar to baking, you cannot change the amount of one ingredient without adjusting the other ingredients if you want to achieve the same result.

Tool B: The onion

Once you have clarified the type of CV profile and available budget, your next big task is to decide which investment strategy to pursue. This task sounds trivial, but we can tell you that it is important to get this right.

You need to ask whether you want to invest close to the parent company or more distantly in adjacent or new businesses. Do you want to innovate from the inside-out or the outside-in? Or both?

Figure 9.3a CV profile objectives and prioritization

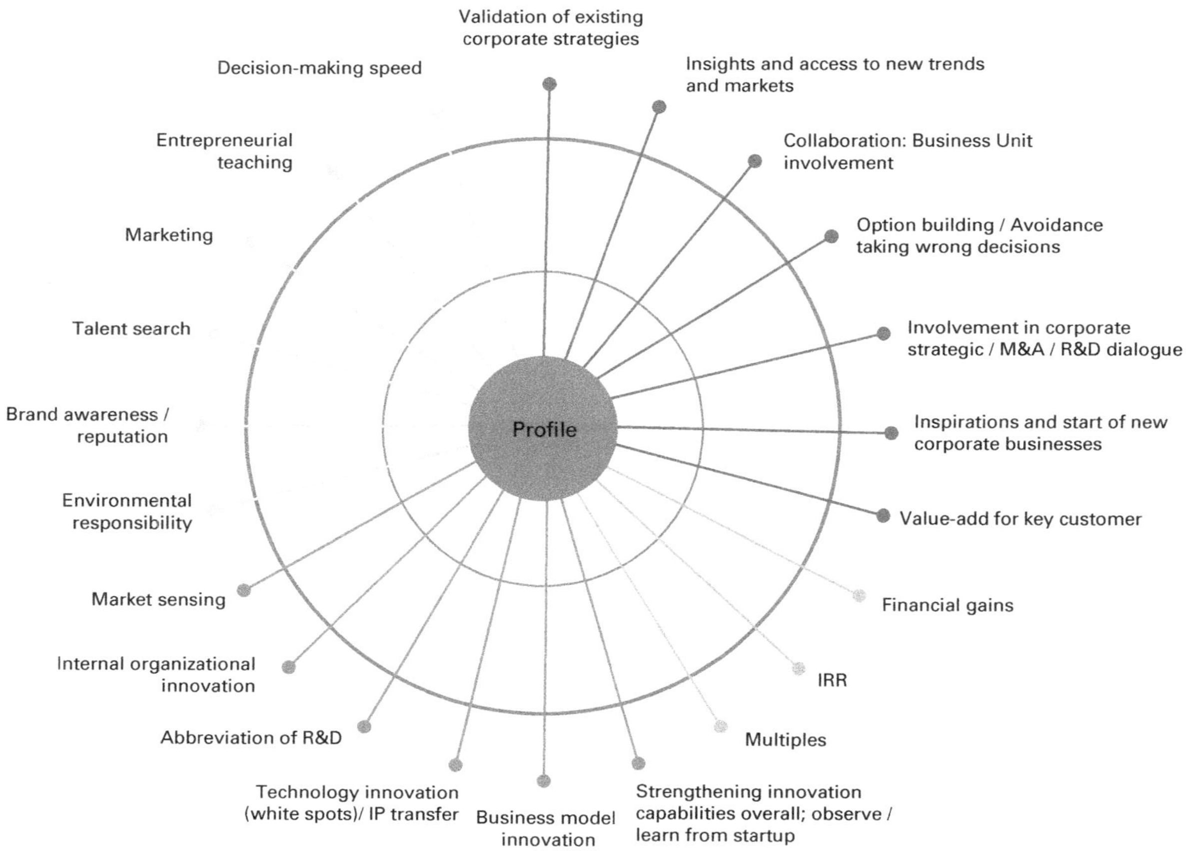

Figure 9.3b CV profile objectives and prioritization example

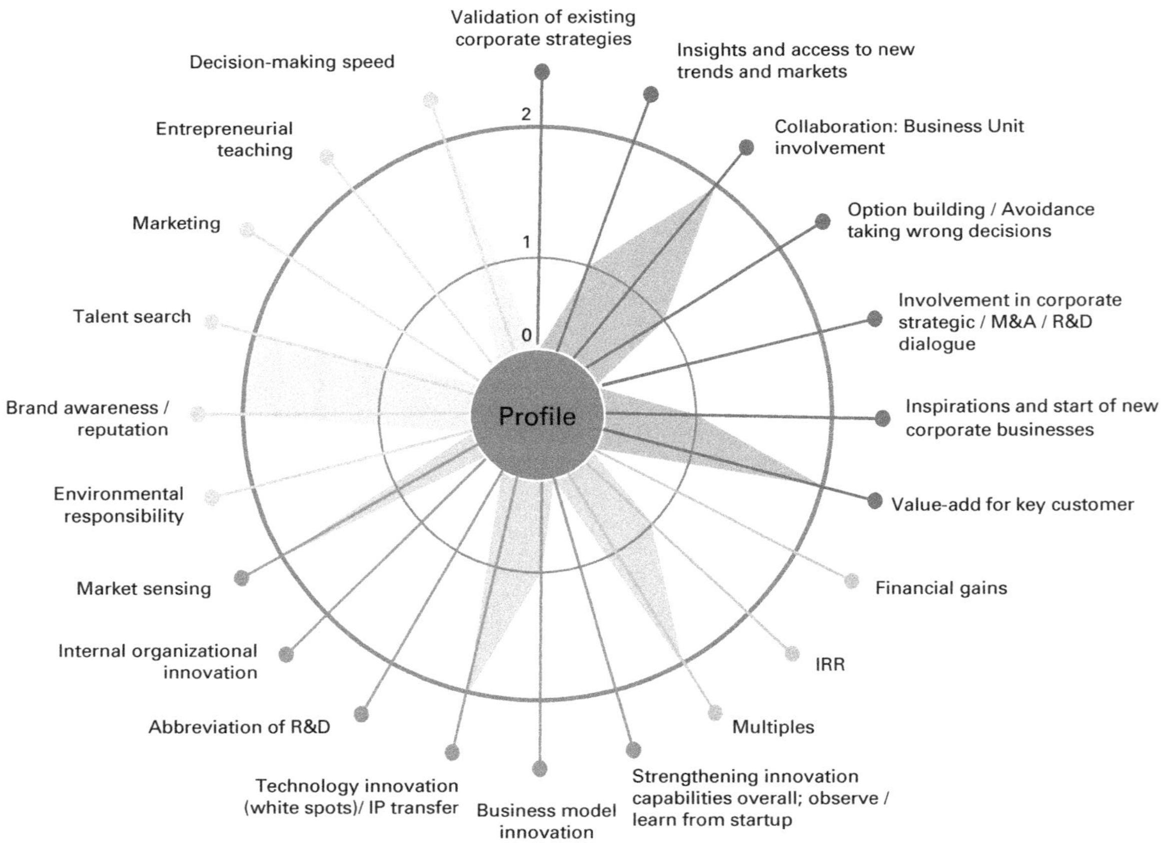

NOTE 0 = Not important or no answer; 1 = Somehow important; 2 = Important

The onion tool provides you with support for the decisions you need to make. Now you might ask yourself why the tool is called the onion. Well, simply because there are different investment layers, namely three in which you will find yourself operating. These are:

- Core business areas
- Adjacent business areas
- New business areas.

Investments in core business areas are very closely related to the parent company with an inside-out innovation approach. In other words, this means that the target ventures will be able to enhance corporate learning because tacit, specific experiential knowledge is applied in a similar, related context. Corporate business is likely to increase the efficiency of strategy execution and ultimately lead to better business performance. Investments in adjacent business areas have a medium distance from the parent company in inside-out and outside-in innovation, while investments in new business areas have the largest distance from the parent company in outside-in innovation. The investments with a greater distance have the advantage of providing the company with new knowledge, market access and growth.

So, both investing in core business areas and investing in new business areas seem to be beneficial and so is the middle ground – companies operating in adjacent business areas. There is no right or wrong on which approach

Figure 9.4 The onion approach

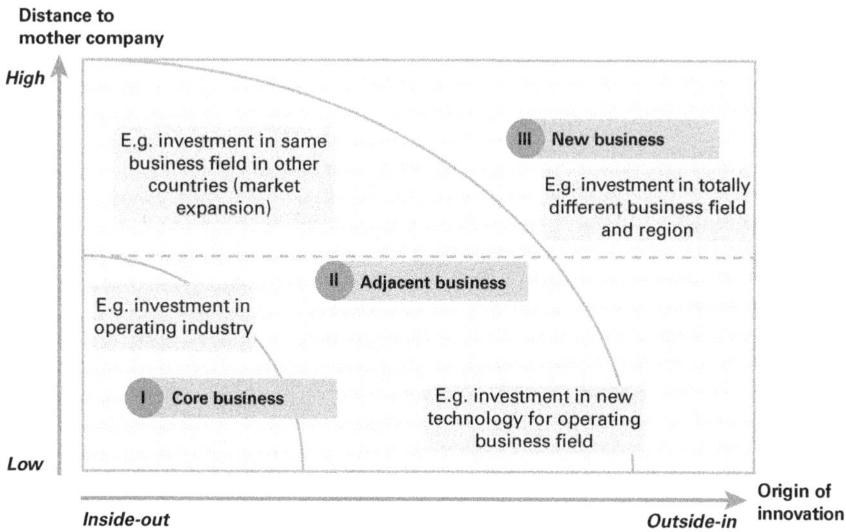

to take, but what you should consider is the level of risk and the timeframe in which you expect to see results. The risk increases the further away the investment is from the core business, due to the lack of expertise of the business unit and the increasing uncertainty of the investment environment – the further the innovation originates outside the company, the greater the potential for loss of control.

Short-term results can be expected when there are investments closer to the core business as spill-over effects and synergies are easier and faster to generate. In contrast, the returns of venture investments further out from the corporate core will be longer in coming. And again, you need to check the profile and budget chosen. What have you decided to aim for, which objectives to follow and what results to expect and when?!

Along the chosen CV profile direction, it is necessary to decide how the business should be developed, what level of risk is acceptable accordingly and which timeline to follow. This is where the double S-curve comes into play again, as described in the Deep-dive in Chapter 4. Always remember that a successful company must manage innovation two-handed, securing the traditional core business and innovating to stay ahead of the curve. CV investments should accordingly be used as a supporting vehicle.

Summary – CV mandate 10

You have now made it this far. You have completed the first section of the CV Navigator. Congratulations! What have you learnt? What insights have you gained? Which ones are you still missing? How does all the information fit together and how can it all be coherent? Fair enough. We will summarize the section for you here and give you a preview of what to expect next.

First and foremost, you have worked out your CV mandate. You have been guided on how to get a clear profile direction by defining your CV profile, following your set objectives and their prioritization. The *Know your profile* tool sets the game. Then, you have explored stakeholders involved in the CV programme and you are aware that it is important to get everyone on the same boat – on the same course. Mutual understanding, trust and good cooperation are obligatory factors. In addition, you have learnt that you have to think about your CV sponsorship – how to achieve high reputation and credibility. Past experience has shown that a top-down approach is most promising. In the event that this is not possible, don't worry about it. Just make sure that your CV programme has enough positive recognition and trustworthiness.

What comes with the stakeholders and sponsorship is the budget. We have introduced you to the conceptual thinking that you need to master in order to determine the funding volume that fits your investment plans. We have also shown the interdependencies between your investment focus, how long your corporation has to commit capital and how your CV mandate is eventually translated into a portfolio.

The budget discussion is the make or break for your CVC unit. It should be taken with considerable care. Keep in mind that top managers in corporations are (often) less familiar with the venture capital and startup ecosystem. Take the time to educate them on corporate VC programmes. Here are some elements to consider:

1 The investments related to a corporate VC programme are actually investments, not expenses. In other words, if we dedicate €100 million to the programme, this does not mean that we spend €100 million, but that we invest, i.e., we get shares in return. The money we actually spend is the money that we put on the table for the personnel of the CV unit and costs related to their activities.

2 Also financially speaking, it can be said that if the CV programme is managed successfully and breaks even, not to mention if it provides tangible returns on investment to the corporation, then you have created a profitable R&D activity. Think about it: you add value to your organization and the products and services, and some of the investments are so successful that they do not only compensate for the losses, failures and bankruptcies in the portfolio but provide a bit of extra profit on top.

3 More activity in the startup space has spillover effects that go beyond what the investments will achieve. One example is the corporation being approached by more startups on a more regular basis. And often it is not even necessary for the company to invest, because it can also become a customer or partner of the startup (which provides indirect funding). Moreover, startup-related activities are very popular with many other employees of the corporation. They are often seen as signs of entrepreneurial openness, risk appetite and out-of-the-box-thinking – they resonate well with existing employees. So, there are two sides to the CV programme: the impact of actual investments, and the impact of non-investment related but startup-related effects on the corporation.

In this context, with the Know your profile tool, you can map out your CV programme orientation. With the onion tool you can find out what options there are for your business. When you apply the tools, you have a clear picture of what your programme looks like or should look like in terms of simulating different scenarios of your CV investment orientation. But that is not all; let's look at the nitty-gritty aspects of the CV rationales.

We've given you some pointers that the right leadership and culture must be in place to make things work. After all, CV is a people business – the people involved set the pace of the process and therefore its progress. And do not forget that this will not be possible if the stakeholders involved are not supported by an appropriate setup with assisting structures and governance. The required structure and governance includes, but is not limited to, org-design, incentive systems and appropriate integration, team and capabilities, communication systems and tools as well as a good ecosystem. But also, processes and methods, systems and tools must be selected and established. All these elements are to be seen as interrelated and interdependent and only contribute to performance when used in unity. Further detail is given in Section 2, the Designing phase.

What does that mean to you now? What is coming up next? We will make you familiar with how to design your CV programme based on the CV mandate established in the Profiling phase and how to develop a well-thought-out rollout plan to meet set objectives and expectations. If that's all set, you have made it from base camp to first camp of your own CV programme Mount Everest. How this could look is outlined in the best practice of AXA shown in the case insights (Figure 10.1).

Case insights: AXA

Figure 10.1 Case insights: AXA

Alexander Behr
Principal of AXA Venture Capital & Strategic Partnerships

Established: First CV activities in 2015 as Axa Strategic Ventures

Parent: Axa

HQ: Paris

Industry: Insurance

(1) Profiling

Axa overall:
- 3 funds + Fund of Funds
  - ASV Diversified
  - AVP Early Stage II
  - AVP Capital II (Growth fund)
  - Fund of Funds (FoF)
- Axa Germany Investments
- ~35 employees
- ~85 investments
- Investment focus: diverse
- ~11 exits

(2) Designing

Mandate (Axa Germany)
- Strategic mandate to bring innovation into the corporate / strategic thesis-driven from corporate strategy

Budget:
- Flexible (balance sheet investments)

Business advancements
- Beyond core business

Structure & Governance
- Organizational: Balance sheet
- Legal: Subsidiary of Axa Germany
- Reporting: CEO office Axa Germany + Business Unit sponsor

Team:
- 4 employees

(3) Investing

(4) Harvesting

Portfolio size:
- ~2–3 investments/yr

Investment focus: Seed and early stage (1-stage-gate)

Ticket size: At first explorative; late stage investments (bigger tickets) – 0.5 – 5m

Collaboration
- Strong collaboration with BUs, already at the venture selection (often sponsor)
- With parent: AXA's distribution networks, client base, know-how / global footprint

Exits:
- ~4

SOURCE Corporate insights via interview and website; Crunchbase

Reference

AXA (2022) Interview with Alexander Behr, Principal of AXA DE Venture Capital and Strategic Partnerships. AXA operates highly dynamically and changes in AXA's CVC strategy between interview date and publication are possible.

PART TWO
Designing

By designing your individual CV elements, you set the framework for the implementation of your CV programme. You will define the structure and governance, your team, communication-related aspects and how to address different players in your ecosystem, as well as your portfolio approach. In the end, your CV blueprint is set and ready to go.

Structure and governance

11

Organizational structure

The structure and governance of your CV programme is crucial to the performance of the CV team and the impact it has on the business. If your fund invests in close alignment with your company's innovation goals, you will tick the strategic box, but you may frustrate the CV team and maintain too narrow a focus. If you give the fund too much autonomy, team motivation and performance may improve, but alignment with technology and innovation issues of strategic importance to your company may be less than you would like. So how is this resolved in the real world?

Through our research and work with CV teams active and investing in the market today, we have identified three popular and commonly used organizational archetypes for Corporate Venturing:

1 Integrated, dependent CV
2 Independent but integrated CV
3 Independent CV.

And yes, of course there are other variations and hybrids of these three models. But let's understand the archetypes first, and then you can put together the ingredients you think are most appropriate to 'cook' the best structure for your organization. In what follows, we will first describe each of the three archetypes of organizational CV models and explain their characteristics. And then, towards the end of this section, we will give you some examples of real CV structures that are active in the market today.

(1) The integrated, dependent CV

In this structure, the CV team is essentially a division or part of a division of the company. All processes and all investment-related decisions are managed and controlled by the corporation. The CV team often reports either to the finance, strategy, product or R&D group of the company, or directly to the CEO.

Control

Operationally, a single manager, a group of managers or an Investment Committee of internal decision-makers (and possibly external experts) makes all investment decisions regarding new investments, follow-on investments, divestments, and so on. Other managers or teams from internal business service groups, e.g., audit, compliance, treasury, human resources, will support the CV team and oversee accounting, audit, tax, compliance, treasury and human resources issues. The company will track standard financial, strategic impact and other performance-related metrics.

Funding

CV programmes in this structure are typically funded from the balance sheet, either on a deal-by-deal/as-needed basis, or with a dedicated annual budget derived from the company's global budget. Often, the corporation will set an overall investment budget for a certain period of time (e.g., €50 million over five years), but reserve the right to update and change the annual operating budget as needed (e.g., to require a hiring freeze, reduced activities such as business travel or conference attendance due to cost reduction programmes affecting all or certain departments of the corporation).

Philosophy

The integrated, dependent CV model allows the corporation to control and monitor all CV activities, without exception and very closely. However, the CV unit can develop into a permanent structure or department. But it can also be easily dismantled or completely changed according to the company's preferences and needs. The staff is usually composed of managers and employees of the company, but with limited visibility to the outside world. Often only the head of the team is featured on websites or in CV-related press statements. Remuneration is also comparable to other teams in the finance group, i.e., the whole CV programme has very few venture capital characteristics.

Challenges

One of the biggest challenges of this model is that the alignment between the CV team and other teams (e.g., R&D) is sometimes too narrow and difficult to achieve. What happens is that the CV team gets a very specific brief and develops a very sharp investment focus (which looks very thoughtful and useful). But by chance, this very specific brief excludes too many potentially disruptive and relevant innovations. How does this happen? Consider someone who signs up to a dating site, but enters very specific preferences (e.g., only this particular hair colour, lives in a specific city and not a neighbouring one, or works in this profession). More often than not, such a person ends up frustrated because (1) there are very few candidates who meet all the criteria, and (2) they still meet the wrong candidates (i.e., no chemistry) and, even worse, they may miss out on candidates who may not meet all their requirements but would actually be much better partners for other reasons and characteristics they possess.

In addition, the CV team is likely to be fed up with the perceived dictatorship of the R&D team, because their investments have to follow the company's lead (i.e., people with an internal focus) and are not based on what the CV team finds exciting and new in the market (i.e., based on their external focus).

Another major challenge is the presumed expertise (and inadequate recognition of biases and shortcomings) of decision makers. This structure gives the company full control over CV activities. But does it make sense to control these activities so closely? How well equipped are company managers in terms of expertise and experience to make CV-related decisions? As one CV professional put it:

> Just because you have watched Shark Tank twice and happen to be the super-smart CFO of a large global organization does not automatically make you a good decision-maker/member of the investment committee for CV activities.

The implication, of course, is that an experienced venture capital professional who has worked on private or corporate venture capital teams is likely to make better decisions. Another CV veteran added:

> Ask yourself this: Would you develop your company's marketing campaigns yourself, or are there people better qualified to do that? And would you question all their decisions? A professional venture capitalist is more used to making risky investment decisions and is likely to have a more long-term view (as opposed to the short-term view of your own top management). Last but not least, the professional will be less biased by your organisation's history or past failures.

(2) The independent but integrated CV

This organizational model, and its associated governance, is somewhat of a halfway ground between a fully integrated model and a fully independent model.

Control

CV teams operating under this structure and governance still have a strong systematic alignment of their activities with the interests of the firm. In terms of investment focus, target company maturity, target geography, etc., they follow the preferences and needs of the parent company. However, such teams also tend to enjoy a somewhat greater degree of freedom to think, make (certain) decisions and operate without having to coordinate every single decision with the parent company. In most cases, investment decisions are still taken by an Investment Committee, the only difference being that one or more senior managers from the CV team may also be active members of this Investment Committee.

Funding

Funding of activities under this structure is often similar to an 'integrated and dependent' CV, i.e., no separate fund entity, but investments are made off-balance sheet. The investment budget is usually approved for a number of years or a series of investments, but the operating budgets are still controlled and audited by the parent company. To the outside world, however, such teams often act as if they were operating under a separate fund entity. And, depending on how it is set up, the CV team will often have more influence on decision making, which also significantly strengthens its position vis-à-vis founders and other investors (and makes their lives a lot easier).

Philosophy

This structure is a typical 'middle ground' approach. The sponsors of the CV programme recognize that the integrated and dependent structure is too controlled, but do not (yet) believe that greater degrees of freedom will make the CV team more successful in the long run. This structure can also be described as a compromise between an independent CV and an integrated and dependent CV.

Challenges

This structure can work well for the company and the CV team, especially if top management strikes a healthy balance between a high degree of freedom for the CV team on the one hand, and a good alignment with the company's interests as reflected in the teams' investment activities on the other. However, this 'in-between' structure also has the potential for frustration. As one CV professional said during one of our interviews:

> You know, the company is often a bit unbalanced, one might say, when it comes to the CV activities of my team. The basic mission is clear and undisputed: Bring innovation to our company and try not to lose money. But if you do, that's ok because internal innovation also loses money on a regular basis. But how this translates into reality is weird. On the one hand, top management wants us to be independent, so that we are not limited by internal biases or personal agendas, e.g., when people fear that a certain startup could replace them and their team. Plus, they believe that we understand startups better than most of their other corporate managers in the organization, which is why they hired us in the first place. On the other hand, however, they want (and feel they need to) to control us. Because we are spending shareholders' money, and so it is their duty to supervise this. And because they feel that while other managers in the organization have no clue about startups, and we were hired as experienced startup investors/builders, they as top managers must also have a say in our investment decisions.

This statement also explains why, for outsiders, a good indicator of whether or not this approach is working could be the frequency of changes in the CV team's personnel and/or investment strategy.

(3) The independent CV

The independent CV structure is somewhat contradictory in nature, one might argue. It is initiated and funded by a company but set up as a team with a very high degree of freedom to operate, which is different from most other corporate programmes and difficult to explain to the shareholders (or owners) of the company. Shareholders may ask, 'How can you use our money to fund an activity that you do not fully control?' Keep in mind that top management has a fiduciary duty to shareholders; managers cannot simply spend the money as they see fit, but they must be able to explain and justify to shareholders how the investment will help to advance the company's agenda and success.

Control

Under this structure and governance, CV teams operate with arguably the highest degree of autonomy. The independent CV is usually a separate legal entity but is still fully (or at least partially) owned by the company. It is also possible for the CV fund management team to set up a separate entity, which is then contracted by the company to manage the fund. Under such a structure, the fund's capital would be pooled in a separate entity. And sometimes that entity is registered with the financial regulators as a 'real' venture capital fund, open to investment from other investors. So, as an example, you would have:

- ABC Fund Management Ltd, in which the fund managers are shareholders
- XYZ Fund Ltd, under which the capital of the fund is pooled
- The company as an investor in XYZ Fund Ltd and a paying client of ABC Fund Management Ltd.

Even with this structure, the strategic interests of the company will still play an important role. If the top management of the company does not see a strategic angle to justify the investment in the fund, then it will pull back from the investment. And then the whole structure can fall apart, so it is in the CV team's interest to consider the strategic interests of the company.

Moreover, if management is concerned about investing a lot of money and giving the fund management team a free hand at the same time (think of the moral hazard or principal agent problems in such structures), they may also require individual fund managers to invest money from their own pockets ('skin in the game') to strengthen the alignment between the company and the fund managers.

Funding

Activities under this structure are in most cases still funded by the company that initiated the CV programme in the first place. However, as described above, funding under this structure can be more formalized, i.e., the fund can be registered as a fund and the company can invest like a regular fund investor ('limited partner'), with limited to no decision-making rights, but investment obligations and certain rights to the proceeds of investment activities.

As explained above, the fund management team may also decide at some point to try to persuade other external investors to invest in the fund. But as more outside investors join the fund, the fund may lose its strategic focus from the perspective of the company. And then the company will become a less reliable investor and supporter of the fund, which the fund management will want to avoid.

Philosophy

Companies that adopt this structure have, on average, several years of experience with CV programmes.

- They believe that the success of a CV programme is not positively correlated with how much control the company can exert over the activities of the fund. In fact, they understand that greater degrees of freedom for the CV team increase the team's motivation and are likely to bring more complementary innovations and technologies to the company.
- They also understand that a more independent structure does not deprive them of any 'insider rights' they believe they would have under a fully controlled structure, because there are no insider rights. Neither in a fully controlled structure nor in an independent structure can the corporation take secrets from the startups in which it invests.
- Last but not least, management may also understand that this structure does not deprive them of all rights. Their influence in this model is simply more subtle. Just like other institutional venture capital investors, the company can decide which fund it wants to invest in (based on which fund and which investment strategy is most aligned with the company's strategy). And by removing the safety net for the CV team (whose members have been acting as employees, i.e., getting paid no matter what the fund does for the company), they will increase both the upside and downside risk for individual team members. And this is likely to lead to more prudent investment management and a high motivation to make the fund a success, both strategically and financially. The team will quickly understand that this fund, which comes with a high degree of autonomy, may be their first, but potentially their last, independent venture fund if it is not successful.

Challenges

There are several challenges associated with this model:

- The company has to accept a lower level of control (compared to the other two setups), but should understand that this can lead to more diverse inputs into the innovation strategy and to a higher motivation of the CV team.
- The company needs to understand that 'control' is a term used for internal processes. Whatever your internal scientists and engineers develop, you could (and probably should) control. But often this only leads to incremental improvements in products and services. But when you work with external innovators, you want disruptive innovation. And then you should give your CV managers more freedom to innovate, because they will need to find innovative ways to make the David and Goliath concept work. Also, stay away from micromanaging your portfolio companies, as this is likely to alienate startups and defeat the purpose of the CV programme.
- Last but not least, the corporation has to realize that it still has influence and power. No one is suggesting that you should not condition your fund investment on a reasonable degree of alignment of the fund's investment strategy with your corporate innovation strategy. Also, insist that if managers are free to make decisions (and be incentivized to perform well), they should be required to invest in their own funds, just like their private venture capital counterparts!

Pick your poison!

Looking at the different models, you may be wondering which one is best suited to your case and situation. The answer is, as so often: it depends. It depends on your organization. Models 1 or 2 are probably more popular with companies that are just starting to run CV programmes. Model 3 is probably more popular with companies that have been running CV programmes for some time. You may also find it helpful to review the setup of your CV programme every 24 months and make adjustments if necessary.

Who uses what setup in the real world?

Let's look at some real-world examples of CV activities and how they are implemented and managed by different parent companies. Each of the following examples is similar to one of the three archetypes, but each group also has some individual characteristics (see Table 11.1).

Siemens Healthineers

Let's look first at the CV activities that are most dependent on and integrated with the parent company. Siemens Healthineers is a DAX listed medical technology company based in Germany.

You will quickly recognize a distinct characteristic of an integrated/dependent CV unit: its name does not correspond to its CV activities. Instead, these activities are conducted by a dedicated team within the Healthineers organization.

Siemens Healthineers was created as a spin-off of Siemens' traditional healthcare and medical technology business, formerly called Siemens Medical Solutions and later Siemens Healthcare. As Healthineers became more independent from the main Siemens business, the CV activities (in Medtech) were transferred to the Healthineers unit and the whole business was spun off and listed on the stock exchange in 2018.

Another feature of an independent/integrated CV team is the undisclosed and off-balance sheet investment budget of Healthineers and the composition of the investment team. When we spoke to the team, we learnt that they operate with a clear and strategic mandate, focusing on supporting the execution of the company strategy, e.g., via investment in new technologies and market segments. Therefore, CV is supporting in core business as well as in adjacent areas.

Financial returns are also an element of the strategic agenda of their CV programme, but financial return alone is not driving investment decisions. In general, the main intention of the CV activities is based on the (challenging) characteristics of the medical technology market. Siemens Healthineers is active in various sub-segments, including but not limited to imaging technologies, diagnostic technologies, radiation therapy, and advanced therapies. In each of these areas, technologies and processes are constantly evolving. And different teams (e.g., in various startups, in larger companies, but also in universities) are working on new solutions, approaches and ideas.

The risk associated with most, if not all, new developments is significant and the technical/engineering aspects are challenging (highest reliability, safety is required). The associated science and medicine are also complex (i.e., can the technology be used safely and effectively in patients?). And then there's the surrounding ecosystem of regulators, hospitals, practitioners, insurance companies, etc., which is also difficult to navigate.

Consequently, CV activities are recognized as an effective means to complement internal technology and business development efforts with external or open innovation. This can involve partnerships with external startups, aimed at advancing projects to a certain level of maturity. Such partnerships enrich the innovation process, bringing fresh perspectives and expertise to the table, and help driving forward both technological progress and business growth.

Swisscom Ventures

Let's go one step further and look at CV programmes that are (more) independent but still integrated, like the CV programme run by Swisscom and Swisscom Ventures.

Swisscom Ventures is the corporate venture capital arm of Swisscom AG, the leading telecommunications and IT provider in Switzerland. Swisscom Ventures is managed by the strategy department with the support of the CEO. Swisscom Ventures acts as a strategic investor on behalf of the parent company and proudly bears the name and corporate design of the parent company. The internal CV arm consists of more than 10 employees who are employed by the parent company, while they are in constant exchange with the business units via their venture partners.

However, Swisscom Ventures is much more 'visible' and 'outspoken' in the marketplace than its colleagues at Siemens Healthineers. For example, they have their own website where stakeholders can find information on the positioning of Swisscom Ventures ('Who we are', 'Our added value', etc.).

More importantly, visitors can find out about the team's investment strategy, which is quite interesting. Only 40 per cent of the portfolio will be dedicated to telecom and IT infrastructure startups, i.e., companies and technologies very close to Swisscom's own core areas. Another 40 per cent will be dedicated to artificial intelligence startups, and a further 20 per cent to cybersecurity companies (Swisscom Ventures 2022).

It is also very interesting to take a closer look at the portfolio of Swisscom Ventures. By flipping through the different portfolio categories, you can also follow the group's strategy development over time, i.e., the portfolio also contains companies classified as 'eHealth' or 'fintech', both of which are areas that are arguably outside the scope of telecom and IT infrastructure, artificial intelligence and cybersecurity (which are defined as the main investment focus).

Perhaps the most interesting structural feature, which puts a big exclamation point on Swisscom Ventures' (growing) independence from Swisscom, is the following: 'With over $650 million under management and advisory, two-thirds of which is funded by 20 institutional investors and one-third by Swisscom, we invest throughout the life cycle of high-potential startups' (Swisscom Ventures 2022). This funding structure implies a certain degree of independence of Swisscom Ventures from its parent company.

Bertelsmann Investments

Looking at Bertelsmann Investments, we see another CV unit that is still integrated, but has otherwise been given a relatively high degree of independence. The Bertelsmann Investments (BI) landing page clearly states that BI is the global venture capital arm of Bertelsmann, and that the BI team follows compliance standards set by the compliance team of the parent company. All of this confirms that the group is still 'integrated' into the Bertelsmann family of companies.

The team manages four distinct funds, each dedicated to investing in startups in a particular region: Bertelsmann Asia Investments (BAI), Bertelsmann India Investments (BII), Bertelsmann Brazil Investments (BBI) and BDMI (investing in the US and Europe). BI also makes fund-of-funds investments in Southeast Asia and Africa, as well as funds focused on new technologies. The group has invested more than €1 billion in over 250 innovative companies.

BI is funded from Bertelsmann's balance sheet, and organizationally the group reports to Bertelsmann's CEO, which is another indication of the integrated nature of the team. It is interesting to note that BI and each fund have the freedom to make investments completely independently, at least to a certain extent. This clearly signals independence.

BBVA

We have now looked at CV programmes that are wholly or partially parent-owned. At the other extreme are independent CV units (or perhaps we should call them VC units, as they are no longer directly controlled by the parent company). An example of such an arrangement (and how such an arrangement occurs) is the Spanish banking group BBVA and its former corporate venture capital arm (now independent venture capital firm) Propel Venture Partners.

BBVA used to run its CV activities through its own corporate venture capital team, BBVA Ventures, which was established in 2009. At the time, many banks were becoming increasingly concerned about the emergence of fast-growing and successful fintech startups and felt the need to establish a more systematic and continuous exchange and monitoring of the world of financial technology ('fintech') startups.

Indeed, the first BBVA Ventures fund worked well. However, according to BBVA staff, they sometimes faced challenges with startups that were reluctant to partner with corporate venture capital funds due to potential conflicts with the parent company. Based on this critical insight and learning, BBVA decided to take a bold step in 2016. They decided to close BBV Ventures, and then they took the existing portfolio of BBVA Ventures, plus the rest of the previously allocated $100 million, and added another $150 million in fresh capital. And then they transferred this $250 million block of assets to an entirely new VC structure called Propel Venture Partners, based in San Francisco and London.

In 2021, BBVA announced that it was renewing its support for Propel Venture Partners and decided to provide the VC with another $150 million in fresh capital, bringing the total investment to a whopping $400 million. Admittedly, it could be argued that a VC firm that has a cornerstone investor (i.e., a limited partner) that invests as much as BBVA in Propel Venture Partners is probably not completely independent of that limited partner. However, if you look at the Propel Venture Partners website and listen to the team, you will also agree that the independence of the fund is not a story, but reality. And let us not forget that Propel has successfully invested in blockbuster companies such as Coinbase, Neon and DocuSign, so something seems to be working for them.

CV organizational structure modes

Legal structure

The legal structure of a CV programme goes hand in hand with the chosen setup. There are two basic options: 'independent entity' and 'corporate entity'.

Table 11.1 CV unit setups

	Integrated (Business Unit alignment)	Independent but integrated	Independent
Positioning in the market	Integrated in parent company; corporate unit; department	Independent positioning but systematically aligned with parent company	Independent positioning and clearly independent from parent company
Strategic industry focus	100% aligned with parent; regularly updated through corporate business; horizon 1 and horizon 2	>50% aligned with parent; regularly updated through corporate business but with flexibility; horizon 1, 2 and 3	Generally aligned; otherwise completely independent; horizon 2 and 3
Team	Staffed with corporate personnel	Mix of corporate staff and external experts	Mostly external experts
Compensation/ incentives	Standard corporate compensation and incentives	Standard corporate schemes and optionally additional VC-like incentives	VC-like compensation and incentives
Investment Committee	Staffed by corporate management	Staffed by corporate management and optional external experts	Selected corporate management and mostly external experts
Restrictions/ specifications	Corporate bureaucracy; use of corporate processes, systems, regulations	Partly corporate bureaucracy if not independent system and processes	Independent system and processes; rather lean and agile
Examples	AXA; Siemens Healthineers; Straumann; Nestlé; Deutsche Bank	Swisscom Ventures; Bertelsmann Investments; Hitachi Ventures; Samsung Catalyst Fund; Shell Ventures	Intel Capital; GV; Sapphire Ventures; BBVA

Independent entity

You can choose to set up a CV programme as an independent entity, fully funded and owned by the company (or partially funded and owned if you can attract additional external investors to fund and co-own the programme). You can then give this entity tailored governance, as well as a unique identity and profile.

A standalone structure has many **advantages**, particularly from an investment and investor perspective. The structure feels more reliable to the CV team itself, but also arguably to partner startups – in other words, this structure is likely to be less exposed to mood swings on the part of the parent company. A separate entity is likely to be able to offer more appropriate economic incentives (such as carried interest payments) to CV team members, as it does not have to adhere to the company's incentive schemes, and therefore attract/retain better qualified personnel. Finally, although this structure requires the company to make a number of strategic, governance and administrative decisions before and during the launch of the initiative, the company will have fewer governance and administrative issues to deal with afterwards because the structure will manage and maintain itself.

The main ***disadvantages*** of a standalone entity are that the company has to set up and launch a structure with a team, a strategy, sufficient funding and a working legal structure and governance, so this means a lot of thinking and work for something that you will own, partially own or not own in the future.

In addition, the structure is indeed independent. Certainly, the partners running the fund will listen to and accommodate many of the preferences of the parent company, but they will also ensure that the company is broadly independent of the parent company, because they will not be able to raise funds from other investors if there is too much perceived dependence on the fund.

Corporate entity

If you decide to launch your CV programme as a corporate unit, you are essentially still positioning the team internally and externally as a 'dedicated group of specialists'. But you are also saying that the team will operate legally and otherwise like any other department or team within the company, without a separate legal structure, governance, etc. So, the whole set-up process will largely follow the set-up process for any other team you would create within your organization, except for the funding.

The *advantage* of this structure is that everything is extremely flexible for the company. The governance of the team is basically the adopted governance of the parent company. If necessary, everything can be changed at any time and with immediate effect, i.e., the team can be changed, the strategy, everything. And there is very little additional bureaucracy and cost, with no need for specific 'officers', no separate accounting or auditing, etc.

Capital can also be made available to this team with maximum flexibility. The company can make direct investments in specific target companies (as identified by the CV team) on a case-by-case basis, investing off-balance sheet. Or it can set up a Special Purpose Vehicle (SPV) that pools enough cash for a single deal, or perhaps even a series of deals. The company can also commit the funds on paper for a number of years, or for a single year (and then renew), or even commit to an evergreen fund, not withdrawing any funds for the foreseeable future.

The *disadvantage* is that this structure feels extremely unreliable, both to the CV team and potentially to external start-ups toying with the idea of accepting an investment from the CV team. The parent company has so much control over its CV unit (being a corporate entity) that there is limited trust given little independence of the CV unit from its parent.

In the market, large companies often start their CV activities with a non-separate unit, which then becomes a subsidiary and finally a separate and increasingly independent CV unit (see Figure 11.1).

Reporting line

What you may want to contemplate is who you put in charge of the CV programme on the corporate side. And the time horizon dedicated for the first wave of the CV programme.

What if you put your CEO/CFO in charge?

We have already mentioned the challenge of putting your top C-level executives in charge of the CV programme. We alluded to the fact that few top managers in a large corporation have significant experience and expertise in startup investment and innovation (the 'shark tank' training).

Figure 11.1 CV setup options and funding sources, based on 500 startups (2019)

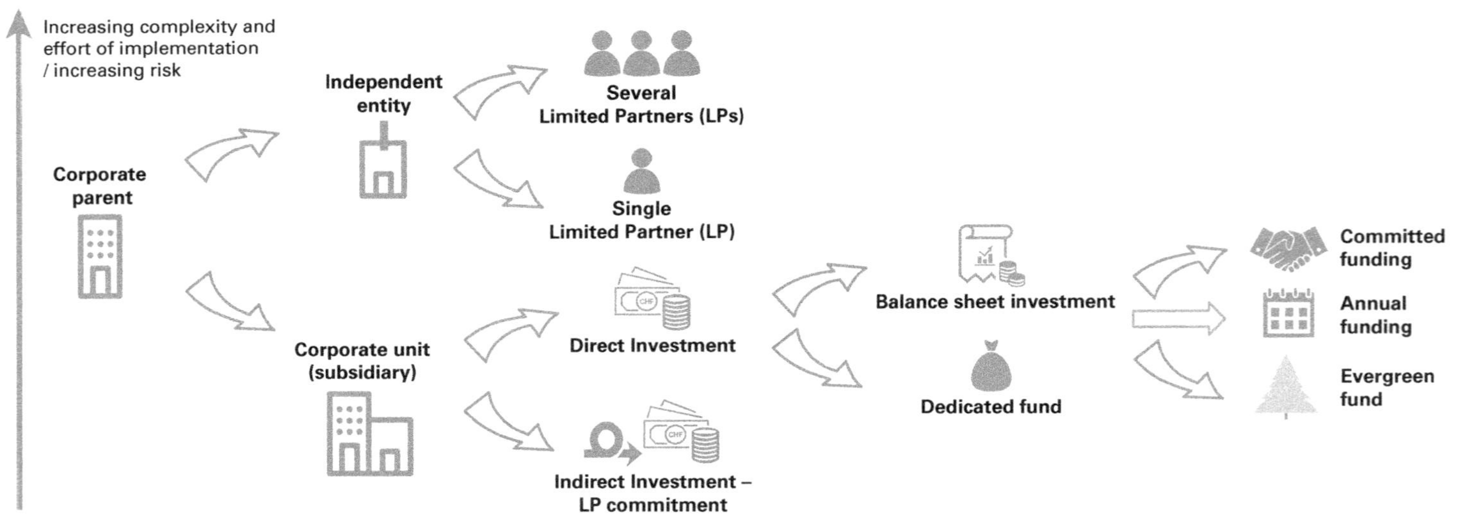

The other fundamental disconnect is based on their own agendas and different time horizons. C-level managers are expected to improve their company's performance from quarter to quarter, from year to year. They are less likely to think in terms of 5–10 years, because neither they nor their company's shareholders care about what may or may not happen in 5–10 years. They care about today and tomorrow. From their point of view, the financial performance of a CV programme slowly but certainly turns into a nightmare.

First, they have to build a team that costs a bit of money (especially if you decide to hire 1–2 senior VCs), but generates no direct revenues or profits, not now and not in the future. And no recurring revenues, just occasional one-off exit proceeds, if you are successful, from time to time.

Second, the programme that these somewhat expensive CV managers run is likely to generate failure stories before it generates success stories. Here's why: let's say you invest in a group of early-stage startups today. Everyone knows that some of them will fail, right? But the ones that fail will fail quickly, as soon as the funding runs out, and they do not get a follow-on round after 1.5 or 2 years. The successful startups, on the other hand, will take 3–5 and sometimes 10 years to mature and reach an exit. So, your fund is likely to generate two, three, maybe even four bankruptcies before the fund generates its first success story. Also, the early success stories are likely to be less exciting because the real money in venture capital is made after longer periods of time with really mature startups that go public or are sold to large corporations at significant prices. So, what may happen is that your C-level management may become frustrated with the (expensive) VC managers they have hired to run the CV programme, because the managers' investments may irritate other teams in the company. They also create failure after failure and keep talking about silver linings on the horizon.

This is why many first-generation VCs in larger corporations are fired after 3–4 years, and why most second-generation CV funds are smaller in size than the first generation.

What if you put your R&D team in charge?

If you put your CV programme under the R&D function of your organization, you are likely to see a much more playful and open-minded way of guiding and working with the CV function. But the risk is that the whole programme becomes less focused. It could be that the scientists and engineers in your organization become fascinated by startups and their innovations, and look at company after company, attend conference after conference, and have meeting after meeting, without a conclusive investment decision, or without sufficiently strong post-investment follow-up and collaboration (because they are already looking at the next hot thing).

As so often, the (arguably) best organizational reporting line may be a mix of finance and R&D. Ideally, you will have a mature finance leadership team and a mature R&D team, with the finance team resisting the temptation to confuse the CV team's financial performance with strategic effectiveness, and the R&D team resisting the temptation to use the CV team as a self-renewing 'buffet' of geeky new ideas, concepts and technologies to play with.

Investment Committee

Let's start this sub-section with some entertaining remarks from the CV partners we interviewed. One CV executive explained:

> Few decisions in the corporate world are made without committees. The beauty of a committee is that you can contribute to a committee or just sit in on a meeting and listen (or sleep). You can also use the opportunity to raise your profile by making astute comments that reflect your business acumen and intellectual skills. But you can also show aspects that your colleagues do not always see, such as your courage, your willingness to take risks, your humour, your expertise. Last but not least, the company and its top managers can make decisions without clear responsibility for the decision, because no single individual will make the decision. At the end of the day, of course, the chair of the meeting is responsible. Sometimes I think it is interesting how decision-makers are reluctant to take decisions...

The same is true in the Corporate Venturing world. The Investment Committee (IC) plays an important role in the CV deal process. It is the final decision-making body on whether to invest in a startup.

The composition of an IC can vary from a very lean committee with only a few executive-level representatives to a large number of executives from different backgrounds and departments. The structure will of course depend on you and your company. Sometimes the number of members reflects the value placed on an initiative. If a particular committee is building a reputation, membership can also become a status symbol. IC membership is a role that requires training, expertise and experience, and certain personalities may be more suited to IC membership than others. IC members can include a range of senior executives from the company, including but not limited to the CEO, CFO and CXO, as well as various senior VPs and VPs, business unit heads, and even representatives from supporting functions such as legal, compliance, and PR and communications.

Going back to the objectives of an IC, the committee aims to validate the strategic direction of the CV team and the CV team's investment activities. In addition, the approval of an investment proposal is also intended to improve and facilitate the ongoing collaboration between the target startup and the corporation. This means that the CV team will later point to the approval of the IC and explain to internal teams that the requirement to work with startup XYZ has been reviewed and confirmed by the IC (which includes key corporate decision-makers).

The roles of IC members often evolve throughout the CV programme cycle: At the very beginning of a CV programme, the IC helps to implement the CV mandate and to sharpen the profile, the design and even the operations. IC members are a target audience for this book.

The IC can be asked to approve the CV team's plan for approaching new investment targets (but such decisions may also be delegated to the CV team). In addition, the IC may be asked to approve term sheets or more expensive due diligence processes (i.e., the IC will preview upcoming investments). Finally, in most cases, the IC will have the final say on investment decisions, follow-on investment decisions or decisions to liquidate or sell an asset. Think of the IC as the governing body that has the final say on (potentially) all major decisions related to the CV team and its activities, unless you are working with an independent CV team that may have its own investment committee.

Typically, IC meetings are scheduled on a monthly basis and then confirmed or cancelled about a week before the date, depending on the CV team's submission of a tentative agenda for the IC meeting and possibly some pre-read materials for the IC members. In addition to these pre-scheduled meetings, IC members are often required to either make themselves available for ad hoc IC meetings to make decisions at short notice, if necessary, and/or have an agreed process for discussing issues and making decisions virtually, e.g., via email or video meetings.

One of our CV executives described the IC experience as follows:

> Experienced IC members understand that their role is not to challenge the presenting CV team members and business experts, but to have a conversation about the overall upside and downside risks of a proposed case.

Prior to an IC meeting, the CV team would share pre-read materials with the IC members so that they could familiarize themselves with the objectives to be presented and discussed. During the meeting, the CV team will walk the IC members through the case, often inviting either subject matter experts from the company to add comments or answer specific questions, or even inviting the founders to make a short presentation about the company so that the IC members can also get a sense of the nature and quality of the founding team.

The IC is often set up with a rather simple governance structure, for example, members are nominated, and decisions are taken by majority vote. Over time, the IC may decide to further refine the governance, assigning a smaller subset of IC members to approve/reject smaller investment decisions.

We also learnt from our interviewees that many ICs have defined certain standard elements of information to be presented to IC members whenever an investment case is submitted for approval. The rationale is that the standardized formats are easier to understand and help the IC to grasp the essence of a proposed deal faster. Such standard elements are often:

1. Key terms of the investment, i.e., ticket size (e.g., ticket taken by the corporation versus tickets taken by other investors), pre-money/post-money valuation, target shareholding on an undiluted and fully diluted basis, type of financing (e.g., equity, loan, convertible note), timing of next steps (e.g., negotiation, signing, closing), key milestones, if any, etc.
2. Key concepts of how the company can or may ultimately benefit from the investment and what steps the CVC team (in collaboration with other parts of the company) plans to take to support the target company and pave the way for realizing the potential strategic/financial benefits of the investment.
3. Key risks and concerns associated with the investments, e.g., commercial, financial, technical, legal/regulatory and ESG/impact. The CV team is required to make these risks transparent. Where possible, the CV team should also seek to quantify the potential impact of risks on the investment and, where appropriate, on the company. The CV team is encouraged to present ideas and concepts on how such risks could potentially be reduced or mitigated.

We have found that most CV teams, whether operating as dependent/integrated or independent/integrated units, have ICs that include high-level company executives and sometimes external advisors to help IC members understand certain complex aspects of proposed investments.

Independent CVs, which tend to operate more like private venture capital firms, typically rely on the expertise of the partners (i.e., the senior managers of the fund) and only occasionally invite experts, i.e., in areas where specific technological, regulatory or other expertise is required to make a sound investment decision.

Advisory Committee

The Advisory Committee (AC) complements the IC. AC members can come from within the company (e.g., a person from the engineering department) or be completely independent of the company (e.g., a serial startup entrepreneur who has successfully launched several companies with a particular profile and focus). They can be functional experts, scientists or industry experts, from the corporate world, from the startup world or even from another venture capital fund (e.g., a retired senior partner). The composition of the AC often varies over time, with both permanent members and members called in as required.

An AC is not mandatory, but they have become increasingly popular in more mature CV programmes, where IC members begin to understand that their own expertise is often limited and that it is valuable to hear other people's opinions on cases as well.

The main role of the AC is to evaluate investment proposals. However, it may also be consulted in the context of deal sourcing and portfolio management, and for specific topics or situations (for example, the company needs a general counsel with a strong understanding of the highly regulated insurance industry, and an AC member with some insurance background is able to recommend/introduce a couple of candidates).

The AC may not need to meet regularly. They may review deal-related materials compiled and shared by the CV team, participate in meetings/interviews with target companies, or meet for a conference call to brainstorm on key issues, strengths and concerns regarding a particular case.

Ideally, the work of the AC will result in several things – either an oral briefing to the IC and CVC team (i.e., the AC represented by a member summarizing its findings) and/or a written summary of the AC's findings (e.g., a popular format might be a risk matrix with commercial, financial, legal, technical and the increasingly relevant ESG/Impact as a 5th sector or separate item).

Regulations to consider

Corporate Venturing is carried out in a wide range of industries, from B2C retail to B2B industrials. However, many, if not most, industries in the marketplace adhere to certain legal standards imposed by sector-specific authorities. There are industries that are highly regulated, such as pharmaceuticals/life sciences or financial services (banking, insurance). And there are sectors with less regulation, such as data security in entertainment software. CV investments need to take into account the applicable industry regulations and standards. In the European banking industry, for example, you will have to deal with authorities such as BaFin (Bundesanstalt für Finanzdienstleistungsaufsicht) in Germany, FINMA (Financial Market Supervisory Authority) in Switzerland or CSSF (Commission de Surveillance du Secteur Financier) in Luxembourg. These institutions are like your parents when you were a child. If you did not follow your parents' rules, you were not allowed to play anymore or you were even punished. A similar principle applies to CV. If your company operates in (and invests in) a regulated sector, the CV programme should consider compliance with regulatory requirements and standards before, during and after the investment. Failure to do so could have negative consequences.

As with many risks, there is an upside to these regulatory risks: Regulatory procedures, test requirements and the underlying laws are constantly changing, sometimes quite dynamically. For example, look at the regulation of cannabis in different countries. Investing in a startup will allow the company to learn more about regulatory requirements (or update its existing understanding), get real-world insight into the money that needs to be spent to comply with certain regulations, meet experts who can help navigate regulatory processes, etc. And this is important. Remember, regulatory requirements act as a barrier to entry, so if your company is better at managing challenging regulatory environments than your competitors, this may enable you to outperform your competitors and potentially protect you from certain newcomers.

References

500 Startups (2019) Unlocking Corporate Venture Capital https://go.500.co/unlocking-corporate-venture-capital (archived at https://perma.cc/E6F9-S79L)

BBVA. Propel changes the financial industry's venture capital model, (2021) https://www.bbva.com/en/innovation/propel-changes-the-financial-industrys-venture-capital-model/ (archived at https://perma.cc/6AMZ-JC6Q)

Bertelsmann Investments (2023) https://www.bertelsmann-investments.com/ (archived at https://perma.cc/73YA-6HJA)

Flaticon.com (2023) Figure 11.1 has been designed using images from Flaticon.com (archived at https://perma.cc/UH4J-3GKA)

Shell (2023) https://www.shell.com/energy-and-innovation/new-energies/shell-ventures.html (archived at https://perma.cc/G8N9-3GGH)

Siemens Healthineers (2023) https://www.siemens-healthineers.com/healthcare-professionals (archived at https://perma.cc/AEG6-CRG6)

Swisscom Ventures (2022) https://ventures.swisscom.com/ (archived at https://perma.cc/J5VG-9N8X)

Your CV team 12

Once you have your CV structure and governance in place, the next step is the CV team itself – the people who make things happen. CV is a people business. People are at the heart of it. The communication skills of your CV team may ultimately be more important than most other skills, as we will see below. Only with the right communication systems and processes in place will the team be able to address the concerns and information needs of stakeholders such as the company's shareholders, employees from other departments in the company, the startups you have invested in or are looking to invest in, and other key partners, such as other investors or strategic allies. The size of the CV team goes hand in hand with the CV structure and governance you choose, as discussed earlier in this book. And, of course, the budget available will play an important role.

CV team structure

CV programmes are often led by a Head of Corporate Venture Capital (or Head of Startup Investments), or by a dual leadership team if the company prefers to separate deal sourcing and deal making from strategic collaboration and portfolio management. The Head(s) of Corporate Venture Capital is/are supported by Principals or (Senior) Investment Managers who focus their activities on coordinating and executing all transaction-related processes (sourcing, screening, due diligence, negotiation, term sheets, contracts and closing, portfolio management, exit and liquidation management). They will also oversee and manage the involvement of other corporate functions such as tax, accounting, legal, compliance, and external affairs and communications. Last but not least, the team will include associates and analysts, often complemented by a few interns. Their main role is to execute or support all activities coordinated by the Principals and Investment Managers. They will also have most of the direct interaction with the founders (as part of the pre-screening process) and will often prepare the essential bones of all transactions, e.g., due diligence reports, term sheets and cap tables.

The number of people in the investment team will also depend in part on the support the team receives from other teams in the business. For example, you could build a lean transaction team that focuses on deal execution only, while deal sourcing, pre-screening and even selection and portfolio work/strategic collaboration are handled by subject matter experts from the department that supports a particular investment.

Individual CV team members

Let's take a closer look at the CV team and the skill sets you may want to bring together by recruiting several team members. As part of our research, a senior corporate venture capitalist shared the following personal insight on recruitment with us:

> Whenever we recruit new people to our team, I focus on two things when talking to candidates:
>
> **(1) Are you a quick and unconventional thinker? In other words, can you quickly understand and reflect on a business concept?**
>
> Many people will tell you that technical knowledge is important. Well, I don't need you to understand the technology immediately. I need you to assume that the technology works, and if you and I don't understand it enough, fine, we'll find two experts to give us their opinion. But if the technology works, what does that mean for your customers and then for the deal? And what should be in the presentation that isn't in the presentation? A lot of people will question what's in the pitch deck, and that's fine. But what is not in the presentation? What other upside or downside risks should we consider? Should we look at the startup from different angles, i.e., founders, customers, investors and our corporate angle, and what do we see?
>
> **(2) Do you keep your cool under stress or when other people lose their nerve?**
>
> The reason is simple. Venture capital can often be stressful. Sometimes it will feel like a living experiment of Murphy's Law. But whatever happens, we cannot afford to lose our temper. We stay polite, friendly and professional with the founders, with other investors, but also within our team – not only because it leads to better ideas, discussions and so on, but also because that is the way I want to work. Not having toxic people around you will lead to a better and longer and happier life.

Let's take a look at the mix of profiles you would often find in a CV team.

Professional background: Traditionally, most members of a VC or corporate VC team have a financial, technical or scientific background. Or, they may have an entrepreneurial career, or a combination of these. Of course, the right mix depends heavily on the calibre of people you have access to. For example, in the pharmaceutical or life sciences industry, team members with a scientific and/or legal/regulatory background are essential. That's the case at M Ventures, the strategic corporate venture capital arm of Merck KGaA, Germany, which works with a highly scientific and experienced team.

Personalities: Many successful CV teams are made up of a combination of people with entrepreneurial/VC expertise and corporate DNA. This is a good way of facilitating mutual understanding between the company and the startups. Often the challenge is to educate and encourage each 'group' to accept the other. A strong entrepreneurial personality can easily be frustrated by corporate policies, bureaucracy and politics. Such a person can also actively frustrate or alienate others, especially senior managers, by completely ignoring the processes and communication expectations of the company. If you bring in a strong corporate manager, this person can easily be frustrated by the somewhat incomplete business setup of startups ('You don't have an audited annual report?') and also frustrate and alienate others (e.g., founders) by insisting too much on standards the manager is used to. If you can get entrepreneurs/VCs and corporate managers to join the team and develop a mutual understanding, you can end up with a power team that incorporates the best of both worlds.

Seniority: Seniority levels depend on the type of fund and the size of the budget. Accordingly, the overall size of the team and the 'partner to manager' ratio is crucial. If you are running a small fund or a very early stage, very broadly diversified fund, i.e., investing in many, many startups, you may work with a less senior team (i.e., pyramid organization chart). If you intend to build a focused portfolio of late-stage mature companies, then you may actually prefer to have more senior people on the team than juniors and assistants (i.e., an inverted pyramid organization chart).

Geography: The geographic location of CV arms is very diverse and often aligned with the investment focus of the initiatives. Some CV teams tend to focus on regional ventures and will have offices mainly, if not exclusively, in the region. Others have a global strategy and have offices or team members in different countries. As a rule of thumb, the CV arm will usually operate in a similar territory to the parent company.

If you look at Swisscom Ventures, the team focuses entirely on sourcing ventures locally (while investing internationally!) and operates from Switzerland. Shell Ventures has a global strategy and operates from the Netherlands, where the parent company is headquartered, but the CV team also has offices in the Americas. The various Samsung funds have offices around the world and also invest internationally, but their operations are managed from Korea.

Diversity: Today, the vast majority of people working in the financial services industry or in corporate finance departments are men. And diversity in finance is also low in terms of ethnicity. CV teams innovate on behalf of companies and in collaboration with external innovators. It's clear that these teams, which can see themselves as the avant-garde of their parent company, should carry the torch of diversity and inspire more diversity in their parent companies.

Recruiting

Having the right people in the right place at the right time sounds trivial, but it is definitely difficult to achieve (and, once achieved, to maintain). As we have already alluded to, Corporate Venturing is a people business. CV teams can recruit like other teams in the company, working closely with the corporate HR team. Or the CV team can work with external head-hunters. In the marketplace, it appears that many CV teams use head-hunters for senior recruitment and internal HR teams for more junior recruitment.

Team remuneration

Remuneration is arguably the most important bait that companies use to motivate and retain employees. And compensation is also an important tool for motivating and retaining the members of your CV team. Retaining team members should be in your company's best interest because, over time, the CV team will settle in, build its network to top management decision makers, and subject matter experts who drive internal research and product development. The CV team will eventually become one of the best-informed and best-connected teams in the organization, otherwise it cannot select targets effectively. CV team members who leave the company not only create additional costs because the company has to recruit a replacement, but resigning CV team members also cause a brain drain – know-how, expertise and familiarity with your secret plans and aspirations will leave your company and, in the worst case, may join your competitor's organization.

Performance incentives

The standard elements of remuneration for anyone working in a management (non-administrative) role in venture capital (private VC and corporate VC) are:

- Base salary
- Bonus
- Other benefits, such as a company car.

Senior private VCs may also receive a share of the carried interest generated by the VC firm on a particular fund (or funds). Carried interest is the share of a fund's overall profits that limited partners (i.e., fund investors) agree to share with and award to the fund manager(s) in order to retain and motivate them.

To help you understand the scale of carried interest and why it is such a powerful motivator for VCs around the world, let us show you a very simple example of a venture capital fund's performance.

Note that we have deliberately chosen to make the example as simple as possible. If you reflect on the example and change some of the numbers, you will find that venture capitalists can potentially become millionaires, which many believe is an attractive opportunity.

Carried interest example

Setup:

- You are the only general partner in a venture capital firm and have two more managers supporting you.
- Your fund investors, the limited partners, have invested €100 million in your fund.
- To keep things simple, you do not invest as a general partner, which you would normally do, and which would lead to additional proceeds for you and your family if the fund performed well.

- Moreover, there is a 5 per cent per annum hurdle rate and carried interest of 20 per cent.
- You are also charging a 1 per cent management fee per annum to your limited partners over the lifetime of the fund.

Fund development:

- You have made only two investments with the fund, each for €50 million.
- Startup A goes bust; the investment is gone, too bad. Startup B is sold after a couple of years for €5 billion, a huge success!
- During the lifetime of the fund, you receive a management fee of 1 per cent, year after year. That is €1 million to pay for your two investment managers, yourself, office rent, and all other expenses of the firm such as computers, travel, conference fees.
- You close the fund at the earlier date of the pre-agreed timeline of the fund or after all assets of the fund have been sold off.

Payout plan:

- Your fund owned 10 per cent of Startup B upon exit, and accordingly the fund has received €500 million from the €5 billion exit.
- From that €500 million, you have to pay €100 million to your limited partners, i.e., the equivalent of their initial investment.
- On top, you have to pay them the hurdle rate over the lifetime of the fund; let's assume that's another €30 million.
- The remaining proceeds left in the pot for distribution are €370 million, which would be the total carried interest. According to the prospectus of your fund, you are entitled to 20 per cent of that, i.e., €74 million (while €296 million also goes back to your limited partners' pockets).
- And then potentially, you share the carried interest 50:50 with your team members, but that's still a handsome €37 million for you, the acting general partner, based on your fund's performance. Not bad, right?

Why are we describing and explaining carried interest at all?

It's true that corporate VCs rarely (if ever) receive carried interest. But one thing you need to be aware of is that if you ever plan to recruit a private VC to manage/co-manage your CV programme, you should be aware that this person's existing incentive scheme is quite attractive, and you will have to make very lucrative offers to attract such a person to the CV programme of a large organization.

The other thing is that you, as the architect of a new CV programme, need to be aware and mindful of carried interest, because you may want to create similar alignments of interest between your CV team and the company. In terms of private VC, the alignment created by carried interest is extremely strong. Basically, it says: 'If the fund does well, the team does well, and I do well. If the fund doesn't do well, I'll still get paid, but I won't do extremely well'.

In terms of corporate VC, many companies try to achieve a similar alignment through employee stock option programs (ESOPs). However, this alignment is less strong and much less attractive: It allows employees to receive shares in the company at a pre-determined price and then benefit from the value appreciation of the stock over time. In theory, therefore, it could be argued that an employee share ownership programme introduces innovation into the parent company, and that this innovation is then reflected in higher expectations of the company's future cash flows, which has a positive effect on the performance of the company's shares. In reality, however, the innovation introduced to the parent company by the corporate VC team will usually take years to become part of the parent company's product portfolio. And it will also take years for the innovation to have an impact on the share price. So, the positive effects enjoyed by the employees of the CV team on the basis of an ESOP may not be due to their own value contribution to the parent company. In addition, the share price may be influenced by other factors. Perhaps the innovation introduced by the corporate VC team is positive, but the effect is offset by further disruption to the parent company's key target markets, resulting in a significant drop in share price.

Last but not least, while private VCs can hope to get their hands on high six-, seven- or even eight-figure carried interest, their corporate VC counterparts enjoying their company's ESOP may only see moderate share price appreciation.

Communication 13

In essence, a CV programme is a bit like a startup itself (even if it is fully integrated and dependent). It needs to position itself and explain its purpose and goals to stakeholders so that they know what to expect from it. Therefore, the team will have internal and external communication activities, targeted and untargeted communication activities and it will use different communication channels, different formats, etc. This is not a book on communication, but we will try to outline the main parts of communication that you need to think about when setting up a CV programme.

External communication

Let's look first at the external communication component, i.e., the messages you send to the startup universe. This universe is populated by founders and investors, but also by supporters such as lawyers, accountants, consultants, universities, think tanks and the press (i.e., the public).

Standard aspects that you may want to cover as a CV unit in your external communications include:

- **Who are you?** Describe who your parent company is, what you are trying to achieve in the long term (i.e., mission/vision) and how corporate venture capital is instrumental in working with startups and innovators in this context. Also indicate what you can and want to offer beyond capital, i.e., based on the capabilities and capacities of your parent company.
- **What is your investment strategy?** Describe the type of companies you focus on, e.g., sector, stage of maturity (e.g., pre-seed, Series A, etc.), your average investment per company, whether you have a geographical preference, and anything else that is important to you (e.g., ESG issues).
- **What does your portfolio look like?** Allow people to discover some or all of your past investments, i.e., companies that have received funding from you and are already working with you (often just logos plus a link to their website). Finally, you can also showcase successful exits so that stakeholders can see that you have also achieved exits from your portfolio.

- **What is your team like?** The team aspect is key for startups, but startups are also very interested in the composition and quality of your team. So, this is where you introduce your team members, talk about their backgrounds. This will also allow external partners to see who they know from your group and approach that person (e.g., sometimes through social networks).
- **Other topics you may cover:** Many private and corporate VCs include other topics in their communications, such as how to contact them, investment team or portfolio company vacancies, portfolio company or investment team news, etc.

The main **formats** for external communication are:

- Corporate or individual website – this is like a virtual business card, especially for people who are contacting you for the first time who will likely look at your website. But they may never come back, and they will check not only the content but also the style of the website.
- Newsletter – not used by all teams, but popular to provide regular updates as the website is first and foremost a business card.
- Short presentation or summary – this is often a slide or one-page document that the team shares with first-time contacts or event partners.
- Boiler plate – this is the shortest form of external communications profile. Examples can be found under press releases in connection with financing rounds (e.g., https://www.prnewswire.com/news-releases/beekeeper-raises-45m-series-b-funding-round-300918249.html) with boiler plates from Swisscanto Invest and Thayer Ventures.
- Longer presentations for follow-up and further insights, e.g., for potential limited partners who are considering investing alongside a fund or even in a fund.
- Flyers or brochures (no longer popular).

The main external communication **channels** are:

- CV team website and/or corporate website
- Websites managed by other players, e.g., social networks such as LinkedIn or Twitter
- Company publications and reports that feature the CV team and its activities

- Publications and reports by other players, e.g., private equity and venture capital associations, industry publications, interviews, etc.
- Corporate or CV team newsletters
- Events organized by the company, e.g., press conferences, shareholder meetings
- Events hosted by external parties, e.g., trade fairs, industry conferences.

Internal communication

For the most part, internal communication will be consistent, of course. Whatever you have put together to address external partners must be consistent with what you tell internal stakeholders. If anything, you will be sharing more insights with internal audiences.

For the sake of simplicity, let's assume that most of the internal communication to the rest of the company will be similar to the external communication, perhaps with a few more names of relevant people surrounding and supporting the CV team, but the most important aspect of internal communication is reporting (which also has an external communication aspect, as we will see in the next paragraphs).

Reporting

We have already discussed that the CV team should not just report to a group of C-level managers, or finance professionals, or R&D professionals, but rather to a mix of people with the ability to embrace the long-term and exploratory nature of corporate venture capital. Let's talk about the actual reporting, which has several aspects.

In general, it is important that you understand that reporting is relevant to three main parties:

1. The parent company
2. The CV unit
3. The individual startups (portfolio).

What all three parties have in common is a relatively low level of passion for reporting activities. Nobody is enthusiastic about reporting, unless you have something extremely positive and exciting to report. Reporting often feels like your organization is feeding off another organization or person.

Reporting is also not rewarding. In fact, most reporting organizations will try to report in a way that does not invite feedback or additional questions, because feedback and additional questions usually lead to more (and not necessarily productive) work.

In the case of an ***independent setup***, you will typically have less frequent (but still quite formal) reporting requirements because you have independent/external investors who have invested capital in your fund. Of course, you will not be able to share confidential information about your startup portfolio companies (e.g., pre- and post-money valuations of your latest investments) with your parent company or your external investors, as you will be bound by confidentiality agreements. However, you will treat the parent company/sponsor as you would any other arm's length investor in the fund by providing them with all the information they need to understand and analyse the performance of the fund.

In contrast, when you are operating a dependent and integrated or independent and integrated setup, you will likely go through a fairly formal reporting process with more frequent but shorter reports. Often, short monthly updates and more formal and extensive annual financial statements will be required by your parent company. In addition, as a dependent and integrated or independent and integrated CV team, you will report on the performance of your individual CV team members as you will be subject to your parent company's annual incentive scheme. Again, you will have to be careful not to disclose confidential information about the startup to your parent company (e.g., what you hear in board meetings of the startup), and you may have to outline how you as a team plan to manage the individual investment moving forward, i.e., your portfolio management or value creation strategy.

Limitations of internal CV reporting

Speaking of reporting and funding, since certain deals of your CV team may be supported (or even funded) by certain business units (BUs) of your company, these BUs (and other BUs in the parent company) may want to be involved in your reporting processes. Keep in mind, however, that much of the information you may gather internally in the CV team about your portfolio companies is, and must be, confidential.

In general, startups are not keen on too detailed reports and/or long distribution lists for such reports from their investors. To better understand this concern, look at CV reporting from a startup's point of view:

1. Let's say your CV investor tells you that he needs to share the reporting with his finance department. This is potentially acceptable as long as the information is limited to the amount invested and possibly the non-fully diluted shareholding in the company. However, you would probably prefer to keep your pre-money and post-money valuations confidential, as these figures could influence future negotiations for future rounds of funding. And you would prefer a limited number of people to have access to the report.
2. Let's say your CV investor tells you that he needs to share the reports with the sales organization of his parent company. This is potentially fine, as long as the information is limited to the gross revenue generated in a given period. However, information about 'best customers' or 'terms and conditions' is something that you as a startup team would want to keep strictly confidential.

And think about this: Sometimes even the parent company may decide that it wants to limit the number of people who have access to the CV report.

If one of the portfolio companies is working on an innovation that is also being pursued, researched and developed by its own R&D team, then you want to make sure that the startup's R&D efforts do not 'pollute' or 'contaminate' your internal R&D efforts in any way. Often there is an ethical wall between internal R&D units and other departments that regularly interact with innovators to ensure that the efforts of the internal team are not contaminated by an external organization or startup.

Who receives CV reports?

The first and most important recipient of reports is the CV team itself. The CV leadership team should discuss the reports, use them to inform investment and portfolio decisions, steer and guide activities, and/or identify areas for improvement, etc.

The second most important recipient of the report is the relevant CV sponsor and supporters on the parent company side, e.g., the Investment Committee top management and sometimes even the board of the company.

The third most important recipient is the company's own finance/accounting/auditing department, i.e., the internal department that deals with accounting for expenses and income, other financial reports relating to the company/affecting the company, etc.

Who does not receive CV reports?

Advisory Committees will not have access to CV reports. This is because the primary role of the members of the Advisory Committee is to act as subject matter experts, advising the Investment Committee (and the CV team) on scientific/technological/regulatory, etc. issues that may not be apparent during the screening and/or due diligence process. However, as the Advisory Committee is not responsible for investment decisions and does not benefit directly from the positive or negative performance of the CV unit, there is little point in sharing CV reporting with them on a regular basis. You can refer back to the role of the Investment Committee and the Advisory Committee in Chapter 11: Structure and governance.

Reporting requirements for startups

Let us now take a look at the reports that the CV team should be receiving on a regular basis from its individual portfolio companies.

As you can imagine, the CV team (and other investors in the individual startups) regularly assess and monitor the development of the portfolio companies. By monitoring the development of the startups, the investors aim to identify as early as possible any significant deviations from the business plan (which the startup had shared with its investors prior to the investment), to analyse and identify the reasons for such deviations, and then to discuss rapid and sometimes radical changes in strategy or operations to avoid or limit the negative impact of such deviations from the plan. As this is important to investors, these reporting requirements are included in the term sheets and in the final agreements ('information rights') signed between investors and startups.

Usually, a standard startup report has to be prepared by each startup on a monthly basis. It is short – 1–2 pages maximum – because it should not be too tedious to produce for the team or too complicated to understand for the investors.

The structure of a particular startup's report will depend somewhat on the sector and maturity of the startup. For example, a startup that is developing (but not commercializing) a specific technology, e.g., a biotech startup, may only report on the progress of its research and development work four or six times a year. And, where helpful, such a startup will report on certain scientific and financial KPIs (e.g., scientific: particle size, throughput, temperature; e.g., financial: burn rate in the reference period and remaining cash available to the company).

On the other hand, an e-commerce startup that is already selling products on the market is likely to devote most of its monthly report to performance figures, e.g. standard financials such as gross and net revenues, key cost items, profits, etc., but also business model-specific KPIs such as customer acquisition costs of different acquisition channels, churn rate during the reference period, monthly recurring revenue (MRR), annual recurring revenue (ARR), number of users, number of transactions completed during the reference period, etc.

The CV team, which receives monthly (or quarterly or annual) reports from its portfolio companies, typically works with the reports it receives in the following ways:

- With regard to their own shareholders and stakeholders, the CV team will aggregate individual (non-confidential) elements of the startup reports and reflect them in the portfolio report that they themselves share with their constituency, so that their shareholders (e.g., the top management of the company) can understand how the individual companies in the portfolio are performing, and thus how the portfolio as a whole is performing.
- In addition, the CV team will analyse the individual company reports, comparing the figures with previous reports and the business plans and projections they have received (or prepared) for the individual company in the past, to see if the company is developing in line with their expectations.

So far, we have talked about report senders and recipients, but less about the CV report itself. As the CV report often looks similar, we have created a deep-dive for you into the four chapters and appendices that many CV teams in the market cover as part of their reports.

Deep-dive: Reporting in practice

A typical CV report is divided into four chapters and several appendices:

- **Chapter 1:** Overview of latest activities of the fund and changes concerning the setup and operations of the fund.
- **Chapter 2:** Portfolio itself a) current short description of all ventures (tabular); b) investment overview of all ventures (tabular: when/how much invested/performance); c) visualization of the portfolio (e.g., by share in portfolio/strategic fit/financial performance, etc.).
- **Chapter 3:** a) Portfolio management plan (high-level summary of intentions to develop each portfolio company plus target KPIs); b) timing of future potential investments (planned follow-on rounds and maturity rates of convertible loans).
- **Chapter 4:** Profit and loss account of the fund (value gain/loss, current expenses, net asset value calculation).
- **Appendix 1:** Non-investment related activities of the team e.g., ventures introduced to parent company but not invested (e.g., partnerships); impact of fund portfolio (i.e., how many FTEs in ventures; how much money raised in total by ventures; how many patents registered; etc.).
- **Appendix 2:** a) Detailed two-page summary per portfolio company (strategic fit/recent achievements/next steps/collaboration with parent); b) Investment-related data (shareholder structure, cash runway, key investment terms and financial performance and budget reporting: report to IC and Leadership parent every 6–12 months (if total investment budget >100 million or if significant to the company)).
- **Ventures**: Monthly reporting (commercial), quarterly (research / development), standard annual report (audited) for shareholders.
- **Special reporting mandates:** Possible but should be minimized (less bureaucracy to be achieved).

Expert insights on reports

In speaking to CV managers in the marketplace, we have received a number of interesting comments that we would like to share with you as we believe they are instructive. One CV manager told us:

> As in private VC firms, I soon realized that our younger team members in a CV team (i.e., analysts, associates, investment managers and principals) are less interested in portfolio company reports. What's important to them is to be involved in the process of making or closing a deal. They assume, I think, that they will probably no longer be on our team when the individual startups exit. Also, they are not likely to get any carried interest. So, they just don't care too much about how the individual companies perform on a monthly basis.
>
> So, as senior members of the team, we have to take the time to go through the individual portfolio company reports and our strategies for the individual companies, and also make sure that the youngsters are not just trying to add another deal to their career track record, but that they really embrace the individual companies as their babies. They also need to learn how to support, nurture and celebrate these companies, and how to spot negative developments early on.

Another CV manager added an interesting and somewhat controversial observation:

> As a startup investor, you will have companies in your portfolio that are struggling. It is simply not possible to invest in startups and not have portfolio companies that are struggling. Very often it becomes clear what is not working, e.g., development is not progressing fast enough, it takes more money than expected to build or reach this or that milestone, or simply the sales figures are not taking off, etc. In some cases, the founders and investors will be able to find solutions to the problems (such as therapies). And then the troubled startup will get better and eventually thrive. Sometimes, however, no solution or cure can be found. And then the startup goes from not doing well to seriously ill to deathly ill. And when that happens, it is important for investors not to get too hung up on the individual case or spend more and more time trying to save the company. In fact, at some point you have to decide to move on and focus on other, more promising companies in the portfolio. This may sound simple and logical, but it is extremely difficult. Our natural instinct as human beings is to help. And a struggling startup is often like a good friend in need. As an investor, you had great days and shared wonderful memories with the founders. And now the

company is in a desperate situation. You feel you owe it to the startup to do everything in your power to save it. But let's be clear: this may not be possible. Two-thirds or more of all early-stage startups fail. You have to accept that, and you should not lie about it, but inform your team members and write off the investment, and also talk to the founders and explain that there is only so much you can do.

A third CV manager made a similar observation and provided further insight into how her team monitors the performance of individual portfolio companies:

For us, there are three main components that we analyse on a monthly basis.

Key performance indicators such as revenue or profit or number of users. These are based on the plans previously communicated by the founders.

Cash left, i.e., how much longer can the company go on and when do they need to start fundraising (which is often interesting in combination with aspect (1)).

Other aspects such as major changes in the founding team, other external news (e.g., macroeconomic crisis with a potential impact on the company), etc.

Based on this, we take the list of our existing portfolio companies and assign a simple traffic light symbol to each company, i.e., a company that is doing well is green, companies that are doing well but with certain struggles are amber, and companies that are struggling on many fronts are red. Essentially, we try to focus on the green and the yellow. Mostly the green ones, if we're honest. It's true that from time to time we may discuss a red, but usually a company does not go straight to red. It starts green, then it becomes yellow, it stays yellow for a while and then it becomes red. By then we have done everything we can to get them back to green, but to no avail. And then we try to discipline ourselves not to spend any more time on the red ones, but simply to monitor their development and focus our energy on working on the yellow and green companies.

Sustainability report

Sustainability and the concept of ESG investing is a vast topic that would potentially allow us to write another book. However, in the context of Corporate Venturing, we believe that ESG investing and sustainability reporting are also important aspects of CV programmes.

By now, most governments, regulators, investors and societies have accepted the fact that fundamental changes (e.g., to better protect the environment and to treat people fairly and equally) require orchestrated efforts by most, if not all, people and organizations. And this obviously includes companies, i.e., all activities in modern companies have to take ESG standards into account when planning and executing their activities, otherwise the company may face repercussions from governments, regulators, investors and people in general. As a result, many companies have launched programmes to improve the sustainability and ESG compliance of their organizations. And this includes CV programmes. However, the term 'sustainability' is somewhat opaque and we think it is helpful to reflect on this a little in the following section.

The vague term 'sustainability'

Corporate and private seed investors are sometimes asked whether sustainability considerations are part of their investment selection process for the companies in which they invest, or even if there is a systematic selection process in place. The question is probably a bit naive, and the answers you get are unlikely to be very helpful. Here's why.

First of all, we already know the answer to some of the most standard questions. For example:

Q: Are you fundamentally opposed to equal pay and equal opportunity regardless of gender, age, sexual orientation, political preference, etc.?

A: Of course not.

Q: Do you support child labour?

A: Of course not.

The same goes for sustainability:

Q: Do you check the sustainability aspects of your target companies before you invest?

A: Of course we do; sustainability is important to our business and to everything we do, including CV activities.

But there are several other things to consider.

1 Professional and savvy investors will not just say they take sustainability seriously, they will take it seriously. Quite simply, if your startup engages in somewhat unsustainable business practices, it will eventually be grilled

by the market. Customers may boycott it. Employees may resign. Backers and investors may withdraw their support and investment, and so on, so not paying attention to sustainability issues in your startups is naive and unprofessional and can cost you a lot of money.

2 How can you really be sustainable in all processes of your (startup) company? If your employees drive to the office in non-electric cars, are you still sustainable? If you do not generate your own energy through PV panels on the roof, are you still sustainable? By the way, are photovoltaic panels sustainable? In other words, the term sustainability is tricky and should be used with care.

3 How much of your business is actually under your control and how much is controlled by others? For example, you might buy off-the-shelf materials to build a prototype, but those materials were produced using non-sustainable processes. Or, you may use source code to improve your software, but the companies that originally produced that source code may not have used equal pay and equal opportunity processes, but your startup does not even know that.

All we are saying is: be aware of the opaque nature of the term 'sustainability' and the limitations of companies to achieve 100 per cent sustainability.

Portfolio strategy 14

You've got your CV structure and underlying governance in place, your team in place, your communications strategy in place, and you know your ecosystem pretty well, but what about your portfolio approach? Let's answer that.

Portfolio size

One of the first things to consider is how broadly you want to invest, i.e., how many different companies do you want to invest in, and how does the total capital available for your CV activity translate into tickets per startup?

Let's say you prefer to 'spray and pray'. This means that in the industry/business/technology area of particular interest to your organization, there are a large number of companies working on innovative solutions. Take artificial intelligence (AI) as an example. Many companies out there claim to be working on AI technologies. Let's say you can identify a sub-category of AI that is of particular interest to you. You may decide that with so many different innovators out there, you prefer to spread your bets a bit. So, assuming you have €10 million available for CV investments, you decide to invest in up to 20 different companies, investing €350,000 per company in the first round (requiring a total of €7 million), leaving €3 million for follow-on investments in the few companies you think will be most interesting after 18–24 months. Or you may be targeting an industry/business/technology area with a relatively small number of startups, e.g., a treatment for a rare lung disease that fits into your portfolio of other drugs for rare lung diseases. Again, you have €10 million available, but you decide to invest €1 million per company in only three companies, and then you have another €7 million for a follow-on investment in the one company that looks most promising after, say, the preclinical phase.

Industry focus

It may seem obvious that an automotive company promoting innovation through CV investments is likely to invest in startups focusing on developments for the automotive industry. However, it may also be interesting for such an automotive company to consider investing in startups targeting the aerospace industry, because it is possible that the aerospace industry, which certainly faces different challenges, may also happen to be interested in extremely light yet tough materials, which could potentially be of interest to car manufacturers.

Geographical focus

Perhaps your company is active in the European semiconductor industry. But is it enough to decide that you want to focus your investments on European startups? You may also need to consider innovative startups from Japan, Taiwan, even China and the USA. And even if the parent company is not active in these markets, it may be advisable for the CV team to closely follow the emergence of such startups, or even to open a branch in that market in order to engage more intensively with the local startup universe.

Investment stage

As a CV investor, you need to define the preferred growth (or maturity) stage for your investment targets (see Figure 14.1). Otherwise, you will be approached by startups at different stages of maturity and it will be unnecessarily time-consuming and frustrating for their team and for your CV team to communicate (and receive) rejections of investment proposals.

The common terminology for the main funding stages is as follows:

- Pre-seed – founders are considering a concept and raising small amounts of money for initial validation of the idea.
- Seed – founders have found a concept and raise small (but slightly larger than pre-seed) amounts of capital to work on a first prototype or alpha version of a product or service concept.
- Series A – early-stage startup, often generating (or close to generating) first revenues or potentially reaching initial 'product-market fit' or other significant development milestones in its journey.

- Series B, C, D (...) – growth stage startup generating revenues and sometimes profits, or a startup that has reached more advanced development milestones for its technology, product or service.

The different stages of maturity also mean different levels of investment risk. As a rule of thumb, consider the following:

- The younger a startup, the higher the risk, and the lower the pre-money and post-money valuation of the company, the higher the potential upside for investors, and the smaller the amounts raised in funding rounds.
- The more mature a startup, the lower the risk, the higher the pre-money and post-money valuation of the company, the lower the potential upside for the investors, the larger the amounts raised in the funding rounds.

More importantly, you need to decide for yourself and your CV programme what level of maturity is most appropriate for your purposes. For example, if you are setting up the first ever CV programme for your organization, you may find it more appropriate to invest in more mature startups (e.g., Series A and later, potentially generating revenue, first customers, etc.). Simply because the risk of failure is somewhat lower for these startups (though still significantly higher than for large publicly traded companies, of course), and more mature startups have more people, more structures and processes in place, are somewhat more familiar to larger companies, and may grow more quickly into true acquisition targets, if that is a potential consideration from your organization's point of view.

If, on the other hand, you are building a new CV activity on the shoulders of previous successful CV activities, and if the primary strategic purpose of the programme is not to build future acquisition targets, but to expose your organization to cutting-edge research that may one day enable you to add more unique features or properties to your products or services, then a CV programme focused on seed or Series A start-ups may be more appropriate for you.

Investment fund volume

To give you some guidance on how to think about the initial capital you plan to allocate to your team's CV activities: Most first-time funds in the private venture capital world start with a volume of between €10 million

Figure 14.1 St. Gallen Venture Growth Lifecycle Model

Funding Stage (Investors' Perspective)	**Seed Stage**		**Early Stage**	**Late Stage**	
Venture level	**Entrepreneur**	**Startup**	**Gazelle / HGF**	**Scale-Up**	**Established Firm**
Lifecycle Phase (Ventures' Perspective)	Birth		Growth		Maturity
Definition	Entrepreneur(s) identifying a problem & ideating a product/ service to solve it.	Entrepreneur(s) with a highly innovative solution for a relevant problem in a large (future) market.	Startups with >20% p.a. average growth in FTEs or revenue, over a 3-year period (Gazelles: age < 5 yrs.)	Scaling Gazelles/HGFs, leveraging EoS in exponentially growing their revenues across (geograph.) markets.	Scale-ups successfully surviving, switching to long-term ownership model, diversifying revenue streams.
Funding Round	Pre-seed	Seed	Series-A	Series-B(+)	IPO / Trade Sale / Merger / MBO
Round Size	€50k – €1M	€1M – €4M	€5M – €15M	€10M – €200M(+)	n
Funding Sources	• Co-Founders • Friends, Family & Fools (FFF) • Incubators/Accelerators • Business Angels	• Business Angels • (Seed-stage) Venture Capital • Crowdfunding • Public Programmes	• (Series-A) Venture Capital • Corporate Venture Capital • Public Programmes	• (Late-Stage) Venture Capital • Commercial Bank Loan • Venture Debt, Mezzanine • Private Equity	• Commercial Bank Loan • Private Equity • Mezzanine, High Yield Bonds • Public Debt, IPO, SPAC etc.
Product	PoC / Prototype	Prototype / MVP	Product / Service	Product / Service (Portfolio)	Product / Service Portfolio
PMF	None		*Initial* Product-Market-Fit	*Scalable* Product-Market-Fit	
Revenue Growth	None	10% p.a.	100% – 300(+)% p.a.	50% – 100(+)% p.a.	40% – 60% p.a.
Literature (University of St.Gallen)	Startup Navigator		Scale-Up Navigator		
	Corporate Venturing Navigator				

Time (>10 Years)

Abbreviations: HGF = High-growth firm; EoS: Economies of Scale; IPO = Initial Public Offering; MBO = Management Buyout; PoC = Proof of Concept; MVP = Minimum Viable Product; PMF = Product-Market Fit; FTE = Fulltime Employee

Author(s): Greger, M.K., Grichnik, D., Hess, M. (2023)

Source(s): Own figure; integrated: Goeldi (2021 & 2022), Alemany & Andreoli (2018), Coviello (2019), OECD (2007), Millers & Friesen (1984)

and €75 million. The ability to raise funds from investors and then invest in startups depends on three main aspects:

1. How promising and exciting is the fund's focus?
2. How compelling is the fund management team, i.e., track record and perceived intelligence?
3. Other factors such as the global economic situation, etc.

In the corporate world, you can also adopt a startup mindset for this setup, i.e., start a little smaller to gain experience and familiarize yourself with how a CV activity needs to be run in or to be productive for your company. And then increase your commitment when you feel comfortable.

Investment per company

You can either invest larger amounts of capital in fewer companies in order to have larger stakes in your target companies, i.e., more influence and potentially a larger discount on future acquisitions, if that is your objective. Or, you can invest smaller amounts of capital in more companies to maximize your exposure to companies competing in the same or similar areas of focus, diversify your investment risk and improve your chances of picking a winner.

You can also consider a simple analogy: If you spend a day at the races, you can choose not to bet on individual horses and bet on all the horses in a single race at once. You will certainly win on one of your bets and lose on the others. And your lost bets will eat into your overall win, unless a complete outsider wins. Or you can prepare very carefully for the race, make sure you see all the horses before the race, maybe even talk to some of the coaches and jockeys, and finally make a very educated bet, and a bigger one at that. Even with this approach you can be wrong and lose. But if you win, your win will be more significant. And if you are able to spot an underdog and place a big bet, your winnings can be earth shattering.

Investment tools

If you have decided to hire a former private venture capitalist to run your CV activity, you should ensure that the team is aware that there are many ways in which collaborations between startups and large companies can be established. Taking a minority stake in a startup is only one way, and will require time and resources to manage the investment. Other sometimes more efficient and equally attractive ways of working together are based on licensing agreements, commercial agreements (the company becomes a supplier or customer of the startup or simply co-sells the startup's products and services), agreements on joint development activities, joint ventures, or the larger company simply providing a loan to the smaller company. Non-financial alliances are also possible, where two companies want to achieve something in the market, but for different reasons may decide to become allies without further financial or legal obligations.

Reference

Greger, M K, Grichnik, D, Hess, M (2023) St.Gallen Venture Growth Lifecycle Model

CV Cockpit II 15

A quick reminder of what the Cockpit is all about: In the dashboard you will find the so-called specs, which summarize important information about the different elements of the CV Navigator. You will find an interface, a Google Spreadsheet, that shows you the choices you need to make by bringing together all the necessary information at once and giving you a good overview of the key details required to run a CV programme. The interrelationships of the necessary elements and their dependencies within and between phases are shown, while the options available are outlined.

Cockpit II (Figure 15.1) covers design, structure and governance, team communication, the ecosystem, the portfolio approach and a rollout plan. It starts with the question of organizational structures, whether the CV programme is integrated and dependent, integrated but independent or completely independent. This is followed by a decision on the legal structure, whether the CV programme will be part of the company or legally operate as a subsidiary/separate legal entity. Next is the definition of the reporting line and the overall decision-making process. You will be asked to indicate the number of directorships sought, the composition of the Investment Committee and the Advisory Committee. At the end, there is space for information on specific applicable regulations or other governance factors to be considered.

In terms of the team, the size of the team, the background of the team and how they are recruited should be clarified. Next, compensation and other incentives need to be determined, rounded out by how the team will be divided and how it will work, as well as other important team factors to consider.

The next decision point is to create clarity around communication: external communication to other investors and founders, or internal corporate communication to stakeholders and employees. Who needs to be addressed by the communication? What communication tools and systems should be used, what language should be used, and what should be communicated and when? Then there is the communication within the CV department, between the CV leader and his team, but also towards the involved BU or other stakeholders. Not forgetting communication factors such as events and general marketing activities that need to be discussed and defined.

When it comes to networks, what networks exist and which ones are actually being used? What ecosystem characteristics and links need to be considered? What expertise is available and accessible and what other factors need to be considered?

Then, you have to look at the portfolio concept, i.e., how many companies to focus on, which industry, which sector, which stage, which investment amount. What form should the partnership take – minority shareholding, collaboration or just strategic alignment? How long should the investment be? What is the venture's unique selling proposition – service, brand, etc. and what other factors of the portfolio approach are important to mention?

At the very end of the specifications, we have created a small implementation plan that you can use to track and review your process along the way. It's a simple tool because it's just about what you've already done and what you still have to do. But believe us, just having an overview of where you are will make a big difference to your progress.

Tool C: RACI

The RACI matrix is a very good management tool to help you work out who should play what role in the CV programme. Why is this necessary? Well, there are simply too many people involved and too many tasks to be done to not have a system in place to provide structure and clarity. Otherwise, if there is no system, the whole CV programme will end up as a game of ping-pong where everyone passes the ball around because no one really feels responsible for anything.

So, what is this RACI matrix all about? Let's start with the acronym RACI. These four letters reflect the roles that stakeholders can play in a given project and governance model. R stands for Responsible; A stands for Accountable; C stands for Consultative; and I stands for Informative. This means that RACI aligns the appropriate roles for a given project by indicating who is responsible and accountable, and who needs to be consulted and informed.

Let's take a closer look at a practical example (Figure 15.2). It shows the four phases that a CV programme goes through over time: Profile, Design, Invest and Harvest with all their tasks. Please note that we have only roughly listed the tasks involved in each phase. Then you will find the stakeholders involved, starting with management, the team and the BUs. Again, this is a very simplified view.

Figure 15.1 CV Cockpit II Design your specifications

CV Cockpit II

Profile | **Design** | Invest | Harvest

Structure & Governance				
Organizational structure	Integrated, dependent	Integrated, independent	Independent	
Legal structure	Subsidary	Within corporate		
Investment Committee	*(please name)*	CEO; CFO; CVC lead		
Advisory Committee	*(please name)*	External advisors / experts		
Certain regulations to consider	*(please name)*	Compliance process, etc.		
Other governance factors	*(please name)*			

Team				
Team size	*(please name)*	E.g. 3 people full time		
Team background	*(please name)*	Corporate, entrepreneurial, etc.		
Individual recruiting	CVC recruiting	Corporate recruiting		
Compensation	Carry (20%)	Corporate	Other	*(please state)*
Incentives	Salary	Carry / bonuses	Corporate stock	Responsibility
	Shadow carry	Award / title	Training	
	Other	*(please state)*		
Team location	*(please name)*	If self-sufficient: Close to mother company; if integrated: Close to C-Level for transparency and awareness		
Other team factors	*(please name)*			

Communication		
Communication externally	*(please name)*	Investors, founders
Communication corporate	*(please name)*	Stakeholders; corporate employees
Communication ventures	*(please name)*	Ventures
Communication CV arm	*(please name)*	Within CV arm, CV team
Other communication factors	*(please name)*	Events; marketing activities

Ecosystem				
Networks available	*(please name)*	Contact to accelerators; research centres; VC firms; business angels; etc.		
Networks used	*(please name)*			
Ecosystem attributes	*(please name)*	Centrality; subgroups; structural holes etc.		
Ecosystem interrelationship	*(please name)*	Personal ties and business connection; embeddedness		
Expertise available and accessable	*(please name)*			
Co-investors	No	Yes	If yes, in lead	If yes, not in lead
Other ecosystem factors	*(please name)*			

Portfolio approach		
Focused number of startups	*(please name)*	<5; 5–10; 11–15;16–20;>20
Focused industry	*(please name)*	Automotive; Pharma; Energy; Retail etc.
Focused area	*(please name)*	GSA; Europe; US; etc.
Focused stage	*(please name)*	Seed; Series A; Series B etc.
Focused investment sum	*(please name)*	<10k;10–50k;>50k;
Instruments (stakes)	*(please name)*	Minority investment; collaboration only; strategic alliance etc.
Holding time	*(please name)*	<3yrs; 3–5yrs;>5yrs
USP for startups	*(please name)*	Resources; brand etc.
Other portfolio approach factors	*(please name)*	

(continued)

Figure 15.1 (Continued)

Rollout plan		
Milestone: Profile overall	**Achieved**	**Open**
Profile / CV orientation set	Achieved	Open
Budget set	Achieved	Open
Stakeholder known	Achieved	Open
Business advancements known	Achieved	Open
Milestone Design overall	**Achieved**	**Open**
Structure set	Achieved	Open
Governance known	Achieved	Open
Team set	Achieved	Open
Communication set	Achieved	Open
Networks set	Achieved	Open
Portfolio approach set	Achieved	Open
Rollout plan set	Achieved	Open
Milestone Investing overall	**Achieved**	**Open**
Dealflow set	Achieved	Open
Collaboration set	Achieved	Open
Evaluation set	Achieved	Open
Milestone Harvesting overall	**Achieved**	**Open**
Termination set	Achieved	Open
Continuation set	Achieved	Open
Performance known	Achieved	Open

Using the example of a standalone but integrated CV model, we have gone through the phases and tasks and considered who is responsible for each task, such as 'setting the CV mandate'. Which stakeholder is then responsible and needs to be consulted and informed? True, this is easier said than done. Sometimes there is no clear allocation, and one stakeholder may even play two roles at once. But the important thing is to sit down with the relevant parties and reach a consensus. Nothing else matters.

Now it's time to roll up your sleeves and get started: download the template and get a clear overview of the responsibilities in your CV programme.

Tool C: RACI – Example of independent but integrated model

Figure 15.2 RACI exemplified

R: Responsible
A: Accountable
C: Consulted
I: Informed

	Leadership	Investment Committee**	CVC team	BU head(s)
CVC program	Project leadership		Project team	Business Unit(s)
CV program **profiling**				
Defining CV mandate	R	I	A	C
Specifying CV objectives	C/I	I	R	A
Determining budget	R	I	A	C/I
Determining promoters*	C	I	R	C
Setting business advancements	C/I	I	R	A
CV program **designing**				
Set up structure	C	C	R/A	I
Set up governance	C	A	R	I
Build team	R/I	I	R/A	I
Install communication systems and process	A/C	I	R/A	C
Establish ecosystem	I	I	R/A	A/I

Note: Schematic diagram for the organizational structure and governance model: Independent but integrated
*Structure follows strategy; **Be aware that in case of the same people, a different perspective is applied

Figure 15.2 (Continued)

R: Responsible
A: Accountable
C: Consulted
I: Informed

	Leadership	Investment Committee**	CVC team	BU head(s)
CVC program	Project leadership		Project team	Business Unit(s)
CV program **investing**				
Investment portfolio strategy / development	I	C	R	I
Deal flow sourcing / DDs / business modelling	I	I	R	R/C
Build and manage external networks for deal sourcing	I	I	R	C/I
Reporting and program performance	I	I	R/A	I
Collaboration startups (active / passive)	I	I	R/A	C/A
Collaboration with BUs / R&D / strategy department	I	I	R/A	A/C
Events / Marketing	I	I	R	C/I

Note: Schematic diagram for the organizational structure and governance model: Independent but integrated

Figure 15.2 (Continued)

R: Responsible
A: Accountable
C: Consulted
I: Informed

	Leadership	Investment Committee**	CVC team	BU head(s)
CVC program	Project leadership		Project team	Business Unit(s)
CV program **harvesting**				
Program termination	R	C/I	A	C/I
Program continuation / follow-up rounds	R/C	C/I	A	C/I
Venture termination / follow-on / M&A	C	R	R/A	C/I

Note: Schematic diagram for the organizational structure and governance model: Independent but integrated

Summary – CV programme 16

Part II is coming to an end. Wow, what a journey you've been on so far. You've set up your CV profile and now you've designed the programme around it. Was it an easy task? We suspect not. There are so many decisions to make, so many perspectives to consider and individual agendas to fulfil, while ultimately, we all want to invest in companies that drive business innovation. So, what have you learnt? What are your key takeaways? We want to keep this book pragmatic and practical, so let's focus on the top three learnings.

First: The setup determines the playground

This is all that needs to be said. Structure is fundamental, and we are talking about organizational, legal and governmental structure. Yes, there is a certain dependence on the mandate, but you have to be careful how you choose the structure to implement the mandate. You have to learn the difference between independence and corporate support and backing. Both have their pros and cons.

Second: Mutual understanding

Mutual understanding is the essential aspect that separates a successful CV programme from one that fails to achieve its mission in a short period of time. Clear communication is the key to creating the necessary understanding. Be aware of the different stakeholders involved, who have very different backgrounds and communication languages. Your top management needs to understand venture capital almost as well as the CV team. And startups need to understand the CV team and how that team works with the parent company. Different worlds collide and very often there is no bridge to connect them unless you build that bridge.

What helps is transparency and continuous exchange between the parties involved. And what we have found is that management buy-in in particular – that is someone at the top who understands what CV means, how it works and what it takes to implement it in the business – is very beneficial.

Third: People business

Yes, Corporate Venturing is a people business, which means you can prepare and plan as well as you can, but to err is human and there will be hiccups in your programme. Certain stakeholders are critical and can become showstoppers. What needs to be done? Communication, as well as appropriate rewards and incentives, and assurances that mistakes and unsuccessful trials will not negatively affect a manager's career aspirations will have to be put in place. Additional incentives are then needed not only to attract the right people, but also to retain them. Recently, some studies have suggested that the average key manager stays in one job for four years. That would be fantastic, because it often happens that people leave much earlier. And then everything changes because a new person has a different agenda and the programme is restructured with a different budget orientation or reporting line, which makes it very difficult to get long-term strategic returns. In other words, better to spend more now to get the right people and keep them than to have to invest later to keep the ship from sinking.

One final word, if we may. We would like to reiterate that there is no one-size-fits-all solution. CV is such a complex innovation effort that there should be variations, changes or hybrid versions that evolve over time, so keep that in mind.

Case insights: Siemens Healthineers

Figure 16.1 Case insights: Siemens Healthineers

Christian Wolfrum
Head of New Business Development and Planning

Established: 2018

Parent: Siemens Healthineers AG

HQ: Germany

Industry: Health Care / MedTech

(1) Profiling

CVC mandate
- Primarily strategic (focus on new technologies and markets); financial returns as basis
- Thesis-driven by business units and corporate strategy

Funding size
- Evergreen

Business advancements
- Core / Adjacent / Far adjacent

(2) Designing / (3) Investing

Structure & Governance
- Organizational: Balance sheet
- Legal: Corporate unit
- Reporting: Head of Strategy & M&A
- Investment Committee: Dedicated Board

Team
- not disclosed

Portfolio size
- not disclosed

Ticket size:
- Primarily Series A and B

(4) Harvesting

Collaboration
- Active support (strategic)
- Board seat / observer seat
- Co-development / -marketing (strategic partnership)

M&A
- M&A as objective

SOURCE Corporate insights via interview and website; Crunchbase

PART THREE
Investing

The easiest and most intuitive way to understand a (corporate) venture capital team's daily operations is to understand the value chain of any venture capital investor. This exercise also helps to point out a few differences between strategically and financially focused corporate venture capital investors.

In the first chapter of this section, we will introduce and explain an overview of the corporate venture capital team's value chain and its individual elements. In the following chapters, we will then elaborate on each element and the underlying processes and design options and challenges for the managers.

These last two elements of the value chain, 'portfolio management' and 'Follow-on rounds of funding & exit scenarios' will be addressed in more detail in Part 4 of this book.

Figure 17.1 Investment Process Overview

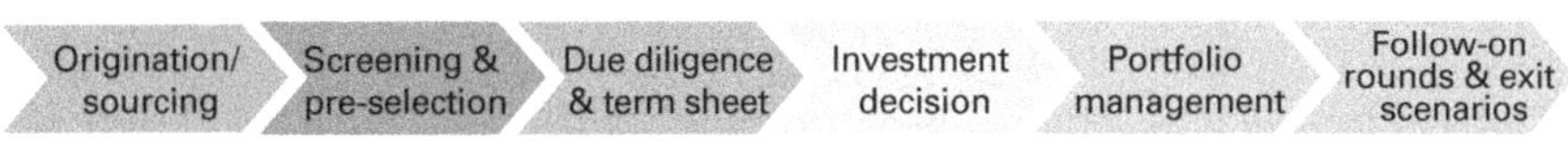

Table 17.1 Investment process key issues

	Process	Key task and challenges	Budgeted time
Origination/ Sourcing	One of the first and most important tasks for any aspiring startup investor is to get access to attractive and promising investment opportunities. Maximizing the number of proposals received is not the goal. Maximizing the quality of the deal flow you receive is. This process is called origination or sourcing.	- Define one or more search profiles, informed by your company's innovation strategy (if you are a strategic investor) or by your investment analysis (if you are a financial investor). - Help stakeholders (founders, other investors, scouts, etc.) understand what sort of startup the CV team is looking for. - Identify, cultivate, and nurture the best deal sources. - Be disciplined and do not waste time, e.g. on sources proven to be useless.	- Ongoing activity, i.e. usually one person or more from your team is assigned to origination activities. - Startup investors are always on the lookout for new deals. Simultaneously, they will always cultivate and nurture their best sources for past deals.
Screening & Pre-Selection	Once you have received deal flow (from your origination/sourcing activities), the CV team needs to analyse the individual proposals and separate 'suitable deals' from 'non-suitable deals'.	- The key aspects for the screening process and system are derived from the search profiles and informed by standard elements/aspects that you would like to understand about any potential investment target. - The CV team will need to develop an efficient process, especially for passive/ inbound deal flow.	- Strive to take not more than two weeks to respond to received proposals. - If it takes your team more than two weeks to give a first signal to a startup that has approached you, this will not help your reputation in the market and, eventually, demotivate stakeholders to share deals with your team.

	Process	Key task and challenges	Budgeted time
Due Diligence & Term Sheet	Once an investment opportunity has been identified as a 'fit', the CV team strives to obtain a comprehensive and robust understanding of the target company's assets and capabilities during the due diligence. In parallel, the CV team begins to negotiate with the pre-selected startup around terms and conditions for an investment.	- Run due diligence systematically, i.e. commercial, technical, legal/regulatory and financial due diligence, and also check for ESG aspects. - Do not just review what has been shared and discussed with you by the founders. Think out of the box about what was never presented or discussed, i.e. gaps. - If you can, reflect mitigations of identified risks in the term sheet. - Keep the term sheet simple.	- Take 8–12 weeks (+/-) as a benchmark for your due diligence and term sheet process. - The due diligence (DD) usually takes 8–12 weeks. Sometimes less (2–4 weeks) e.g., if another investor has already conducted a DD that can be reviewed and proves to have sufficient quality. DD can take more time if the parties do a pilot project or test first.
Investment Decision	The investment decision is taken based on four aspects: 1. Startup is likely able to survive standalone. 2. Fit with the investment strategy, aligned with goal(s) of the corporation or whatever financial strategy the team pursues. 3. No unacceptable red flags in the due diligence (green and yellow are ok). 4. Acceptable terms and conditions for the investment.	- Beware of biases of unexperienced decision makers, and of linking investment decisions to other topics in the corporation, i.e. cost reductions must not impact startup investments. - Document the decisions of the Investment Committee. - Prevent overthinking and the fear that wrong decisions could negatively impact career prospects of Investment Committee members.	- Give the Investment Committee enough time to familiarize itself with the case. - Send pre-reads (short deck, max 10 slides or 1–2 text pages per company) to Investment Committee at least two days prior to IC meeting. - Per IC meeting, do not spend more than 60 minutes per target. - Submit minutes of IC meeting to IC members in the 48 hours following the meeting.

(continued)

Table 17.1 (Continued)

	Process	Key task and challenges	Budgeted time
Portfolio Management	For financial investors, the portfolio management is done by the investment team alone. For strategic investors, the investment team will work with the startup and also with other internal teams to align activities and achieve pre-determined milestones or goals.	- Internal teams may argue that working with startup XYZ is not part of the goals for the year (or the budget) – overcome bureaucracy and have internal teams commit to joint activities prior to making the investment. Present deal in the IC together, for instance. - Educate internal teams on how to work with startups, e.g. avoid corporate arrogance and false expectations or micro management.	- This is an ongoing effort with monthly or quarterly check-ups. - Ideally, the corporation and the startup will discuss what they aim to achieve together and how a collaboration could work prior to the investment, so that both partners benefit. - If that has been done, the portfolio management is merely the execution of this plan, and the ongoing monitoring of deviations from the plans.
Follow-on rounds of funding & exit scenarios	The CV team will require a general strategy on follow-on investments. And then it will take decisions on individual follow-on investments if and when they present themselves, while taking into account the development of the individual portfolio company up until that point, both from a stand-alone point of view, and – for strategic investors – from the point of view of the corporation.	- Understand that the corporation's continued strategic interest in a startup is not the only reason to invest in the next round of funding. - It is also expected from early-stage investors to continuously support the startup irrespective of your strategic interest. Performance is, however, a valid reason not to invest.	- Follow-on rounds usually happen 1–2 years after the previous round. - Ensure that portfolio companies start to engage in fundraising preparations and efforts at the latest six months before they run out of cash. - Commit to a follow-on round early in the process, if possible, as it will facilitate the fundraising for the startup.

Sourcing 17

In the context of investment opportunities' origination or sourcing, we should distinguish between passively and actively generated deal flow, also called inbound and outbound sourcing or deal flow.

Passively generated deal flow

Passively generated deal flow or *inbound* deal flow is what startup investors call investment opportunities that are received without prior targeted activities from the CV team to generate that deal flow. In other words, founders, other investors, or scouts (see below) proactively approach you because they consider the CV team a potential investor, due to one or several characteristic elements of your CV unit, e.g., your disclosed investment preferences, expertise, reputation/brand, and/or abundant capital resources, infrastructure and network, etc. Often, founders read about your CV team and then they approach you.

Here are some examples as to what may motivate them to approach you:

- *Investment preferences:* A deeptech startup could potentially approach Samsung's Catalyst Fund because the founders have read on the fund's website that the fund invests in deeptech startups.
- *Expertise:* The same startup could decide to approach Samsung's Catalyst Fund because the founders believe that Samsung has very good deeptech expertise, e.g., based on their existing range of products.
- *Reputation/brand:* The same startup could also approach Samsung's Catalyst Fund because each of the founders love the Samsung brand and Samsung's reputation for good consumer electronics, as well as the global visibility of the brand. So, in a way, the founders may hope that by adding Samsung to the shareholders, Samsung's positive reputation may provide leeway for the startup.

- *Capital resources:* The same startup could also approach Samsung's Catalyst Fund because the founders know that Samsung generates more than $200 billion revenue per year and so the founders assume that the fund will have more than sufficient capital for this and future rounds, or that Samsung may even become a potential acquirer of the startup.
- *Infrastructure:* The founders could also decide to approach Samsung's Catalyst Fund because Samsung's organization is capable to sell (through resellers) on a global basis, i.e., it has a global manufacturing and distribution and administration/management process which may become something that the startup wants to use or explore too.
- *Network:* And last but not least, the founders could decide to talk to Samsung's Catalyst Fund because they see that the fund has done a number of investments with other investors or corporations and they believe that the fund can provide substantial network support.

In essence, here's what this means to you and your organization: The startups are more likely to approach your CV team if they believe that you have or may have one or two things that they do not have but would like to have (see the previous bullet points). Sometimes, they approach private investors or big corporations for the wrong reasons, for example, they misunderstand what you are looking for. The better known your corporation is, the more deal flow you are likely to receive even without engaging actively on startup conferences, etc. This is not a bad thing per se, but you have to find ways to manage inbound deal flow efficiently.

Quality of passively generated deal flow

On average, the quality of the passively generated deal flow tends to be rather low, that is in terms of 'fit' with your investment strategy. This is mostly due to the phenomenon that we have described above – a founder may ignore what you state to be your financial or strategic investment approach, like what you put on your website or say during startup conferences. The founder may just send you an email inviting you to speak (and invest) because the CV team looks like a potential fit. Or, the founder believes that your CV team will change their perspective if they get to know the startup better, and then potentially deviate from their investment strategy. Whatever the motivation may be, founders approaching the 'wrong' investors, i.e., investors with no fit or just a very limited fit, will be rejected by the investors.

Note that sometimes, a rejection may not even be caused by the startup. Players like Samsung may refrain deliberately from talking to companies working on certain technologies because the same technologies are under development by Samsung. Or there is another barrier keeping the corporation from even talking to you. For example, think of political sanctions against individual states; if a startup is headquartered in a state that is sanctioned, investors may not talk to you at all.

Rejections

If startups approach the 'wrong' investors, they will quickly receive a negative response. Investors, especially those with tons of inbound deal flow, use very effective screening and selection processes to navigate efficiently through the deal flow jungle. As a result, unsuitable investment proposals are very quickly identified, and rejected.

When submitting their rejection message, investors will often use generic and polite phrases such as: '*Thank you for reaching out to us. Unfortunately, your business does not fit our current investment strategy.*' The reason why professional investors reject investment proposals politely and a bit vaguely is that they are fully aware that any specific assessment from their side might be wrong and that their rejection might be held against them at some point in the future, either by the startup or internally by someone from the corporation. The rejection above is therefore very common as it does not comment on any specific aspect of the startup itself, except that it states that the startup does not fit the current investment strategy of the corporation.

Wrongful rejections are actually much more common than one would think. If you have a bit of time, go and visit the anti-portfolio website of Bessemer Venture Partners (https://www.bvp.com/anti-portfolio/). Bessemer is a top US venture capital firm, and they have shared some of their most famous (wrongful) rejections of startups on their website. It's an entertaining read, and quite educational in terms of how often even really good investors can be wrong about the prospects of certain companies. Bessemer has rejected proposals from companies like Meta, FedEx, eBay, Tesla, Airbnb, Apple, etc.

Adverse reactions of founders

Generic rejections like the one quoted previously can, however, frustrate founders nevertheless. Based on such a message, frustrated founders may strive to take the fight to the next level. They may send direct messages to individual members of the top management or even the board of your corporation. That does sound plausible, right? When you are not satisfied with the service of an agent of a company, you go to the next level to complain more. Sometimes, such founders will just present their startup again. Other times they will complain that their proposal was rejected, misunderstood, or that they were otherwise treated badly by the corporate venture capital team. This may, in turn, motivate the top management member on the receiving end of this message (and always concerned about reputational effects) to forward the startup's email to the CV team with an added question mark. And this question mark may then cause some stress on the side of the CV team, as you can imagine, and then even lead to a second examination of the case.

However, CV teams (and top managers) should not get nervous or have reason to be nervous about rejections. Startup investors reject, on average, 95–99 per cent of their inbound deal flow. Top management should support and trust the CV team and not question or interfere with individual decisions. And the CV team should not be afraid of founders approaching the corporation's top management if they do not do what the startup wants or expects. In fact, if the startup starts to believe that approaching top management was helpful and forced the CV team to revisit the case and eventually engage in investment discussions, they may threaten to walk the same path again.

Keep in mind: your CV team should decide where to spend time on more screening, DD and term sheet negotiations and where not to spend time. And it needs to be able to position itself towards the founders as strong decision makers, not as puppets of the corporation's top management.

Actively generated deal flow

Actively generated deal flow or outbound deal flow is the result of the CV team's *active* search for investment opportunities in the market, i.e., informed by their own investment strategy and executed with the support of databases, the investment team's own network (including universities and other investors), or the support provided by specialized external experts, so-called 'scouts'. Actively generated deal flow plays an increasingly important role in the market due to the higher quality, i.e., better 'fit' of the targets with the investor's investment criteria. It's obvious, isn't it? You yourself know best what you are looking for.

The initial rejection rate for actively generated deal flow is, naturally, much lower than for inbound deal flow. Nevertheless, actively sourced deals get rejected a lot but at later stages, e.g., because the scouting team or investment team misunderstood aspects about the startup or find some red flags during the due diligence. But on average, deals that you have sourced yourself following your own investment principles and strategies have a much higher likelihood to 'fit'.

Increasing transparency of the startup universe

But isn't the startup sector too opaque and granular and isn't it impossible to find the right startups by yourself? Since the beginning of the new millennium, the transparency of the startup sector has improved dramatically. In the early 2000s, after the burst of the internet bubble, the startup sector was still very opaque. At that time, 'prominent' startups, e.g., in the e-commerce field or in social media, that could boast success stories and had business models that were easy to understand (and/or accessible for the readers, too) received most of the attention of the press and, hence, the public. In contrast, there was very limited visibility related to startups working in highly complex and hard-to-understand fields, e.g., in deep tech, biotech, chemistry. During that time, the startup ecosystem in the USA was already relatively well established, with numerous large startup investors and good exits for individual startup companies. In Europe, Asia, South America and the rest of the world, startup ecosystems were still in their infancy stage.

In the two decades following the burst of the internet bubble, this gradually changed. More and more 'general' investors with no specific startup focus or expertise (e.g., family offices, private individuals, private equity funds) began to recognize the startup space as an attractive investment segment, even if only as a small complimentary element of their asset allocation. In the early 2000s, such investors could only get access to 'good and promising startups' through co-investments with established VC firms, often based on prior investments into the funds of such VC firms.

Over time, however, database providers such as CB Insights, Pitchbook, Crunchbase or Dealroom, started to recognize the sector's growing demand for higher transparency. The startups and their existing investors wanted to gain more transparency and insights on potential co-investors for their next rounds of funding. And the (new) startup investors wanted to get access to existing startups and their main investors without being forced to follow the footsteps of individual VCs. So certain database providers started to build huge databases and began to sell data on startups and funding rounds to investors, startups, and other stakeholders of the ecosystem. They effectively enabled family offices, etc. to search internationally for startups that would fit their respective investment criteria by setting startup-specific search parameters (e.g., maturity level, geography, industry segment and sub-segment, previous financing volume).

We can assume that the trend for increasing transparency will continue in the coming years because it serves the interests of founders and investors alike. Transparency grants less obvious investors (e.g., investors from different regions or different industries) better access to new investment opportunities, which is in the interest of founders and existing investors. Also, transparency makes markets more efficient and may lead to an effective and efficient secondary market, where startup investors focused on early rounds can sell their shareholdings in certain companies to investors focusing on later rounds of funding.

Generate deal flow with the support of scouts

Much like historical scouts in the Wild West, startup scouts know (or pretend to know) poorly mapped and opaque areas much better than their clients. In addition, scouts emphasize that they have special tracking skills that enable them to trace down even those startups that may not want to be found or are very hard to find. Scouts are often hyper-connected (former) venture capital investment professionals with unique communication skills who have traced down startups on behalf of investors (i.e., corporate or large VCs) in their respective startup scene for years. Scouts are either generalists or specialists.

- Generalist scouts offer their scouting services without reservation to the topic on the basis of an in-depth briefing by the client.
- Specialist scouts offer their scouting services with particular focus on certain topics, often with high complexity and require a unique understanding (e.g., Crypto Currency Scouts, Biotech Scouts, Artificial Intelligence Scouts, Longevity Scouts).

Similar to the Wild West, most specialized scouts deliberately limit their search activities to specific geographies (e.g., their home country or a region like EMEA) which they know best and where they can leverage their network of contacts that they have built for themselves over many years. As most specialized topics transcend geographic regions, specialized scouts sometimes operate across borders on the basis of an international network of contacts. Like investors, scouts frequently use databases to complement their activities with second approach. The costs for a scout usually amount to €5,000–20,000 per month, depending on the scout, the topic, and the region (and probably also the client).

Feeder funds and accelerators

Feeder funds and accelerators constitute other popular approaches to deal flow generation. One underlying strength that both feeder funds and accelerators share is the fact that they allow investors to monitor early-stage startups over longer periods of time *before* deciding to make a more substantial investment. This is quite helpful, as you may imagine. If you have to assess an employee or student, would you have more confidence in your decision after seeing the person on 2–3 full days and during a number of calls, or after seeing the person on 40–50 days and in various situations, with many more additional calls? The same is true for startups. Longer observation periods generate more data on the thing that you try to assess, and so it is helpful to find ways to observe startups over longer periods of time before you invest, because the observation will tell you a lot about the startup's dynamic, communication style, openness to entertain discussions around alternative ideas and approaches, and its ability to execute strategies and programmes.

Operationally, Feeder Funds can be implemented in different ways. Economically, a Feeder Fund is, in its simplest form, just a small virtual pocket of money taken from the overall budget of your CV activity that you dedicate to quick and small investments (e.g., up to €150,000) per company targeting very early-stage startups. Obviously, you would still follow the idea to invest in startups that somehow fit your financially driven or strategically driven investment strategy. This small portfolio is then monitored over 12 to 18 months, and then the most promising companies are selected and 'fed' into the actual corporate VC fund as investment opportunities that come with additional insights. In essence, this will allow you to explain the following to your Investment Committee:

> 12 months ago, we made a small investment in startup xyz, that is focused on the development of a new AI software for facility management. In the past, the startup was able to achieve milestones A, B, and C, as discussed prior to our investment. Moreover, we found the collaboration between the startup and our in-house facility management team extremely easy and without frictions. In fact, we were able to lower our cost for facility management activities by x%. We therefore recommend to use our CV Fund program to invest €2 million as part of the next EUR 4m round of funding. (…).

Alternatively, the corporation can also set up an Accelerator Programme. Such programmes often run over 3–4 months per badge of 5–10 startups. The startups applying for admission to the Accelerator programme have to meet certain criteria (e.g., tech focus, maturity stage) as put forth by the sponsor of the Accelerator Programme (and often derived directly from a corporation's general CV strategy).

Accelerator Programmes can be run two to three times per year. Often, corporations commission specialized service providers such as Plug & Play, TechStars, MassChallenge, etc. to run the Accelerator Programme on their behalf, mostly because these organizations have a lot of experience stemming from the different Accelerators which they run in collaboration with different major corporations in different regions. Moreover, the visibility of Accelerator Programmes run by such international companies often allows them to attract more startups from various countries and regions, and allows the participating startups to showcase their activities from investors working with the organization in different countries and regions.

Startups selected for the Accelerator Programme receive highly structured and systematic support as well as training from experts on how to build, grow and fund their companies. Most Accelerator Programmes are funded by one large corporation (or sometimes a university). In some cases, several corporations will come together and jointly fund and run an Accelerator Programme. Some Accelerator Programmes entail small investments from the organization that runs the programme (funded by the corporation(s) sponsoring the programme). Over the different batches processed per year, and over the first 1–3 years, this then leads to a small portfolio that starts to resemble a Feeder Fund. For example, each startup selected for an investment based on its good performance during the Accelerator Programme receives €100,000. Per badge, 3–4 out of 6 participating companies receive such an investment. The Programme is hosted three times per year. So, in total, the sponsoring corporation is (through the Accelerator Program Company) invested in 9–12 startups with tickets of €100,000 per company.

Normally, other VCs operating in the same region and/or focusing on a similar industry are involved in Accelerator Programmes as coaches or jury members. The VCs often appreciate such involvements because they get a chance to monitor a couple of pre-selected startups over a longer period of time without paying for the Accelerator Programme. The Accelerators also benefit from the VC's involvement because they can offer the participating startups real-world training, e.g., on how to approach professional VCs successfully. Furthermore, Accelerators often leverage their VC networks by asking the mentoring VCs to send new fresh applicants to the pre-selection process for the next Accelerator.

So here is how this can work in practice: a VC is invited to meet with students at the local university to give feedback and inputs on some startup presentations prepared by the students. During those presentations, the VC believes that they have discovered 1–2 talents with promising ideas, but their concepts are pre-seed stage, i.e., extremely early-stage and too early to invest right now. So, the VC suggests to the founders to develop their idea a bit more, and then to consider applying to the Accelerator Programme. The VC will explain that the Accelerator enables the founders to get additional training and support from various investors and coaches. The Founders eventually decide to follow the VCs advice and they are selected to participate in the Programme.

In the end, everybody is happy:

- The VC is happy because they can now monitor the team over a longer period of time and eventually invest, if they are convinced they have found 'the right team and the right company'.
- The Accelerator Programme is happy because the startup was introduced and pre-selected by the VC, i.e., a professional startup investor, arguably with a good eye for promising businesses. Furthermore, the Accelerator can reflect in its success statistics that 3 out of 5 participating startups receive funding after the Programme, which helps them become more attractive to other startups, which will enable them to attract high quality companies, which will please the sponsoring corporation more and potentially secure the continuation of the Accelerator programme.
- The corporation that is sponsoring the Accelerator is happy because it can network with the VC, and it can benefit from the (potentially) good scouting effort of the VC and invest in the startup that is also coached and supported by the Accelerator.

- And, last but not least, the startup is happy because what started for the two students as a somewhat improvised presentation of a pretty good idea has developed in less than 12 months into a cool startup that has received coaching, support, investments from the VC and the corporation, and has already increased its visibility to the market significantly by participating in the Programme.

We should not forget that Feeder Funds and Accelerator Programmes are somewhat expensive to host. Depending on the organization, the hosting of an Accelerator Programme will cost €1–5 million per year (or more, depending on the number of badges, the facilities provided for the Accelerator, etc.).

To justify this cost, such Programmes must prove that they have strong, potentially global visibility and are able to attract 'top-tier' startups. And they have to prove that they can 'produce' well-run and promising startups with a good strategic fit to the corporation on an ongoing basis. And they have to prove that startups participating in the Programme have a good chance to get funding from either the corporation and/or other investors supporting the Accelerator.

Inherently, Accelerator Programmes are at risk of attracting 'second-tier' startups because one can argue that top-tier startups (with serial entrepreneurs and a bit of acclaim upon announcing their launch) can raise capital and grow without taking money or support from Feeder Funds or Accelerator Programmes. But Accelerators are nonetheless popular. And corporations are not sad about pictures of their top management in somewhat quirky Accelerator facilities with nerdy founders in pleasant conversations.

Startup conferences

Startup conferences are a popular tool to generate inbound deal flow. But they also reflect an attempt to increase the quality of inbound deal flow. Moreover, startup conferences may help CV teams to identify new sources for deal flow and new co-investors.

The idea is simple: your CV team attends a startup conference that is completely on whatever topic your CV activity is focused on. Let's assume your CV Team is focused on e-mobility and other innovative mobility concepts. You attend a startup conference focused on 'mobility concepts of the future'. And obviously, after a panel discussion where one of your CV team members was able to describe the focus of you CV activity, or after a seminar or workshop that you host as part of the startup conference, you are likely to receive many more investment proposals from startups focusing on this topic.

The good thing is that most of these proposals triggered by your attendance of the conference will have a pretty good industry fit, because mostly startups focusing on this segment will come to the conference, and potentially, the founders have listened to whatever your CV team had to say during the conference and believe that their company could be a good fit for the CV Fund. However, some founders may still overlook your stage focus, i.e., they may turn out to be too-early-stage or too-late-stage companies. And some may overlook other aspects that are important to you but that were not well understood during the conference, e.g., that you only invest in revenue-generating startups, not in pre-revenue startups.

Another benefit of startup conferences is that they enable your CV team to engage and liaise with other investors and stakeholders interested in your particular area, e.g., in our example from above, new technologies related to mobility. It is not unlikely that other top managers from large corporations working in the same industry may also attend the conference and act as key note speakers. You may know them already, but this is still a good opportunity to catch up and renew the contact. Or perhaps a high-ranking representative of the government is attending the conference to speak about the plans of the ministry for traffic and mobility. Whoever you meet, if your team builds a meaningful relationship, such people and organizations may share deal flow and opportunities with you. Because they see you as a potential (co)-investor, as a potential strategic partner, or as a potential acquirer of the startup.

Startup conferences are, however, also a major perk of the job of a venture capitalist. And they can be very distracting. You may even hear from your CV team that they would like to postpone a certain meeting with your top management or the Investment Committee because they prefer to attend a two-day-conference in Helsinki where they have a feature called 'the Investor Sauna'. And as much as it makes sense to network and scout, it is also important to note that investors should be disciplined around startup conferences:

- Focus on conferences that fit the investment strategy of the CV Team
- Focus on conferences where your team members will not just sit in the audience, but be featured on stage, e.g., as part of a panel discussion, so that they can increase the CV's visibility towards the aforementioned groups

- Send a small number of team members (max 1–2) per conference, except if you plan to have a booth which usually requires 4–10 people
- Assign clear tasks and targeted outcomes of the conference, e.g., meet startups A, B, C, and commence conversations around their next round of funding. Also, meet investors D, E, F, and agree on a separate call to discuss collaboration in the context of scouting and investing.

Reference

Bessemer Venture Partners (2023) The Anti-Portfolio https://www.bvp.com/anti-portfolio (archived at https://perma.cc/VJ9A-U7RA)

Screening 18

The selection of target companies is a critical success factor for startup investors. This is true for business angels, private VCs and corporate venture capital investors alike.

Speaking about success in the startup world, arguably *investment* success in the world of venture capital hinges on three factors:

1. How well the investor 'buys', i.e., makes new investments
2. How well the investor supports existing investments and help them gain a lot of value in a relatively short period of time
3. How well the investor 'sells', i.e., supports exit plans of the startup.

You may want to add 'sheer luck' to that list, but maybe that's helpful for any list of success factors. You may also contemplate that success does not necessarily mean financial success. Maybe an investor would only count 'unicorn status' as real success for startup investments, but for the founders, employees, their customers and all of their families, even a mildly successful company can be extremely meaningful and a core element of the lives of certain people.

Perhaps you want to note that the optimization of the terms and conditions, for example, the successful negotiation around the valuation of a startup or the liquidation preference, is missing in the list of three points above. This is because in most cases, even the most sophisticated term sheet and investment agreement cannot make up for a poor selection of investment targets in the first place. Think about it: if you selected the 'right' company, you may never need the liquidation preference, because there will be no liquidation. And even if you were not able to negotiate the exact pre-money valuation for your investment, this may not be as important, because it does not make a major difference if you own a 12 per cent share or 15 per cent share in a startup that is now worth more than a billion dollars. What really matters is that you acquired that 12 per cent share for an initial investment of $5 million and that share has a value today of $120 million.

Would it be better to have 15 per cent, and the value would be $150 million? Certainly. But would you consider $120 million less of a success?

On the other hand, if you selected the wrong company, and you owned 15 per cent of it, and you were able to negotiate for a liquidation preference working in your favour, the liquidation proceeds may still be way too small to compensate for your initial investment. And then the size of your shareholding becomes irrelevant, because there are not even enough liquidation proceeds to pay back the initial investment.

The ongoing support of startups is mostly considered slightly (only slightly!) less important than the selection due to the minority shareholders' limited influence and limited capability of VCs to manage startups better than the startup founders. This is certainly not true in all cases, i.e., some investors have outstanding expertise and are able to not only prevent their portfolio companies from committing beginners' mistakes, but also to lift them up to a higher level. However, it is also true that certain investors never moved a finger for their portfolio companies and still ended up generating extremely high returns on investment, partly because they selected the right target, partly because the founders were so brilliant, partly because other investors supported the team effectively, or partly they were just lucky in the exit process.

Speaking of which, even the exit-related activities are considered less important than the selection because good startups will almost automatically attract the interest of several potential exit partners. And unsuccessful startups will not be attractive for any buyers or only very few buyers, even if you put the effort of all members of your investment team behind the case.

Screening-challenge: Not-invented-here syndrome

Talking about the screening of the right startup, the not-invented-here syndrome or myth needs to be managed. There are often internal groups of corporate employees, who hold critical opinions and rejection of external innovations, as they assume that they lead to a loss of capabilities and at the same time create dependency, and conservative ambitions get in the way. The critical opinions of internal experts are usually not the conscious result of a defensive attitude on the part of the experts toward the startup, but the result of years of their own experience and influence in a particular business field. This has often been the case in long-established companies such as

Nestlé in the past. As a result, the incorporation of open innovation is not recognized or rejected, if not CV is called 'dumb money' as highlighted in the research paper by Huang & Madhavan (2021). However, by setting incentives to push innovation further as well as holding the right communication in place, this initial defence towards innovation and thus transformation can be avoided and diminished.

Startup investments are about the future. Investors try to assess whether and to what extent the founders' optimistic assumptions about the future are understandable and plausible. This is because at the time of investing in a young company, there is usually little reliable 'evidence' that the project will actually fly. The lack of data regarding the company's past and future and the resulting uncertainty lead observers of the startup to make do with assumptions or to closely scrutinize the founders' assumptions. This process, in which investors develop their own assumptions to ultimately arrive at an opinion pro/con of the investment, is usually influenced not only by facts, but also by biases, moods, and incidental trivia already built into the investor/viewer.

It happens relatively regularly that startups compete with novel concepts that, from the group's point of view, are actually or supposedly inferior to the products or prototypes developed in-house, but possibly also clearly superior in one or more parameters. Let's imagine that Tesla were to present itself to an established automaker in its startup phase and solicit an investment. There is a good chance that the Tesla presentation or a first prototype will be literally taken apart by the company's in-house experts – '(...) not well-thought-out product details, inadequate build quality, incomprehensible performance data, excessive product cost calculation, etc.' It is easy to overlook the fact that Tesla has strengths in the areas of zeitgeist (keyword: supposed environmental protection through electro-mobility), performance/acceleration/driving feel and possibly also design, which are at least equal to or even superior to the company's own vehicles.

The critical opinions of in-house experts are usually not the conscious result of any defensive attitude on the part of the experts toward the startup, but the result of years of their own experience and influence in automotive engineering. In a corporate group, there are the highest quality standards, which a startup usually cannot meet right from the start. And possibly the in-house expert also combines his own frustrations in connection with his own first attempts in the startup: 'We already experimented with electromobility in the 1980s, but it was neither then nor is it now a real option...'). Subliminally/unconsciously, the scepticism of in-house experts may also be driven by the fear of jeopardizing their own position in the company in the medium term if an engagement with the startup comes about. Therefore, it is important to create criteria catalogues that allow you to define how, where, when, and for what to screen to find promising investment prospects.

Requirements and screening catalogue

Corporate and private startup investors often use a clearly defined **criteria catalogue** and **system** to screen and pre-select startups.

For most *corporate VCs*, at least one out of the three following general aspects should be true for a valid investment hypothesis:

1. The startups can help the corporation to become more successful (i.e., this would be a key requirement for strategic investors).
2. The corporate can support the startup in a way that will enable the startup to grow much faster (i.e., this would be a potential requirement for strategic and financial investors).
3. The startup looks extremely promising and the investing corporation sees tremendous growth potential, even without significant support of the startup from the corporation (i.e., this would be a requirement for a financial investor).

Table 18.1 shows an example of a typical *requirement catalogue* (i.e., what is the investor actually looking for) and *screening criteria list* (what other aspects the investor will examine even during the first interview to decide whether or not a given startup is potentially an investment target).

The screening process or selection process is based on a preceding thought process in which the investor must reach a clarity about what he/she is looking for. In corporate groups, investment strategies and criteria catalogues are often developed in collaboration between the strategy department, the investment team, top management, and subject matter experts from R&D departments and sometimes even customer-facing departments.

Table 18.1 Requirement catalogue and screening criteria

Typical requirement criteria catalogue (exemplary), i.e. what startup profile the corporation is looking for...	Typical screening criteria list (exemplary), i.e. what the corporation will examine to determine investment suitability of a given startup...
Geography: Americas or Europe	Executive summary
Industry: Software	Team
Segments: SaaS/B2B (ERP, CRM)	Product or service
Turnover: Turnover >EUR 100k p.a.	Market
Phase: Seed to Series A, not later	Competition
Preferred ticket: Max. €2 million, min. €500,000	Sales and business model
Preferred %: Min. 10%, max. 40%	Financials (historical, current, future)
	Legal
	Investment case
	Strategic roadmap
	Sustainability aspects
	Timing

Typical requirement criteria catalogue

In determining the requirement criteria catalogue, the investor defines which startup types or which basic criteria/characteristics of individual companies he considers suitable. Typical criteria include:

- **Geography:** for example, the corporate investor may prefer to invest in companies located or active in the regions where the investor has or plans to develop business activities, too. The thinking behind this is easy; being 'close' to the startup may facilitate collaboration between the startup and the corporation, may lead to fewer language and culture problems, and may automatically mean that the startup is familiar with the corporation's home market and local regulation, etc. Of course, this point can be refined arbitrarily (e.g., America could mean only USA and Canada, but not Central and South America). Typically, this criterion weighs a little bit less than other criteria, in such that companies from other regions may also be included in the shortlist, provided that they plan to develop activities in the target regions (e.g., a Chinese company that is planning to set up a branch in France may be considered a target for a French corporate VC).

- **Industry and segments:** a broadly positioned group with a large portfolio of products, services, catering to different customer groups in various countries and dealing with diverse challenges, can choose to define its target industry or tech segment very broadly and then potentially refine the requirement criteria over time. For example, Shell Ventures may define renewable energies as a target industry, but over time, they can set certain focal points within this industry cluster, e.g., alternative fuels and photovoltaic innovation. Or it can deliberately exclude other areas which it deems less strategic, e.g., all renewable energies and related technologies except wood combustion.
- **Turnover and startup phase:** In essence, 'turnover' and 'phase' represent maturity criteria. The investor may deliberately exclude companies that have not yet achieved market entry (i.e., they do not generate any revenue). Alternatively, the investor can focus, for example, exclusively, on Series A companies, no matter if they generate revenues or not. This decision can be driven by risk considerations, supposing that revenue-generating companies represent a somewhat lower investment risk. However, this decision can also be driven by a strategic motivation, supposing that the investor intends to invest in companies that could potentially be acquired in 2–5 years to contribute sales and profit to the parent company.
- **Capital requirements and preferred % shareholding:** These criteria are determined by the investment strategy of the investor, i.e., considerations such as:
  - What total investment volume can I invest or do I want to invest in a single startup? For example, €5 million versus €50 million per company.
  - How large is my target portfolio? For example, should the portfolio comprise only 10 or at least 20 companies after 3–5 years?
  - How high is the first and second investment allocation (i.e., first investment and, a few years later, follow-up investment) that I plan to make available for each investment, subject to performance?

The preferred percentage target shareholding is basically a statement against 'spray and pray' or 'symbolic' investments (with 2–3 per cent), and in favour of meaningful investments with conviction (e.g., with at least 10 per cent, which would also provide a noticeable discount if the corporation would decide at some point that it would like to acquire the startup).

Again, please keep in mind that the above requirement criteria merely represent examples. No individual criteria is a must have. In fact, you can also run a completely opportunistic CV programme, if you think that makes sense. Few people do, but it is possible. Just remember that the investor can define additional or fewer criteria, or even define unique criteria in a completely different way. The criteria will make life for your screening team easier; each additional criteria will reduce the number of potential targets that make it to the screening process.

Sometimes, an investor may feel that it makes sense to re-examine the criteria catalogue after the first screening sessions. Maybe you want to refine certain criteria a bit, or add a new one like 'the company should be incorporated as a Ltd or Inc or SA or GmbH'.

Lastly, it may make sense to give your team members a little bit of room to manoeuvre. Let's say a person from your team finds an extremely promising startup team with a perfect strategic fit, but the team does not have revenues yet, however it will enter the market in the next month. Then maybe you want to encourage that person to still include the company in the screening, even though it may not meet one or two of the requirement criteria. In your team, you will be surrounded by intelligent people. Do not force them to act stupidly.

Screening approach

The **screening approach** provides a framework that informs how the CV team will 'examine' startups systematically. It serves as a guideline for the investor to ensure a professional, rigorous and holistic analysis of the target company and to avoid any kind of a subjective and/or feelings-based screening process that may even disregards some important aspects.

Think of the following analogy: imagine you come to an emergency room. The attending doctor does not ask you about your age, weight, blood type, allergies, intolerances, previous illnesses, etc., but addresses your problem directly, e.g., your bleeding hand. While this may cut to the chase – after all, your bleeding hand is why you have come to the emergency room in the first place – the omitted questions may pose a fatal threat if you do not survive the treatment due to intolerances or different blood types.

In the following section, we want to exemplify (without being conclusive!) which questions investors typically raise in the context of individual screening aspects and kick-off meetings with startups.

The investors may ask an infinite number of additional follow-up questions within each segment of the screening process. Nevertheless, the investor should not confuse screening and due diligence.

One of the veteran CV managers told us the following story:

> (…) so, I have a meeting with our Chief Marketing Officer. She tells me that she has just met with startup xyz in Tokyo, and that the meeting has lasted for eight hours. 'Eight hours, really?' I asked. She smiled at me proudly, as if there was a positive correlation between time spent on a screening meeting and information gathered. Apparently, they had discussed all sorts of things in these eight hours. But ask yourself the following: what does a Chief Marketing Officer, with all due respect, understand about how our tech department is assessing the startup's technology, and if and how they would be working with the startup? And how much does she really understand about startups based on her previous career as a consultant or marketeer? I believe it makes much more sense to have shorter, more focused sessions with the founders, to see them in different situations, and to include your subject matter experts, too, so that the questions you ask are not too generic. On the other hand, I believe that people less experienced in dealing with startups are easily [impressed] by a young team of smart and well-presenting founders. So not surprised that she was super excited about the meeting. Who wouldn't be? But I also think that this behaviour did not help our negotiation position. If you camp outside of your BMW dealership and take pictures of your favourite BMW model, do you think this will help you in negotiations with the BMW sales team? If the startup starts to believe that your organization has already fallen in love with what they do, how strong is your walk-away threat?

The goal of the first in-depth interview between investor and company (often lasting 1–3 hours) is just an opportunity for the investor to gain an initial but somewhat comprehensive understanding of the startup. Of course, this process may provide the investor with clues for subsequent due diligence, if applicable, and the investor should document such clues.

Table 18.2 Startup screening questions

Executive Summary • What 'problem' is the company addressing? • How good is the product-market fit (customer feedback)? • Is the solution provided superior to other solutions and can it be quantified how superior it is?	**Team** • What skills and experience do team members bring to the table? • How complementary is the team set up? • What sort of personalities are in the team, i.e. how is the intrapersonal fit with the CV team?	**Product or Service** • How does the product or service work? • Is the product defendable, what's the IP strategy? • How does the product differ from the competition? • What are the product risks? • What are underlying unit economics?
Market • Which clients does the product address? • How big and how fast growing is the market? • What portion of the market is actually addressable?	**Competition** • Is the competition fragmented or focused? • What are the major players? • What are the barriers to market entry? • Is the competition dynamic or sleepy?	**Sales & Business Model** • Channels: Online? Offline? B2B, B2C, B2B2C etc.? • Prices? Margins? • How do customer acquisition costs relate to customer lifetime value?
Financials • What are key drivers for costs and revenues? • Which KPIs have been achieved so far? What is the 3–5 year plan? • How has the company been financed so far?	**Legal** • What are the key legal frameworks relevant to the business? • What IP or regulatory aspects need to be considered? • Do any of the previous investors have special rights?	**Investment Case** • How much capital do you raise? • What is the valuation? • Who else is investing in this funding round?

(continued)

Table 18.2 (Continued)

Strategic Roadmap	Sustainability	Timing
• How is the collected capital going to be spent? • What constitutes the next main activities? • What are key milestones, e.g. market entry, break-even, finalize phase 1 tests	• From the startup's point of view: Which aspects of the business, if any, are relevant or critical from an ESG perspective and how are they managed today? • From the investor's point of view: Which aspects of the business are relevant or critical (potentially) for the investor's company?	• Why is the time perfect for the startup's approach? • What are the key milestones the startup is targeting? • How much time is available for due diligence, signing and closing? • How much time will the startup have before the money from this present round runs out?

Ultimately, the screening culminates in a preliminary investment decision. The two choices you have at this point are:

'Yes, we would like to continue the process.'

or

'Thank you, we will refrain from pursuing this opportunity any further, because...'

Factual challenges in the context of criteria catalogue and screening and due diligence

In the course of the screening and the subsequent due diligence, the investor strives to obtain as complete an overview of the current situation of the target company as possible, including its main drivers of upside and downside risk. Let us first look at the purely factual level of screening and due diligence. Following an old paradigm developed by former US Secretary of Defense, Mr Donald Rumsfeld, we can divide the investor's knowledge and knowledge gaps into four 'buckets'.

a Known knowns: These are facts or information that investors are aware of and understand. They are things that they know that they know.

b Known unknowns: These are gaps in knowledge that investors are aware of but do not yet have the information to fill. They are things that they know that they don't know.

c Unknown knowns: These are facts or information that investors possess but are not aware of. They are things that they don't know that they know.

d Unknown unknowns: These are things that investors do not know they don't know – unexpected events, surprises, or unknown problems that may arise and catch them off guard. They are things that they are unaware of and therefore cannot anticipate or plan for.

Let's think about these four 'buckets' for a moment.

- **Known knowns** are the most specific and handy category of information. The investor must query the startup to acquire and/or confirm this information and ensure the obtained information is complete and correct through independent evaluation.

- **Known unknowns** are a very interesting category of information. It is clear from the outset that the investor may not attain full certainty regarding these aspects, no matter how much time and energy is invested to investigate. Nevertheless, dealing with this category, using methods to develop estimates, etc. can inspire useful conversations with the founders and improve the understanding of this positive/negative risk.
- **Unknown knowns** resemble known unknowns in that they are a very interesting category of information. Founders and investors may not yet know who can provide good information on these areas. However, founders and investors can strive to improve their understanding of this information category, for example by launching quick pilot projects. You may know, for instance, that 10 per cent of all US domestic flights get cancelled. You may not know, however, if your specific flight from Denver to New York is going to be cancelled. And you may only find out in a week or so, when you board the plane. But you can improve your understanding on how likely your flight is going to be cancelled. And somebody may know if the flight is going to be cancelled some time before you and other passengers know, so maybe you can find that person.
- **Unknown unknowns** are probably the most unspecific and, arguably, least significant insight category. Can investors gain valuable insights that inform their investment decisions by spending more time and energy on this category? Probably not. This would cause investors to assess, and to seek remedies for acts of God such as natural disasters, political upheavals, or macroeconomic crises.

Psychological challenges in the context of the requirements, screening and due diligence

The process of startup analysis and investment decision is a cognitive process in which the investor strives to develop a robust understanding of the startup to ultimately take an investment decision based on the understanding of what the startup aims to achieve and how likely it is that it will be successful.

One key challenge that investors face is to limit ego-related elements of human perception, and to analyse, evaluate and decide as objectively as possible. In other words, the human mind, facing an opaque information or situation, will quickly come up with assumptions and heuristic estimates. And sometimes you do not even realize that your brain is handing you an assessment which is not necessarily based on a solid understanding of the underlying matter. So as a golden rule, investors should not prioritize their gut feelings, but prioritize the search for facts. And then once you have gathered, discussed, and assessed the facts, as a second priority, you can still consult your heart, guts, or whatever part of your body you believe to be instrumental in your assessment process or decision-making process. But remember, a sober analysis of facts and information has priority.

A veteran private VC commented on this saying:

> I think it is funny how unintellectual the community of startup investors can be from time to time. By and large, we happen to be a highly educated and somewhat enlightened and smart bunch of people. However, I remember attending lectures or key notes from other experienced investors were intelligent people seemed to suggest that because the success of a startup cannot be predicted with certainty, it is advisable to follow your gut feeling. How is that advisable, I wonder? Let's assume you climb a mountain. I agree that you may not be able to predict with certainty what the weather conditions will be like 24 or 48 hours from now. And you may not even be able to decide today how you will change your path tomorrow if and when weather conditions deteriorate. But wouldn't you at least research the different routes to the summit that you can take, mark places where you can seek shelter, make sure that you bring enough food and water to potentially wait out a thunderstorm?

This – prioritization of objective assessment – is easier said than done. After all, it is in the nature of human beings to succumb to cognitive biases. Let's take a look at a few practical examples to illustrate where and how problematic situations typically arise.

You may or may not have witnessed how a startup and the founder team can make a ***subjective-negative*** impression on an investor for non-objective reasons. Here are some typical examples:

- During the conversations between founder and investor, the founder may unintentionally make the investor feel intellectually or professionally inferior. Subsequently, the investor may feel, consciously or unconsciously, insulted, paraded and even humiliated. In essence, a communication problem or a connection problem may hamper the investment process. The founder may attend a meeting driving an expensive car or wearing an expensive watch. This may cause the investor to question, consciously or unconsciously, whether the founder raises funds to grow the company or to finance a lavish lifestyle. In essence, resentment and envy may hamper the investment process, even if these concerns seem irrational.

- The startup may present a product innovation that does not directly appeal to the investor. For example, the startup may present a new video game to an investor who does not play any video games. While gamification may be the right tool to incentivize users to use the startup's software application, the investor may ignore this because her/his own preferences differ greatly from the target customers'.
- The startup develops a cryptocurrency or metaverse innovation, but the investor is fundamentally suspicious of cryptocurrency or metaverse projects because a friend of the investor has lost a lot of money on a cryptocurrency investment. As a result, the investor may disproportionally consult overly negative/disastrous articles about such projects. Selective perception and confirmation bias have hampered the investment process.

In reverse, a startup can also make a ***subjective-positive*** impression on the investor for non-objective reasons. Here are some typical examples:

- An investor may immediately feel a connection with a founder who grew up in the same region, went to the same university, or communicates in an entertaining or flattering way.
- Some founders try to play with the investor XYZ's 'fear of missing out' (industry-jargon: FOMO). So, let's say the founders present a cryptocurrency innovation to Deutsche Bank. It could be worthwhile for them to mention to Deutsche Bank that they have already signed contracts or co-development agreements with HSBC, UBS, and Bank of America, so that Deutsche Bank feels more comfortable working with the startup team, but also starts to discuss if they can reject the startup's proposal, given that some of their most relevant competitors have apparently signed up for this.
- The startup may appeal to the investor's ideals, values, virtues, etc. For example, the investor may deem the startup's purpose and orientation so important for the good of the planet that the investor overlooks and/or underestimates or simply ignores crucial shortcomings in a conscious or subconscious attempt to promote or defend the startup's ideals.

Almost all investors (99 per cent) will claim that they decide purely on the basis of objective facts. Nobody likes to admit the inconvenient truth that personal and emotional aspects play a decisive role in the decision-making process. However, most investors may remember at least some situations that resemble the aforementioned examples.

Putting in place the right processes can protect investment decisions against personal biases, for example:

- The investor may put in place an Investment Committee or a dual control principle, i.e., group of experienced investors and/or entrepreneurs, ideally with subject matter expertise, who can support or challenge decisions to invest/not invest.
- The investor may also put in place an Advisory Committee of independent/external subject matter experts.
- The investor may also put in place a process that determines that team members and partners/senior executives who have worked with a company for a long time are excluded from the decision process or voting because they may be biased.

The investor may spend time, money and energy on training people and making them aware of the risk of biased decisions.

Reference

Huang, P and Madhavan, R (2021) Dumb money or smart money? Meta-analytically unpacking corporate venture capital, *Strategic Entrepreneurship Journal*, 15(3), 403–429

Due diligence 19

A due diligence process is essentially a 'deep dive' that complements and substantiates the screening process, but also covers certain areas in much more detail. If one thinks of screening as a comparatively superficial startup analysis, one should think of a due diligence process as an in-depth examination – a deep dive of sorts. Due diligence usually encompasses the following aspects: Legal, Financial, Technical/Operational, Commercial, and Sustainability. We will elaborate on each aspect in the following subchapters.

In parallel to the due diligence, the negotiations between founders and investors around the terms and conditions of the investment begin. These terms and conditions typically cover the amount of the investment, the company valuation, conditions to closing, and, last but not least, the preference rights that the investors will have after the investment. The investors often take 4–8 weeks (and sometimes longer) to run their due diligence and understand the business of the target company in its various facets as precisely as possible.

For corporate investors, the corporation may decide to initiate a joint pilot project or a test collaboration over 1–6 months to substantiate the due diligence with concrete data points. Especially in the corporate venture capital space, the pilot project approach plays a major role because, ultimately, the corporation must demonstrate that it can work with a startup in the intended manner and achieve concrete goals.

Often, corporate investors hire external specialists to support the due diligence process. This has the advantage that it suggests to the corporation's own shareholders that the due diligence is managed professionally. Moreover, it can help to overcome the fact that many corporate investors lack the expertise and capabilities to conduct a fully-fledged due diligence in-house. Topics like IP and freedom to operate (FTO) analysis are often outsourced, as are most aspects of the financial due diligence (such as review of previous annual reports and tax declarations), or technical aspects (like test results generated so far, previous interactions with regulators and received comments or approvals).

Due diligence aims to identify and quantify the negative *and* the positive risks of the target company as precisely as possible. In other words, the investors strive to find out what external or internal factors could jeopardize the success of the company, and what internal and external factors could boost the growth potential of the company. It is extremely important to never forget the forward-looking and optimistic attitude. As one veteran CVC investor explained to us:

> With startups, it's always the same. The longer you look at them, the more risky they appear. At some point, you should gather your courage and jump, i.e., invest. You must never forget (or allow others to forget) that the investment in startup xyz is not driven by the belief that this will definitively work. Not even an investment in a listed company can guarantee success. A startup investment is driven by the belief that their technology or process or approach may work, and we have reasons to believe that it will. And if it does, it will be very successful (and potentially strategically relevant for the corporation and financially rewarding for its existing shareholders).

One must carefully define the scope of the due diligence in advance by assigning responsibilities (i.e., is the due diligence conducted in-house or with external specialists?) and by specifying a time line and financial budget (in what time and at what cost does one want to complete the due diligence process?). Documentation is essential throughout the due diligence.

Legal due diligence

As part of the legal due diligence, all agreements that affect the legal sphere of the startup are reviewed. This includes patent/IP agreements, licenses, binding supply or purchase agreements and pending legal proceedings. In some cases, patent/IP due diligence and freedom-to-operate analyses can even constitute a separate due diligence chapter for which patent attorneys are called in. Corporate groups often go beyond the scope of private financial investors in that they investigate whether legal restrictions may impede a potential M&A process in the future (e.g., antitrust concerns) and whether existing contracts may impact the corporate group post-acquisition. Leases, existing insurances, employment contracts as well as the police clearance certificates of key employees are also checked. As part of the legal due diligence (and sometimes commercial due diligence and/or technical due diligence), one also checks whether the business has all the necessary permits, certificates and other approvals or licenses to carry out their business and whether they are all valid in all geographies now and in the foreseeable future.

Commercial due diligence

As part of a commercial due diligence, the target market and the company's business model are scrutinized. The target market is analysed in terms of market growth, market volume, competition intensity, competition structure (many small versus few large competitors, or a combination thereof) and customer segments. The business model is analysed in terms of the product and/or service, the pricing of the product and/or service, manufacturing costs, margins and unique selling propositions, all of which are evaluated in terms of importance from the customer's perspective. Sophisticated investors would also look into churn rates (how quickly/easily customers can change to another supplier and how often they change), re-purchasing rates (customers returning to the business to buy the product or service again), average basket size and potential development thereof (which individual products or services a customer buys today, and which additional services and products a customer may buy in the future), sales cycles, competitive advantages and disadvantages and how to work on them. The distribution of products and services is also under review.

Technical/operational due diligence

The technical/operational due diligence focuses on a detailed analysis of the technology developed and used and commercialized by the startup, including the supply chain and the production process and potentially elements of the distributions process, too. Depending on the startup's sector, this due diligence process varies greatly. For example, while hardware startups demand rigorous supply chain analyses, software startups call for rigorous analyses of data processing, data protection and systematic software architecture documentation. A biotech startup, on the other hand, calls for a careful analysis of data that stems from proof-of-concept studies, pre-clinical studies, clinical studies, and the strategy to obtain more approvals from the regulator (phases 1, 2, 3 with the FDA, for instance). These days, a separate IT due diligence is also often carried out, involving analyses of IT processes and data protection, because cybercrimes may impose a significant business risk, even for small innovation companies.

Financial due diligence

Financial due diligence typically includes a review of the company's current assets, historical and current income statements, historical and current balance sheets, historical and current cash flows, and a detailed analysis of current shareholders and creditors and capital structure. Larger groups frequently hire external consultants (e.g., from audit firms such as 'the Big Four') for the financial due diligence, to better understand tax risks and balance sheet provisions (like bad debt, amortization).

Sustainability due diligence

Sustainability due diligence focuses on aspects relating to the sustainability of the company. First, the startup's impact on the environment in terms of energy demand, waste generation, and/or greenhouse gas emissions is examined. Second, social aspects such as diversity, human rights, and consumer protection are reviewed. Third, corporate governance aspects such as decision-making processes and fair remuneration of employees is evaluated. And last but not least, the due diligence may also reflect on how an investment in a startup (or an acquisition at some point in the future) may impact the sustainability level of the corporation.

Business valuation 20

Business valuation is an integral part of investment decisions that precede the term sheet. In recent years, venture capital investors and founders have tended to de-emphasize (a little bit!) the importance of business valuation for very early-stage investments, i.e., pre-seed and seed stage. This is due to the fact that if one believes that the value of a company should be determined by its future cash flows, in lack of a more reliable and less controversial basis one also has to acknowledge that projections around the future of the company (and its cash flows) are likely to be wrong – at least to a certain extent. And so why argue endlessly (or even risk the investment) if the valuation cannot be determined with certainty?

Valuation is important because it determines how large a share in the company an investor will get based on the cash invested. In general, many investors believe that only a reasonably large stake in a target company (10 per cent or more) at a reasonable price can ensure that the investor keeps a significant stake in the company after dilution through various rounds of funding. And we will dive deeper on these aspects in a moment.

So, the company valuation determines the share that an investor acquires in a startup based on his cash investment – great. How does this work 'mechanically'?

- Let us assume a startup is looking for an investor to invest €500,000 in a startup.
- Let us further assume that the startup sets a valuation of €2 million pre-money and €2.5 million post-money. By the way, the difference between pre-money and post-money is always the total ticket invested, i.e., €2.5 million post-money minus €2 million pre-money is €500,000, which is the invested amount. And accordingly, €2.5 million post-money minus investment of €500,000 gives you a pre-money of €2 million. Importantly, this ticket could be served by a single investor or multiple investors.

- Let us look at this from the other side as well: Pre-money is the valuation of the startup today, before any investor makes any investment in the context of the current round of funding. Post-money is the valuation of the startup tomorrow, after the investor(s) have injected cash into the company. Again, pre-money plus investment gives you the post money.
- Let's further assume that the investor believes that the pre-money valuation of the startup is not €2 million pre-money (and €2.5 million post-money), but rather €1 million (and €1.5 million post-money).

The ratio of investment amount (here: €500,000) and post-money valuation (€2.5 million if the startup convinces the investors, or €1.5 million if the investor convinces the startup) determines what percentage shareholding the investor will hold in the startup in the future.

Table 20.1 illustrates and explains how the parties will behave in the negotiations:

- Both parties, startup and investor, agree on the ticket, because both share the same view on how much money is needed to take the company to the next level over the next 12–18 months. So, the ticket is not disputed.
- The founders, however, will try to keep the valuation as high as possible to limit their own dilution (20 per cent according to their own valuation and 33 per cent if they accepted the investor's valuation).
- Investors, in turn, will try to keep the valuation as low as possible to increase the share of the company they acquire based on their investment (i.e., 33 per cent if the startup accepts their lower pre-money valuation and 20 per cent if the investors end up accepting the higher valuation requested by the startup).

Table 20.1 The points of departure for negotiations

	Startup assessment	Investor assessment
Pre-money	€2,000,000	€1,000,000
Investment ticket	€500,000	€500,000
Post-money	€2,500,000	€1,500,000
Resulting share of investor	20%	33%

In the next financing round, the former negotiating opponents, founders and investors, are united in negotiating together for a high valuation 'against' the new investors. And again, these new investors will try to negotiate for a lower valuation.

It is also important in this context that founders and investors must ask themselves whether the capital raised in the current financing round is sufficient to take the startup to the next level (i.e., significantly increase revenues, number of customers/users, etc.). Because when the money that is raised in the present round runs out, the company will have to raise fresh funds, preferably at a higher valuation, but then they will have to provide more proof that their approach is working. In other words, with the money we get right now, we have to demonstrate in the next 1–2 years that this is working in the market. This also means that if a portfolio company of the CV team can raise money to increase its runway to two years, in many cases this can be very helpful. If the runway to the next round is too short, the startup may not be able to show a dynamic development, may struggle to attract new investors, and may struggle even more to negotiate for a higher valuation. And under a so-called down round scenario, founders' and existing investors' shareholdings will be diluted much more heavily.

By the way, to clear up a still widespread misbelief: the valuation of a company and thus the share to be allocated to an investor based on the investment is *independent* of the capital invested in the startup company so far. Here's what we mean by that: sometimes founders ask whether investors who plan to make a large investment (e.g., €1 million or €5 million) may 'accidentally' acquire the company, because the proposed investment exceeds their previous capital contributions (for example, €25,000 made by the founders) by a factor of 40. The clear answer is: ***No.*** Professional investors value the company on the basis of expected future cash flows and returns on investment. They do not value the company on the basis of previous investments, cash contribution, or acquired assets (e.g., tables, chairs, and computers). As a result, a startup with a capital contribution of only €25,000 can certainly be valued at €10 million, so long as the investors' expectations on future cash flows are positive. And isn't this a nice Segway into different methods of business valuation?

Business valuation methods

Literature distinguishes numerous methods for the valuation of businesses. Some of them are more useful in the context of startups, some less. In this book, we want to introduce you, on a relatively high level, to three groups of valuation methods: *substance-oriented valuation, market-oriented valuation, and capital-oriented valuation.*

Note that no method will provide you with a reliable, non-disputable value for a business. Accept that different people value the same company differently – which is quite intuitive, if you think about it for a moment.

1 Obviously, founders of a startup as well as existing investors will often tend to overestimate the valuation of the company, because the higher the pre-money valuation is, the lower is the dilution that they will experience in the context of a new round of funding. In other words, they have a built-in initiative to overestimate business valuations. And the same is true for new incoming investors; they tend to underestimate the valuation of the startup because the lower the pre-money valuation is, the more shares they will get for their investment.
2 If you look at public markets, each day different investors have different assumptions regarding the business prospects of a listed company. Think of a giant blue-chip company like Microsoft, for instance. Certain investors will calculate and update their personal valuation of the company on an ongoing basis. And as long as Microsoft is trading below this valuation, they will hold on to their existing Microsoft shares and potentially acquire additional ones. Other investors will value Microsoft differently. At the exact same moment, they might be taking a different view of Microsoft's future cash flows, and therefore get to a different valuation of the company. So, they will sell their Microsoft shares because they believe the company is currently trading above its valuation. This is why you have investors buying and selling shares at the same time in the market and as soon as you have more investors wanting to buy a certain stock, you see an increase in share price. Once you have more investors wanting to sell a certain stock, you see a decrease in share price.

Substance-oriented valuation, e.g., replacement or liquidation value

Substance-oriented valuation methods value the *existing* assets of the company. Under the replacement method, you would assess how much money it would cost you to build an identical twin of the company, i.e., how much money you would have to spend to replace the assets of the company. Under the liquidation method, you would assess how much money you would receive if you were to sell all assets of the company in the market today. Both approaches do not account for any growth potential and profit potential, and also tend to underestimate immaterial assets such as software developed by the company or other IP. Therefore, substance-oriented valuations lead to relatively low company valuations and are deemed unsuitable for most startups.

Market-oriented valuation

Market-oriented valuation methods value startups by comparing them to 'somewhat similar' startups or other companies in the market. In essence, you are comparing assets to assets, and then deriving the value of an asset A from the value of an asset B, which you believe to be relatively similar and of which you know the price.

One easy way to apply market-oriented methods is to look at comparable key performance data of publicly traded companies. Unfortunately, few startups resemble publicly traded companies, as they are way smaller and often use different and new technologies (which is what they hope will make them more valuable than comparable publicly traded companies at some point in the future!). Moreover, you can look at previously done transactions (trade sales or IPOs or other M&A transactions) of companies somewhat similar to the startup you are trying to assess. Again, the comparability might be low, and you may end up comparing apples and oranges. However, this method is much more popular in the market than substance-oriented valuations.

Capital-oriented valuation

The most popular capital-oriented valuation method is the discounted cash flow (DCF) valuation method. Among most investment bankers and private equity professionals, this is considered the most useful method, and also the most commonly used method. DCF models are, however, looking into the future and therefore take into account estimates, which makes them less reliable, unless you are able to actually look into the future. Few people are. But as we will see, DCF models are also an interesting tool to understand better the company you are analysing and valuing.

The DCF model takes a company's sales and profits (leading to cash flows) from the past, projects/extrapolates them into the future to show future cash flows and derives the net present value of these future cash flows by discounting them at a rate that takes risk, your own cost of capital, and time into account.

Deep Dive: Net Present Value calculation – The Discounted Cash Flow Method

Setup:

- You are the CFO and co-founder of a start-up with high growth ambitions. You want to hire staff, buy supplies, and expand your office. Overall, you estimate that your capital requirement is $10 million for the next two years.
- You approach venture capitalists and pitch your start-up to them. Unfortunately, the first two-dozen conversations do not gain momentum, but you gather a lot of feedback which you use to refine your pitch. Finally, an investor appears really interested. You feel that your conversations have reached the next level.
- The investor says, 'I believe in the prospects of this company. I've also taken the liberty to evaluate your company. And as of today, I value your startup at $40 million pre-money. This means that if I invest $10 million today, we're talking about a post-money valuation of $50 million today. And the share in your company that I would receive in return for my investment of $10 million would be 20 per cent, assuming no other investors invest any additional amounts. This is because my $10 million represents a share of 20 per cent in the total value of the company of $50 million after the investment, i.e., post-money.'
- You have to chew on this a little bit. You are not happy with the investor's concept. Giving away 20 per cent of your company? That is hard for you. And you agree not to part ways with so many shares without putting up a fight. Therefore, you decide to run a discounted cashflow (DCF) model to challenge your start-up's valuation as put forth by the investor. You know that DCF models tend to over-value the company, which would produce an effective counterproposal.

Method:

- Based on your knowledge of your startup's current expenditure and revenues as well as your upcoming challenges and opportunities, you estimate that the cashflow of your startup will most likely be ***$4 million*** in Year 1, ***$1 million*** in Year 2, ***$6 million*** in Year 3, and ***$24 million*** in Year 4.
- After Year 4, it becomes too difficult to predict your future cashflows, so you simply assume an indefinite growth rate. You know that the growth

rate will impact your start-up's valuation a lot. To stay realistic, you assume an ***eternal growth rate of 2 per cent per annum***.

- You further estimate that the ***discount rate***, which reflects the risks of your investment, is ***6 per cent per annum***.
- Based on your assumptions, you calculate the Net Present Value (NPV) as the sum of all discounted cashflows (DCF) plus the terminal value. The terminal value is the next cashflow (i.e., the previous year's cashflow increased by the growth rate) divided by 'discount rate minus growth rate' and discounted to the present value.

Figure 20.1 Cashflow estimations

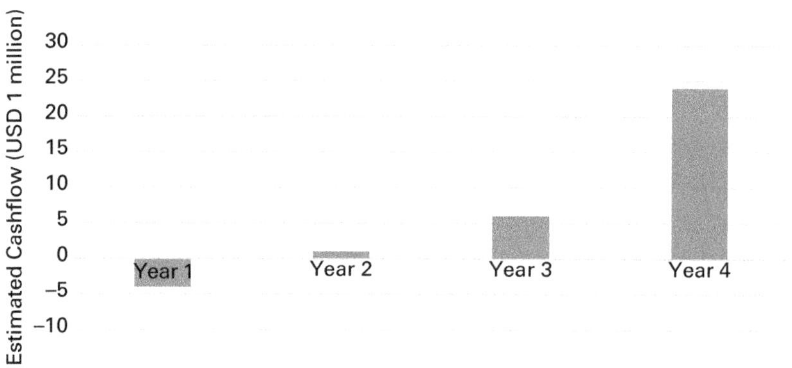

Formula:

$$NPV(DCF) = \sum_{t=1}^{n} \frac{FCF_t}{(1+r)^t} + \frac{FCF_n * (1+g)}{(r-g) * (1+r)^n}$$

Where:
FCF_t = Free cashflow in period t
r = discount rate
g = terminal growth rate
n = maximum number of projected cashflow periods
(The left term equals all discounted free cashflows from period $t = 1$ until $t = n$. The right term equals the discounted terminal value.)

Result:

- Applying the formula, you calculate that the NPV of your DCF from Year 1 to Year 4 is $21 million. Further, you calculate that the discounted terminal value from Year 5 onwards is $612 million. Summed up, your start-up has a pre-money valuation of $633 million.

- You return to the investor with this result. Reviewing it, the investor disagrees with your valuation wholeheartedly. 'First and foremost,' he explains that even, 'you have to understand that it would be somewhat difficult for me and my investment committee to agree to a company valuation (pre-money) of a whopping $633m today, given that your company will only generate meagre free cash flows of –$4 million in the next year and only $1 million in the year after that. And needless to say, even these cashflows are uncertain and unreliable. The startup could also end up incurring even lower free cash flows. Nobody knows what the future will bring, right?'
- But the investor wants to find a compromise. He proposes to review the assumptions of the model a bit more carefully. He points to the fact that the NPV of the startup for Years 1 to 4 (based on the founders' DCF model) is only $21 million. So, the main distortion of the valuation is a result of the terminal value, which is 2 per cent per year for all eternity, which is not realistic. After all, what have you ever seen that grows by 2 per cent indefinitely? This terminal value adds more than $610m to the pre-money valuation of the startup.
- The investor then suggests a slightly different approach: 'Why don't we drop the terminal value entirely because it messes up our model. Instead, maybe we can calculate the NPV for the next five years, and then take that as a proxy valuation basis?'
- You agree because you know this will result in a higher valuation than what was initially offered. But above all, you agree because you have no other options.
- Note that the investor could have also negotiated a higher discount rate, or weighted average cost of capital (WACC). The WACC should reflect the risk-free rate of return that an investor could get in the market (and hence expects as a minimal outcome of any project he/she agrees to do) if they did not go for a project. In other words, the investment project must return at least the weighted average cost of capital or more to be deemed 'viable' and 'attractive' for the investor. Sometimes, investors can also apply a much higher WACC because they want to reflect the high risk involved in the project. Or they can decide to inflate the WACC

for negotiation purposes, i.e., the investor may in fact agree that the WACC to be applied should be 10 per cent, but then he applies a higher WACC of 25 per cent which leads to a lower valuation, and confronts the founders with this calculation, to see if he can convince them to accept a lower valuation of their startup.

A lot of professional investors argue that DCF models make little sense for early-stage companies due to limited availability of historical data (or even a proof of concept or proof of market for the company's products and services). So, projections of revenues and free cash flows rely a lot on the quality of the crystal ball you are using to look into the future.

Having said this, investors who apply DCF models in the context of startup investments often argue that it enables them to gain deeper insights and a much richer knowledge about the startup's business. After all, the precise understanding of the company's financial planning, which is essential for the creation of a DCF model, allows the investor to test its understanding of the startups business, identify key revenue and cost drivers, and potentially come up with new hypotheses on how the group can support the startup.

Here are some exemplary aspects to consider:

- **Sales forecast** – the sales forecast always follows the simple formula 'quantity × price', i.e., the price you will get from your customer per product or service delivery, times how many times the customer(s) will purchase. One interesting aspect in this regard is 'price'. A lot of founders determine their prices using cost-plus pricing when they really should use value pricing. For example,, they tell you that it will cost them $10 to manufacture and deliver the product, so that charge the customer $12 or $15, or even $20. However, they could also look at what value this product or service creates on the customer side, and price their product with a discount on that value. For example, let's assume the same product represents a value to the customer of $100, then the startup could price their product at $50, which leaves a nice margin for the buyer, but is still significantly higher than the $12 or $15 or $20 that they contemplated before.
- Similarly, a lot of early-stage founders determine 'quantity' in terms of an addressable market based on numerous hypotheses, i.e., total size of

market, the market attainable to them, etc. Here investors can chime in and bring fresh thoughts to the table, and suggest a bottom-up analysis, for example, based on your online and offline channels, let's try and project how many customers we can reach, how many we believe we can convert, and then use that as our estimate for 'quantity' or at least compare it with the top-down approach.

- **Sales cycles** – how long does it take for the startup to sell its product or service to customers (of different sizes and scope) and until the cash comes in? Investors can raise such a question to probe whether the startup has exhausted all potential ways to sell, e.g., online and offline channels, with certain price initiatives. Maybe certain channels and certain campaigns can be tested to see which approach is most successful in the market? Sometimes, a startup may not have tested the sales channel 'call centre/telephone sales' because it is deemed old-fashioned and 'unsexy', but in certain cases the startup may find that this channel is actually quite useful.
- Investors can also try to advise the startup on how to collect money from customers faster, for example by suggesting implementing a different payment process or a new approach to manage open receivables. Moreover, they talk to key customers with significant monies payable to the startup, to accelerate the payment.
- **Cash flows** – an interesting point to discuss between startup and investors is the evolution of a customer-supplier relationship over time. What effort must the startup make to acquire a customer (e.g., training of employees, prototype installation, waiting for six months to receive test results)? And what cash flows result from a customer relationship over what time periods? When do customer relationships end (and why)? Would the startup be able to sell more products or services to the same customer over time? Key indicators in this context are customer acquisition cost (CAC) and customer lifetime value (CLV), but also unit economics of the product and/or service in terms of profitability. This perspective is naturally intertwined with sales forecasts and sales cycles.
- **Lock-in effects** – Do customers integrate the startup's technology so deeply into their own business or life that they can hardly switch to other providers? You may be familiar with enterprise resource planning (ERP) software and how such a software from SAP or Oracle, etc. is considered a key tool in large corporations. Switching to another ERP provider would be extremely costly and time-consuming, especially for large, internationally operating

companies, so that is a value that you may want to discuss as a startup with your investors (how reliable your revenues are).

- Conversely, to what extent does the startup have to anticipate customer churn (churn rate)? Who uses the company's products and services only occasionally and then switches to other providers or has no lasting need for this solution? And how can the loyalty of customers be improved, potentially?
- **End Game** – Is the startup able to generate additional revenues and profits as it grows? We are all familiar with the Economies of Scope and Scale models where the cost of goods sold (COGS) per unit decrease as economies of scale increase. Beyond that, some companies develop a so-called end-game, e.g., they generate data from their business activities and then find other players in the market that are interested in the analysis of such data who would pay for it. Or, there can be cross-selling and up-selling potentials that are not obvious. Certainly, there are interesting conversations to be had between founders and investors.

As you can see, a DCF model almost automatically triggers questions and considerations that challenge or confirm existing structures and processes of the startup. And isn't entrepreneurship based on inspiration, but then also on continuous refining and improving? So, the questions that you can derive from the thoughts reflected above are, for instance:

- Can we make other assumptions regarding the **sales forecast**? Is the target clientele larger or smaller than what we have in the plans so far? Is there perhaps a reason to make different assumptions on the expected consumption per customer per year, or can we increase prices over time?
- If the startup goes through long **sales cycles** with large companies, how can we shorten these cycles? Should the startup focus its sales strategy on medium-sized companies first? Or use other sales channels? And taking a step back and then looking at sales cycles, is the current level of funding sufficient, or should more capital be allocated now, so that the startup has sufficient time to achieve a robust proof of market?
- Regarding **cash flows,** we can question whether the distribution channels used so far are the right channels or work efficiently. Perhaps the company is not yet selling online and should test this sales channel. Or, the company is using a call centre provider for sales, but this provider is only moderately successful. Perhaps it would be worth considering switching the provider. In the context of the churn rate, we can discuss whether and how the

startup can change its business model from significant one-off revenues to smaller recurring revenues. For example, with a subscription model or a pay-per-use model, which might even the startup's products and services more accessible due to the initially smaller financial outlay.

- If the startup does not observe any **lock-in effects** with its customers, how can the startup strengthen customer loyalty? Can the startup grow its product scope to become even more important and central for the customer? Or, if the company is running a B2C model, should it introduce a loyalty programme and other incentives to bind customers more closely and permanently to the startup?
- In the context of the **end game,** can alternative business models be considered? Can additional revenue sources be explored in the future? For example, UBER is an on-demand private limousine service for passengers, but could the drivers not transport other goods and items too?

All these questions illustrate how corporate venture capitalists use DCF models as a point of departure to examine the company valuation but also the business structure and concept from various conceivable angles.

In addition, a corporate venture capital investor can look at the revenue and cost projections from a different angle and analyse them, namely: where can the investing corporation possibly provide support? For example, with its own sales channels, with its sales reps, by sharing procurement advantages for certain materials with the startup, or by allowing the startup to partially use costly test facilities that the company already owns and uses, can we make life for this portfolio company easier?

Hedging against 'wrong' company valuation

The startup investor community – private venture capitalists, business angels, but also corporate venture capitalists – has long recognized that they can be (and will be) completely wrong when determining and negotiating a startup's valuation. No matter what valuation method they apply. Consequently, investors have sought out different methods to mitigate their risks to the wrong valuation.

- Contractual risk coverage
  - Contractually agreed liquidation preferences give the investor a preference right over other shareholders to have the investment repaid before others in case of a liquidity event (e.g., exit or insolvency).

- Contractually agreed anti-dilution-protection, i.e., a compensation of an investor by means of shares in case of a 'down-round' (i.e., the startup conducts a financing round based on a valuation that is lower than the previous valuation at which the investor participated).
- Staged investments, i.e., commitment of an investment to the startup, but the amount will be paid in various instalments that are subject to the startup reaching certain goals ('milestones'). The valuation can be adjusted with each milestone achieved.

- Other protection
  - Co-investing with other investors will lower the financial risk for your CV team investing in a startup, and comparing the valuation of your co-investors to your valuation will also be a helpful acid test for your team.
  - It can be an option to use convertible loans or convertible notes and not invest directly into equity of the company. That enables you to postpone the valuation and to accept the valuation negotiated by other investors coming in at a later stage, and then invest the monies with an attractive 20–30 per cent discount on that new at-arm's-length-valuation.

Negotiation of deal terms

21

In many ways, term sheets can be considered a 'draft contract' or 'preliminary contract' in that they are generally not legally binding (except for certain articles that are explicitly defined as binding). As a rule, the following articles are legally binding:

- **Confidentiality** – the parties agree to maintain confidentiality about their negotiations and the term sheet for a mutually agreed period of time.
- **Exclusivity** – for a period defined by the parties, the startup will talk about an investment exclusively with the investor presenting the term sheet, not with other investors.
- **Break-up fee** – if one of the parties unilaterally breaks off the negotiations within a mutually defined period, it pays the other party an agreed compensation, often in the range of €20,000–€50,000. This regularly applies to founders who unilaterally break off negotiations. To some extent, this also applies to investors, provided that these investors have committed the target company to an exclusivity period within which the startup is not allowed to negotiate with other investors, so that the startup suffers a loss in this respect if the investor breaks off the negotiations within the exclusivity period.

By design, term sheets outline all key parameters of the investor's participation in the startup, including investment ticket, company valuation, investor's preference rights, governance-relevant aspects such as board seats, etc. Individual aspects of the term sheet can and will appear in the final documentation of the investment in different contractual documents. For example, the shareholder agreement contains the preferential rights of the investors, and the transaction agreement contains the ticket size and company valuation. Other aspects may be reflected in the Articles of Association of the company.

Why even bother working on a term sheet? Wouldn't it make sense to jump directly into drafting the final contracts? A term sheet is just a pragmatic way to allow negotiators to focus exclusively on the content and not on formal legal aspects. Ultimately, the lawyers assigned to accompany the transaction will 'translate' the term sheet into contractual documents, many of which are subsequently notarized (legally required or optional). But, the term sheet enables business people, entrepreneurs and investors, to discuss among themselves and without lawyers, which is often cheaper, faster and less tedious.

A senior corporate VC was laughing when she shared the following with us:

> Usually, we try to convince the startup that neither they nor we will involve lawyers in the negotiations of the term sheet. Because, you know, lawyers' business models are based on time. So, the longer a process takes, the more money they make. Which does not necessarily incentivize them to be pragmatic, fast, and solution oriented… So, in essence, we try to negotiate as long as we can without lawyers. And then we send the term sheet to one lawyer we trust, often the lawyer of the startup. And then we review the final draft with our lawyer. I remember working with a startup once, and they had (and we had) lawyers involved at a very early stage. Too early, for my taste. And then our lawyer called me up one evening and told me that he had a long discussion with his counterpart around liquidation preference. And that's when I told him not to call the other lawyer without my consent. And also, not to engage in any discussion without somebody present who can actually take a decision. Don't get me wrong, lawyers are important. Highly trained specialists and all. But at the end of the day, let's face it, they are service providers to the startup and to us, and should behave as such. And the founders and the investors should sit in the driver's seat, not the lawyers.

Two main term sheet types

The two most common types of term sheets for startups are:

1. Convertible loan term sheet for loans that can be converted into shares of the company.
2. Equity term sheet for direct participation of investors in the share capital of the startup.

In addition, there are various other participation forms (i.e., varieties of these two participation forms) such as SAFEs (Standard Agreement on Future Equity), plain loans, revenue-based financing structures, venture debt, etc. We will not go into detail on the latter here. Professional templates for term sheets for equity and convertible loans relevant for Switzerland can be found here: https://www.seca.ch/Templates/Templates.aspx.

Convertible loan term sheet

Convertible loans are a popular form for startup investments, especially in early-stage startups (pre-seed and seed stage). One important reason for the popularity of convertible loans in very early rounds of funding is that they spare the parties lengthy discussions about the valuation of the startup. Particularly in the very early development phase of a startup, company valuations are regularly based on financial plans and business plans. And such plans are, of course, highly debatable, especially if none of the parties has a magical crystal ball that can reliably predict the future.

A convertible loan offers an elegant alternative. Investors and founders accept the company valuation as agreed upon in the *next* (larger) financing round (Series A). The advantage is that the company valuation can then already be based on more empirical values and figures, and is therefore a bit more robust and reliable. In addition, the convertible loan investor can rest assured that the equity investors joining in the next big round will fiercely negotiate the company valuation with the founders, serving both investors' best interest.

Another positive aspect of convertible loans is that the startup need not coordinate all investors participating in a financing round to adhere to a joint schedule for signing and closing, as is the case with an equity round. Instead, potential investors can sign convertible loans continuously within a specific time window, such as between January and July of a given year, and all parties can retain a bit of flexibility.

Sometimes, convertible loan investors define floors (to protect the founders) and caps (to protect the investors) for their convertible loans. This means that the convertible loan (plus interest) is converted at a minimum valuation of X and a maximum valuation of Y. Normally, the investors will convert into equity at a discount on the next round's valuation, often minus 20%, which reflects the fact that the convertible loan investors came in much earlier and should be rewarded for taking that risk.

The basic mechanism presented earlier in the context of company valuation also applies here, by the way. For the same investment amount, a lower valuation leads to a higher investor share (hence the floor protects the founders from too much dilution), while a higher valuation leads to a lower investor share (hence the cap protects investors from too low a company share). This ensures that an equity investor who negotiates too softly and accepts a valuation that is 'too high' will not shrink the participation of the convertible loan investor beyond a minimum participation. Similarly, any unforeseen positive developments of the startup that catapults the valuation into the sky will not shrink the participation of the convertible loan investor beyond a minimum participation, either.

Typically, convertible loans come with an interest rate of 5–15% per annum or the reference interest rate (LIBOR, EURIBOR) plus 5 per cent. However, the parties refrain from repayments of the convertible loan principle amount or the interest on the loan *before the* end of the term of the loan because the goal is to provide the startup with growth capital and not to drain cash from the company.

Normally, the amount of the loan (principle) and the accrued interest are converted together into equity. In the process, the lender is assigned preferred shares of the target company (i.e., the loan converts into the share class that the new investors joining in the next round also claim for themselves). This is conclusive insofar as the convertible loan basically has a 'built-in' liquidation preference (i.e., it is serviced first in the event of liquidation, unless otherwise agreed, before the shareholders). In this respect, it is only logical that the convertible loan investor also converts into preferred shares with a liquidation preference, so that the investor is not substantially worse off.

The same modalities also apply to convertible loans 'between financing rounds' (i.e., bridge loans). Here, investors provide additional capital to the startup to bridge a liquidity gap because they assume that the next financing round is very likely to materialize. The investors use the convertible loan because they do not want to provide funding via equity and thereby accidentally set a new valuation. Because that (interim) valuation would then serve the new investor coming in in the next round as a reference valuation. So, the preference is to inject money in the startup, but not set a new valuation, so that the founders can negotiate with the new investors freely.

Inexperienced investors may easily misunderstand convertible loans because the word 'loan' may be perceived as an investment that would give creditors a collateral, i.e., additional security. Such investors may mistakenly assume that they could recover a large part of the investment in the event of liquidation. However, convertible loans are typically not collateralized and are classified as subordinated loans, sometimes without any repayment option at all.

It should be said again, we feel, that the proceeds of liquidation proceedings for a startup are often insufficient to repay all creditors in full, especially after the costs of the liquidation proceedings. Convertible loans thus resemble equity investments from a financial point of view (not from a legal point of view) and are by no means 'safer' than equity investments in startups.

Equity term sheet

At least in Europe, equity investments – and thus equity term sheets – are still the prevailing form of investments in startups, particularly in mature startups that are entering their Series A and subsequent financing rounds.

In contrast to convertible loans, equity investments will usually come along with preferred shareholder rights, such as information rights with respect to the business development, voting rights in the general meeting, participation rights in the business profits, preference rights (in the case of 'preferred shares') including a seat on the board of the startup, liquidation preference, veto rights, etc.

Formally, equity investments are handled differently than convertible loans in that the equity investors become shareholders and are recorded and registered as such in the commercial register.

Above a certain investment amount and in certain jurisdictions, the startups must, in many markets, also meet know-your-customer requirements imposed by financial regulators and report the shareholder's identity ('ultimate owner') and additional personal information to a (public) registrar.

It should also be stated that equity participation agreements (transaction agreement, shareholder agreement, articles of association, etc.) usually require notarization.

Generally, all investments in startups become public eventually. In many countries, convertible loans are not recorded and published in the commercial register. However, the startup usually wants to talk publicly about a good and reputable investor to gain credibility and respectability. Nevertheless, it is at the discretion of the involved parties to agree to maintain confidentiality about an investor's identity or the amount of the investment. The risk of an investor to be disclosed as a startup's investor increases with the number of people who are informed about the corporate investment, and the maturity of the startup.

Misperception: 'Risk reduction'

It is important to note that the activities described in Sourcing, Screening, Due Diligence, Business Valuation, and negotiation of Deal Terms are all connected in one way or another to deal with risk reduction – and Corporations like to look for ways to reduce risks! But can one prevent all negative impacts of a failing startup in advance?

Established companies are obsessed with success. A popular saying among veteran corporate managers is: 'Success has many fathers and mothers. Failure does not even have a dead grandparent'. The concept of 'failure' as a perfectly natural aspect of research and development activities, is something that corporates can only accept at the project level, but terms such as 'bankruptcy' or 'in liquidation' regularly cause nervousness in the executive suites. There is fear that the failure could negatively impact the career of a corporate decision maker or even the entire corporation.

Startup investments are associated with high risks. Young companies face market risks, product risks, technical risks, financial risks and legal risks. They are notoriously underfunded and often work with incomplete teams, limited resources and sometimes unreliable investors. A corporation may try to reduce the risk by discussing an investment target with assumed specialists, such as a world-renowned consulting firm. After all, consultants solve so many problems for the company, don't they? The company may also strive to involve as many internal subject matter experts as possible in the decision-making process. So, the more people you ask, the better (and clearer?) your decision will be, right? Or, the company tries to use contractual risk reductions, e.g., liquidation preferences, participation at board level, a long catalog of transactions and activities requiring approval that cannot be carried out without the group's ok, etc. Well, in fact other investors do use the same contractual risk reductions and still 80 per cent of early-stage startups fail!

You have to understand, accept, and educate colleagues around the fact that risk reductions are often toothless tigers if a startup fails. The insolvency proceeds from a bankruptcy of a software startup are usually small or close to zero. But remember, you did not decide to invest in a startup because you aspire to generate a major return on investment. Your R&D projects are expensive, too. And they often fail, too (or they are not really innovative in nature...). And if your internal R&D fails, your money is lost in very similar ways than in a failed startup investment. Conversely, in a startup failure founders may still be able to sell it to somebody else at an attractive price – plus, you were not the only investor funding the development of the startup. As such, you only carry a fraction of the losses (but also proceeds). Bottom line: despite all the 'risk reduction' measures described in the preceding chapters, investments in young firms remain risky.

Reference

SECA Term Sheet Templates (n.d.) https://www.seca.ch/Templates/Templates.aspx (archived at https://perma.cc/YA9S-2Z2D)

CV Cockpit III 22

Again, a quick reminder of what the Cockpit is all about. In the dashboard, you will find the so-called specs, which summarize important information about the different elements of the CV Navigator. You will find an interface, a Google Spreadsheet, that shows you the choices you need to make by bringing together all the necessary information at once and giving you a good overview of the key details required to run a CV programme. The interrelationships of the necessary elements and their dependencies within and between phases are shown, while the options available are outlined.

Cockpit III covers the Investing phase of your programme. It helps you to define how you do sourcing and screening across your team and your organization and specifically how you collaborate with ventures, with your business units, or how management is involved. You may also define elements such as shared resources. However, most importantly, the content and tools mentioned in part three of this book should help you to define your investment decision.

- In Chapter 18, Table 18.2 aids at helping you asking the standard but important questions when screening startups.
- The Swiss Private Equity & Corporate Finance Association (SECA) provides you with term sheet templates that help you negotiating deals as discussed in Chapter 21. https://www.seca.ch/Templates/Templates.aspx
- Chapter 20 has given you a primer in business valuation of startups.

After all, in your investment phase while screening and negotiating deals, you may also want to keep in mind who your promoters and enablers are within and beyond your organization that support you and how you keep track of things such as 'collaboration' as well as how to measure this. We have tried to give you a formal guideline on those aspects in our spreadsheet reflected here in Figure 22.1. Talking about collaboration logically relates to potentially shared resources or joint investment themes across your organization or the frequency of information exchange with different units.

Figure 22.1 CV Cockpit III Internal and external collaboration

CV Cockpit III

Profile | Design | **Investing** | Harvest

Dealflow & Portfoliomanagement

Screening process	Active	Passive
	Topic based (IoT, Digital...)	Thesis-backed (testing hypotheses)
	Parent business advancement-based	
Screening stages	2stages; 3stages	Other *(please name)*
Approval process	*please describe*	
Screening process duration	<1month; 1-3month	Other *(please name)*
Portfolio development / monitoring	*please describe*	

Collaboration

With ventures	Observer seats	Board seats
	Access to partnerships and networks	Co-investor search
	Access to R&D or technical expertise	Other types of financial transactions
	Marketing and public relation	Others *(please name)*
With Business Units	Information exchange on business needs / development	
	Regular update of venture development / integration into the business	
	Financial involvement	
	Others *(please name)*	
Involvement of mgmt.	Information exchange on business needs / development	
	Regular update of CV development	
	Regular involvement in CV progress	
	Others *(please name)*	
Other parties	Other parties *(please name)*	

Shared resources / Syndication

Access to partnerships and supplier/ consumer networks	Support in hiring talent
Access to R&D and technical expertise	Information on capabilities/ opportunities / threats
Access to infrastructure	Information/ knowledge flows
Marketing & PR	Training/ coaching on topics/ skills
Others *(please name)*	

CV Value-add

Evaluation elements

Tracking tools	*(please name)*	G-suite: Google studio
Reporting frequency	*(please name)*	Monthly; quarterly
Form of reporting	*(please name)*	CV specific reports; Business development reports
Reporting tools	*(please name)*	G-suite: Google studio
Robustness check: alignment with set objectives	*(please name)*	Tools in place
Other evaluation aspects	*(please name)*	

Measurement of objectives

	Measurement conditional (Yes/No)	Measurement non-monitary (number)		Measurement monitary (in EUR)
Strategic renewal	Status	Planned	Achieved	As a consequence of objectives in general
Validation of existing corporate strategies	Yes	*Number corporate strategies to validate*	Yes	*Revenue from new introduced or old elevated products / services*
Insights to new trends	Yes	*Number new trends to cover*	Yes	*Revenue from customers dealing with startup product / services*
Access to new trends	Yes	*Number new trends to access*	Yes	*Cost savings through collaboration*
Insights to new markets	Yes	*Number new markets to cover*	Yes	*Employee Turnover Rate (ETR)*
Access to new markets	Yes	*Number new markets to access*	Yes	*Employee Net Promoter Scores (ENPs)*
Inspirations and start of new corporate businesses	Yes	*Number new businesses to start*	Yes	*Employee and Manager Satisfaction Score*
Option building / Avoidance of taking wrong decisions	Yes	*Number wrong decisions to avoid*	Yes	
Involvement in corporate strategic	Yes	*Number meetings; number involvement themes*	Yes	
Involvement in M&A	Yes	*Number meetings; number cross-themes*	Yes	
Involvement in R&D dialogue	Yes	*Number meetings*	Yes	
Collaboration: BU involvement	Yes	*Number meetings; number investments*	Yes	
Value-add for key customer	Yes	*Customer satisfaction rate of XXXX*	Yes	
Financial returns				
Financial gains	Yes	*XX (EUR) return to achieve*	Yes	*Profit gained (EUR) (new business generated; savings, time efficiency)*
IRR	Yes	*IRR in % to achieve*	Yes	*Share price*
Multiples	Yes	*Multiple of XX to achieve*	Yes	
Innovation				
Strengthening innovation capabilities overall; observe / learn	Yes	*Number new innovations; innovation cycle time; enablement of new business for the corporate*	Yes	*Innovation rate = revenue share of innovations / total turnover * 100; revenue/profit growth from new products; revenue from new introduced products / services; revenue from old elevated products / services; number of new products launched in XX amount of time; ROI of innovation activities*
Business model innovation	Yes	*Number business model renewals*	Yes	*Innovation portfolio = ABC analysis*
Technology innovation (white spots) / IP transfer	Yes	*White spots to cover; enhancement of existing product developed by the corporation; new innovation applications / patents*	Yes	*Patent income*
Abbreviation of R&D / M&A	Yes	*Number R&D / M&A actions originating from a CVC investment*	Yes	*R&D saving; annual R&D budget as a % of annual sale; total R&D headcount or budget as a percentage of sales*
Internal organizational innovation	Yes	*Number innovation meetings / active projects*	Yes	
Market sensing	Yes	*Number markets to screen (selected focus areas); insights to share with BUs*	Yes	
Culture				
Talent search	Yes	*Number interviews; new staff*	Yes	
Entrepreneurial teaching	Yes	*Number teaching units and participants; knowhow and skills gap covered; award; number culture conflicts*	Yes	*Educational budget used*
Decision making speed	Yes	*Number meetings per project planned; errors made; number culture conflicts; Agility (lean time scales, reduced customer complaints, better quality;scores; operational support needed*	Yes	*ROI; project budget saved*
Brand awareness / reputation	Yes	*Customer satisfaction; Net promoter score*	Yes	
Marketing	Yes	*Number of startup events hosted / participated; number of netions (social listening for reputation); Number of 'likes' / 'followers' / 'mentions' on social media*	Yes	*Marketing budget*
Environmental responsibility	Yes	*Number environmental projects; % of innovations that include sustainability goals; % sustainability awareness training penetration; acore energy / emission / emission footprin*	Yes	*Environmental costs or budget; percentage of environmental targets achieved; CSR index*

(continued)

Figure 22.1 (Continued)

Measurement of enablers

		Planned	Achieved	
Budget				
Budget used	Yes	*XX amount to use*	Yes	*XX EUR*
Capabilities / Skills				
Top mgmt. support (companywide acceptance of CV)	Yes	*Planned mgmt. representation of CV (events; announcements; etc.)*	Yes	*Income through new IP generated*
Expansion of network	Yes	*Number network parties; specific relationship secured through investment*	Yes	*Employee Turnover Rate; Employee Net Promoter Score; Employee and Manager Satisfaction Score*
Scouting, startups under review	Yes	*Number startups screened*	Yes	-
Targets evaluated in detail	Yes	*Number DDs*	Yes	-
Investments negociated and signed	Yes	*Number new startups*	Yes	-
Startup used / knowhow or skills incorporated	Yes	*Startups knowhow / capabilities incorporated*	Yes	-
Milestones met on time	Yes	*Number milestones met*	Yes	-
First mover advantage	Yes	*Number one on the market; press*	Yes	-
Risk acceptance	Yes	*Number risk taking; number project failures*	Yes	-
Talent available	Yes	*Number of hires with venture background*	Yes	-
Collaboration with ventures				
Observer seats	Yes	*Number meeting participation*	Yes	*Cost savings through collaboration; revenues generated; (time saved)*
Access to partnerships and networks	Yes	*Number usage; number new customers / contacts through collaboration*	Yes	
Access to R&D or technical expertise	Yes	*Number usage; Usage of startup technologies/*	Yes	
Marketing and public relation	Yes	*Good press*	Yes	
Board seats	Yes	*Startup involvement*	Yes	
Co-investor search	Yes	*Number co-investor search*	Yes	
Other types of financial transactions	Yes	*Number transactions*	Yes	
Collaboration with Business Units				
Information exchange on business needs / development	Yes	*Number of meetings/ roundtables*	Yes	*BU savings through collaboration; revenues generated; (time saved)*
Regular update of venture development / integration into the business	Yes	*Number of updates / briefings*	Yes	
Joint investment theme developed	Yes	*Number of themes developed*		
Financial involvement	Yes	*Number involvement*	Yes	
Involvement of mgmt.				
Information exchange on business needs / development	Yes	*Number meetings; announcement of support*	Yes	*Revenues, savings, risk reduction, customer satisfaction, etc.*
Regular update of CV development	Yes	*Number updates; frequency of engagement*	Yes	*Anecdotal parent business impact success stories*
Regular involvement in CV progress	Yes	*Number invoviements*	Yes	*Mutual benefit metrics such as startup contract value /valuation)*
Collaboration other parties				
Other parties	Yes	*Number of partnerships or co-development effort; partnership engagement*	Yes	

Similarly, while you are in the investing phase it is important to keep in mind the objectives of your CV profile with which you started out. Figure 22.2 serves as a reminder that – of course – your investments need to pay into these objectives and our spreadsheet provides further guidelines on how to measure these. While financial motives are, as you know by now, easily measurable, strategic renewal relates to measuring the collaboration across the investees and your organization, such as the involvement of business units accessing different trends and insights.

Figure 22.2 CV Cockpit III Investment value adds to your CV profile

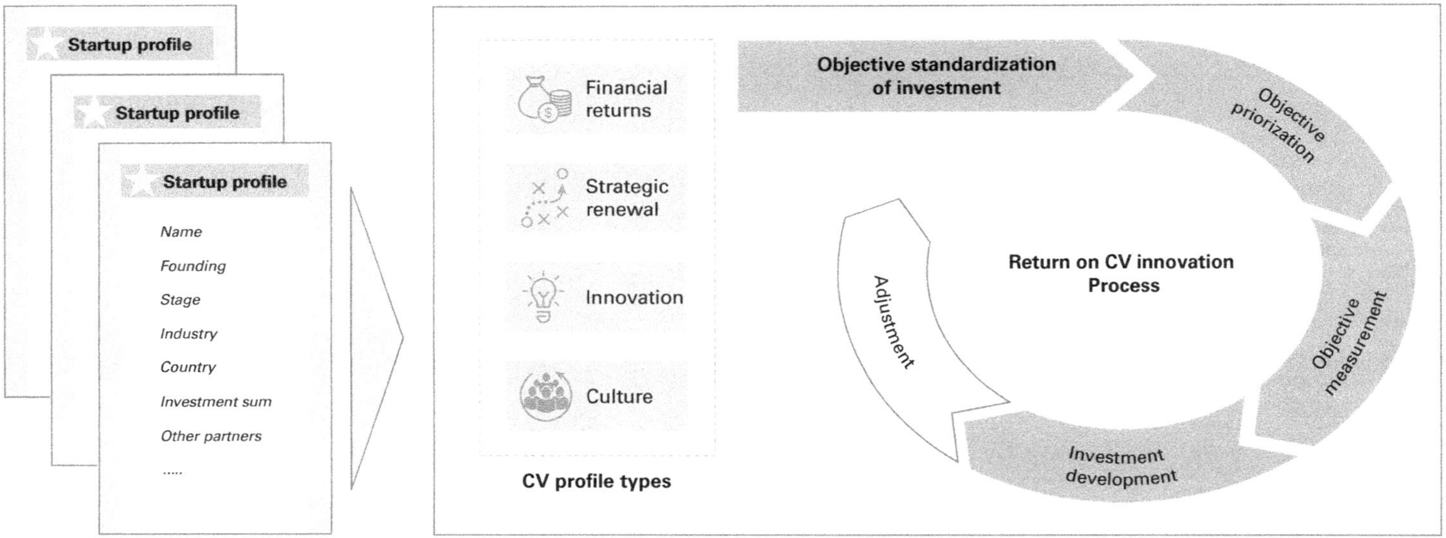

Summary – investment decision

23

We have spoken about the composition and role of the Investment Committee in a CV setup in previous chapters already. In the actual investment process of a CV team, the Investment Committee represents the institutionalized and formal dual control principle or four-eyes-principle. For a large corporation, this means that the members of the Investment Committee are often people from the group's top management. Their role is to check whether the investment proposal submitted by the CV team is in line with the agreed strategy for the programme, i.e., acting as a financial investor or as a strategic investor. Ultimately, the Investment Committee decides in favour or against an investment.

The Investment Committee may take into account four main perspectives (and potentially more):

1 **Conformity with strategy:** Does the startup's profile match the fund's investment strategy? In case of a financially oriented fund, this means: do we have reason to believe that the investment can generate above-average returns? Or, in case of a strategically oriented fund, this means: does the startup fit the fund's priorities in terms of innovation, strategy and investment focus?

2 **Stand-alone success:** Can the target company be successful even if the collaboration with the investing corporation does not develop as planned? Are other investors on board who confirm this view?

3 **Leverage:** In case of a financially oriented fund, this means: How do we plan to support the portfolio company after the investment, i.e., is there anything we can and plan to do to give the startup an 'unfair advantage' or 'growth hack'? Or, in case of a strategically oriented fund, this means: How to we plan to collaborate with the startup, i.e., what milestones

have we set for the startup and ourselves (e.g., prototype stage of the technology), have we planned how our corporation will work with the startup team, i.e., who is assigned from our side, with sufficient time and budget?

4 **Why invest and not choose another path to engage:** Is 'investing' in the startup the best way to engage, or could other ways of engagement be easier, simpler, more cost efficient, for instance, we become customers, or we sign a co-development agreement, or we make a pre-payment on future products and services to enable the startup to deliver?

Implicitly, the Investment Committee's task is to prevent investment managers of the CV team making ill-informed investment decisions because they have 'fallen in love' with an opportunity. In other words, the Investment Committee is the acid test for the work of the CV team. The CV team usually consults the Investment Committee and requests a decision at the latest when the investment decision is 'ready to be taken', i.e., the deal is ready to be signed. This is usually the case when the due diligence has been completed, the main positive/negative risks have been clearly identified and reflected, and all contracts related to the investment are ready to be signed.

In many private VC companies and in corporate VCs, the Investment Committee is also consulted at an earlier stage, e.g., before the start of the due diligence and before entering into the negotiation of the investment contracts with the support of lawyers. This is to prevent unnecessary spending of money and time for investments that are not deemed suitable, and also to give the Investment Committee a heads-up on the deals in the pipeline.

One CV manager shared the following anecdote with us:

> You know, the Investment Committee's reputation is a bit like the reputations of other teams assigned to projects from the corporate headquarter: Nobody in the field understands why they are involved in decisions that they don't necessarily understand. This is our favourite joke in this context: 'There are three main lies in life. (1) I will always love you. (2) The money is in the mail. (3) I'm here from Headquarter to help you.'. On the other hand, you have to give the Investment Committee credit, because they will never be popular with their investment teams, but their role is quite important. And if they play their role well, i.e., not assume you are better startup investors than your startup team, but also don't be shy to ask questions that you would ask as an owner of the corporation, then this can be very helpful.

After the investment decision is taken by the Investment Committee and properly documented and filed by the corporation, a couple of things will happen:

1 The decision of the Investment Committee is communicated to the target company, other co-investors, the legal team(s) supporting the deal, as well as internal teams on the corporate side instrumental for closing (e.g., internal audit and accounting, treasury). The legal teams will prepare and schedule the signing and closing process.
2 Actual signing and closing: Often, the deal is signed by all parties, then certain 'conditions to closing' may apply. And then once these conditions are met – e.g., transfer of monies, and confirmed by the legal teams and the notary – the deal can proceed to closing. The closing notice, sent out by the notary, indicates that the 'deal is done' – the signatures are done, the monies are transferred, remaining conditions to closing (sometimes called conditions precedent) are met. Subsequently, the notary will distribute closing binders containing all deal-related contracts and documents to the shareholders. Closing binders are send out in a paper version and in an online version.

Following the investment decision, the CV team will enter the Portfolio Management and, eventually, the next-round-of-funding or exit-stage. Both portfolio management and exit are elements of the value chain of a CV team, but we have decided that they deserve to be addressed in a separate section that we call Harvesting. But don't worry, the Harvesting part follows right after this chapter (Part IV), so stay with us!

Case insights: Shell

SHELL VENTURES is one of the oldest corporate venturing programmes and also one of the largest, with $1.4 billion in committed budget for six years from the end of November 2021. The fund is a separate entity 100% owned by Shell and was established to support early and growth stage ventures and is in line with Shell's commitment to achieve net zero emissions by 2050. In addition, Shell Ventures (SV) also operates Funds of Funds (FoF) (~10% of SV activities; investments in 9 funds; 1/10 of budget) to access investment deals and have co-investment rights. Its mandate is a thesis-driven one with a clear strategic-orientation but also financial obligation. Investments target the seed to growth stage in the parent companies' focus areas such as

Figure 23.1 Case insights: Shell!

Geert van de Wouw
MD Shell Ventures

Established: 1996

Parent: Royal Dutch Shell

HQ: The Netherlands

Industry: Oil & gas

(1) Profiling | **(2) Designing** | **(3) Investing** | **(4) Harvesting**

Mandate
- Thesis-driven investments (clear strategic-orientation but also financial obligation)
- Global footprint with local presence

Funding size
- USD 1.4 billion (for 6yrs; fund committed)
- Also Fund of Fund investments

Business advancements
- Stage: Seed to growth stage
- Sector: Power, mobility, emission management, resources and digital
- Region: Global (unique; mostly rather local investments)

Structure & Governance
- Organizational: Fund; reporting to leading business (renewable energy solutions; ~50% of business field) + reporting to downstream business
- Legal: Separate entity / totally independent fund (100% Shell-owned)

Team
- ~40 employees globally (SF, Boston, London, EU, CN, IND)

Portfolio size
- 95 ventures; 36 lead investments

Ticket size:
- USD 0.5–50m (increased because of growth fund); seed to growth equity

Collaboration
- Active syndicates
- Active board management
- Implementation management discipline (connect ventures with business at Shell)

M&A
- Exits: 10

>>To accelerate the energy transition and the mobility transformation at Shell (tip of the spear of transformation)<<

SOURCE Corporate insights via interview and website; Crunchbase; *renewable energy solutions energy, mobility, emissions management, resources and digital. Accordingly, SV has a global footprint with a local presence. Currently the CV entity holds 40 employees in the main innovation hubs such as US, UK, EU, CN and IND.

That is SV in a nutshell. But what makes them unique? How could the CV programme survive that long? We have talked to Geert van de Wouw, the MD of SV and gained some very interesting insights.

This time we'll start with what you've learnt, because honestly, isn't that the most important part for you anyway?

1 **Thesis-driven investments:** what's the point of driving a Ferrari on the German autobahn if you don't know where you're going? Have a clear direction and stay in touch with the market to inform the business about what is actually needed.
2 **iTeam:** You need to hire professional VC staff from the market with a great reputation and network in the VC + PE world. You want to be the best, hire the best! Don't even try to educate corporate personnel. That does not do any good. But of course, over time, you should grow your team internally.
3 **Presence in key venture ecosystem:** You have to be local because you have to be able to know what's going on in local markets; you have to be one of them! Hence, get into markets where innovation has its origin.
4 **Manage legal and reputational exposure carefully:** Separate your duties and investment flow between SV and Shell. Otherwise, ventures will never trust you (role of investor versus customer)!

Overall, you must understand the rules of the game and behave in line with VC standards.

As for the CV operations phase, there are a few things that set SV apart. Let's start with the venture sourcing. There is a broad range of sources. Source 1: the VC approach of doing deals with VCs that have already looked at ventures (pre-selection process) or through FoF, which provides access to investment deal flow. Source 2: the thesis-driven approach that addresses ventures accordingly. This is a rigorous process to split the funnel, but of course not a religious one. But let's talk briefly about the Investment Committee (IC), which is special at SV because there is more than one. The IC is divided according to different areas, e.g., mobility and transportation, renewable energy and renewables, early-stage deals and China due to the different time zones. The IC consists of SV's leadership team, which is composed of six of the company's own employees. Some other Shell representatives have standing invitations but no voting rights. The reason for this is to enable quick decisions (the goal is VC speed). The CV head, part of the IC, has high decision-making power (95 per cent independent) and only needs to involve the parent company when it comes to tickets over $15–20 million. That is an essential asset to drive innovation fast and efficiently. Now looking back at the sourcing, there is a three-stage-gate process.

First, a potential venture and the match of strategy/thesis are reviewed. If so, second, a transaction team is formed where a finance and deal manager contacts the venture to submit a proposal to commence negotiations (PCN). And third, the PCN negotiations take place, followed by the term sheet. At SV, it is not often that a term sheet is on the table and the deal is not closed. Of course, the venture must agree, and there must be final negotiations and due diligence by other investors. But term sheets at SV are plain vanilla and simple: no rights (standards and VSA-like terms), no corporate 'textortion', which is the death knell for the CV!

Overall, what definitely needs to be highlighted: have a thesis to quickly narrow down the choices – usually offers via personal connection/network offers are the best quality. And that brings us to the next point: collaboration and network!

Collaboration with the parent company, Shell: SV does not need any investment approval by the business as it makes independent decisions. However, the Business Units (BUs) are always present in the IC as early alignment and commitment from the business are a prerequisite. A call to attention: don't stick to an investment list dictated by the BUs, because then you will surely become a tactical investor in late-stage deals. At the same time, you would lose out on more long-term disruptive venture opportunities, as BUs are short-term oriented and need to make their numbers! What SV does instead: you listen to the business, but you don't literally take it over; you work with the external ecosystem and look beyond the next 5–6 years.

And what about the link to corporate strategy? To be honest, this sounds like an 'ideal connection' because corporate strategy is actually too high-level for CV to be precise enough. CV is in touch with the market and informs the company about what is actually needed. There is no real cannibalization at Shell as the playing field is too big. Funnily enough, SV even invests in its competitors, often in the form of strategic collaboration and often in markets where there is no presence yet. Further, SV holds close collaboration with R&D, which focuses on new process development, and runs good collaboration especially in the venture due diligence process.

In addition, there is cooperation with the ventures – SV acts as an active supporter and has a seat on the board of the startups. But unlike most CV programmes, SV has five Implementation Managers (IMs), who connect the ventures to Shell's businesses and further promote and stimulate collaboration. Each venture has one IM. The IMs receive special training to ask critical questions in board meetings to help the company grow, raise more money, and introduce them to competitors and internal business units. They are a kind of matchmaker, helping to navigate the complex organization and figure out who to talk to. Maintaining a network is critical. That's why SV hosts regular networking events at various venues worldwide, where presentations are given by the company and the ventures, and food is served (~100 people). Personal relationships are very powerful because adding value to a business is in the eye of the beholder.

Let's talk about value creation for a moment. SV stands for both financial return – i.e., the generation of income from the fund – and strategic value – real value in the form of long-term growth for Shell. To capture the financial return, the market value of the portfolio is measured on a quarterly basis (distributive and non-distributive returns). In terms of strategic value, SV considers how much cost or additional free cash flow could be generated through the application of technologies or business models introduced by the portfolio and how much carbon emissions could be avoided. Twice a year, there is a conversation with the Executive Steering Committee, which monitors progress in realizing value. However, there are instances where it is difficult to quantify the value created, so there will be a presentation for values that are difficult to quantify. There is increasing interest in capturing and measuring strategic value, although the full potential has not yet been realized.

References

Shell (2022) Interview with Geert van de Wouw, Managing Director Shell Ventures

Shell (2023) https://www.shell.com/energy-and-innovation/new-energies/shell-ventures.html (archived at https://perma.cc/3NQQ-G7DJ)

PART FOUR
Harvesting

The harvest is the moment of truth, when you prove to your colleagues, your competitors, and the capital market that all plans and promises bear fruit. As with the harvest in the agricultural sense, the fruits can take on very different forms and shades. At the same time, the general conditions, such as the (investment) climate, have a significant influence on the quality of the vintage.

Choosing the right Harvesting path

24

Perishing the moment of truth

The entire venture and private capital industry is based on the premise that investments must pay off at a certain point in time. Again, internal (readiness) and external factors (market conditions) are the key influencers that determine the value of the harvest.

The same is true for corporate venturing: all the sweat and blood put into corporate ventures only pays off when the profits can be realized. Startup and corporate venturing have two other features in common. First, the failure rates of corporate and startup ventures are comparable and surprisingly high for many who are running a venture for the first time or have a corporate background. Therefore, any harvesting decision must take into account the assumed risk.

Second, and as a corollary to the first point, the successful creation of startups and companies requires a portfolio mentality and approach. When risk appetite is limited, building a portfolio rather than individual companies is the key to avoiding large losses. Therefore, any decision to harvest must be aligned with the overall portfolio strategy.

However, amidst the many similarities between startups and corporate venturing, there are two important differences to keep in mind. First, there are many more influencing factors to consider when deciding to harvest in a corporate as compared to a venture capital setting. It starts with a variety of expectations the parent company has: Should the venture deliver financial and/or strategic value? How important is learning and exploring? Is it considered a cost or an investment? In addition, the risk appetite of the owners may change over time as it is influenced by market sentiment, among other factors. Finally, internal politics can play a critical role in decision-making, so harvesting decisions sometimes follow different logics. Second, and related to the first difference, harvesting can take many more forms in corporate venturing than in venture capital, which typically involves only transactional harvesting, i.e., selling shares in a venture to the public or private market (secondaries). In corporate venturing, 'harvesting' can mean many different outcomes at different levels.

Apart from the fact that relevant experience is gained with each individual harvesting decision, we will distinguish between four main paths that a corporate venture programme can take (needless to say, in many cases a combination of the four archetypal paths is not only possible, but even advisable): Portfolio Optimization, Integration, Exit, Rejuvenation & Incubation (Figure 24.1). In each of the options, harvesting takes on a different meaning.

Figure 24.1 The approaches to harvesting

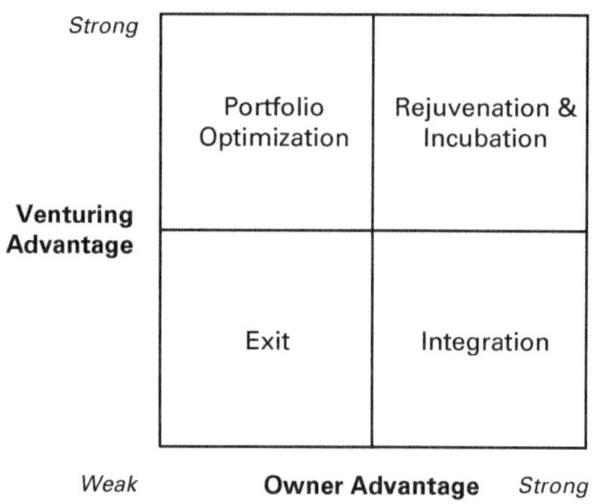

How to choose the best possible path? The answer depends to a large extent on the parent company's assessment of two advantages:

- **The venturing advantage:** this advantage refers to the two modes a company can be in – the 'building business' or 'running business' mode. A company that is in the 'building business' thrives best when it follows the rules of venturing, while an established company requires a very different framework. The extent to which the venture still fits best into the venturing mode at its current stage ultimately determines the extent to which it still enjoys a venturing advantage.
- **The owner advantage:** The owner advantage refers to the question under which the owner of a company can best thrive in its lifecycle phase. Because owners differ in both their expectations of and the contributions

to the business, they may be better or worse suited. Therefore, the business owner must be able to articulate and justify its advantages over alternative ownership structures of its business. As soon as this is no longer possible, the owner advantage has vanished.

Assessing the venturing advantage

It is in the nature of ventures that they grow and eventually (hopefully) become an established company. In this case, they gradually resemble the organizations that the corporate intended to complement through the creation of corporate ventures, namely the established companies. As a result, the approach to managing these companies must also adapt to be as effective as possible. Therefore, corporate venture founders must constantly evaluate which of the two approaches is most effective: the 'building' or the 'running business' mode.

How do the two approaches differ? The two management modes can almost be considered opposites in the dimensions described in Table 24.1.

Table 24.1 Management modes

Build business mode	Focus	Running business mode
Ambiguity	*Risk profile*	Clarity
Agility	*Culture*	Continuity
Exploration	*Activity*	Exploitation
Entrepreneur	*People*	Manager
Investment	*Finance*	Revenues and costs

Since there is no clear point in time when an organization transitions from a building to a running business, it is up to the decision makers to anticipate the optimal time and honestly declare that the venture advantage is gone. This can be a very emotional decision, as those representing the risk benefit may feel insulted or even redundant. Moreover, such decisions are partly subjective, given common decision biases (Deep Dive 1), and often depend on who holds the ultimate decision-making power (see Deep Dive 2), i.e., those trained and conditioned to build or run a business.

It is therefore important to establish clearly defined decision-making procedures that ensure that all key stakeholders are consulted and it is clear who has ultimate decision-making authority. Since the results of such decisions are usually not shared by all due to their partly subjective nature, it is crucial to aim for a fair process. This means that the process must be perceived as fair and transparent so that even those who disagree understand the reasons and do not oppose or even sabotage the process. This also requires open and honest communication and appreciation of individual points of view.

Deep Dive 1: Common biases in venture harvesting decisions

There are several common biases that can impact venture capital harvesting decisions:

1. Overconfidence Bias: This is the tendency to overestimate one's own abilities and probability of success, which can lead to taking more risks than necessary.
2. Confirmation Bias: This is the tendency to look for information that confirms one's preconceived notions, while ignoring or discounting information that contradicts those beliefs. This can lead to decisions being made based on incomplete or biased information.
3. Availability bias: This is the tendency to rely on readily available information rather than seeking more comprehensive or accurate information. This can lead to decisions being made based on incomplete or biased data.
4. Anchoring Bias: This is the tendency to rely too heavily on the first piece of information received when making decisions and to use it as a reference point for all subsequent decisions. This can lead to decisions being made on the basis of inaccurate or outdated information.
5. Sunk Cost Fallacy: This is the tendency to continue to invest in a venture or project because of the funds already invested, even when it no longer makes sense to do so. This can lead to decisions being made that are not in the best interests of the company.
6. Hindsight bias: This is the tendency to overestimate one's ability to predict outcomes after the fact, which can lead to overconfidence in future decisions. This can lead to decisions being made based on incorrect assumptions and inaccurate predictions.

Assessing the owner advantage

The second advantage that corporate investors enjoy by definition from the outset, and which must be constantly questioned, is the owner advantage: is the parent company the best owner of the investment? This is the question of whether the owner of an investment is in the best position to make the investment flourish. There are five ways an owner can contribute to the success of their investment (Hilb 2020a):

- **Capital:** The owner may have unique access to capital that would be difficult to access through other sources, such as the capital market.
- **Customers:** The owner may have a large customer base that they are willing to share with the company.
- **Contracts:** The owner may have interesting contractual rights, such as intellectual property, that prove valuable to the company.
- **Credibility:** The owner may enjoy a good reputation in an area relevant to the company.
- **Capabilities:** The owner may have developed strong capabilities in a particular area that the company can leverage, such as a distribution network or manufacturing skills.

While the venture had one or more of these advantages at the outset, this may change over time as a) the needs of the venture, b) the strengths of the owner, and/or c) the strengths of alternative owners may have changed.

As with the benefits of starting a business, an honest self-assessment is required, from the perspective of the business. Moreover, this assessment is made not only in comparison to two options, i.e., building or operating the business, but in comparison to a range of alternative owners. Alternative owners could be a venture capital firm, another firm, the entrepreneurs, or even the public market. Since each of the options involves a variety of actors; the number of alternative options could be almost infinite in certain cases.

How can one get an overview of all the options? Since this is often unfamiliar territory for both corporate leaders and corporate entrepreneurs, it is advisable to tap into the knowledge of established personalities in the various ownership areas, either by partnering with them through joint deals or by appointing them to one of the different types of corporate venture boards (see the next Deep Dive).

Deep Dive: The pivotal role of corporate venture boards

Corporate boards play a crucial role in the smooth functioning of venture ecosystems (Hilb 2020b). They connect and align the different interests of owners and entrepreneurs, which are likely to evolve over time. They also ensure that relevant expertise and experience can be leveraged, as companies and their teams often lack both. Therefore, they can be considered the glue in such an ecosystem, holding everything together and ensuring a certain stability in a very fragile context.

Figure 24.2 Venture boards as an integral part of the venture ecosystem (Hilb 2020b)

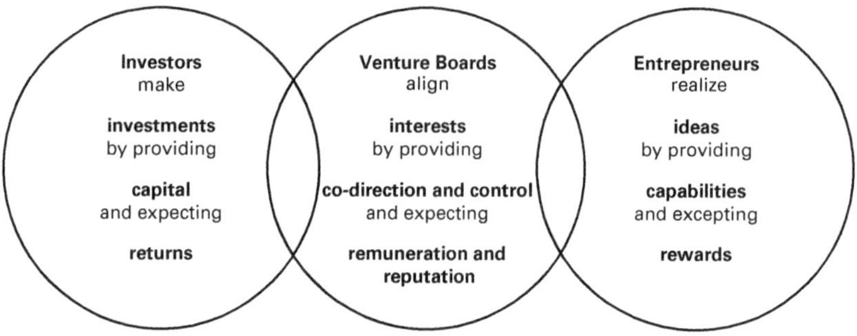

A well-structured and well-staffed corporate venture board also pays off in the context of corporate ventures, as aligning sometimes divergent interests and closing gaps in expertise and experience are often key challenges.

In the context of corporate ventures, it is important to distinguish between four types of boards that perform different tasks:

- **Corporate venture advisory board**: Since corporate ventures often do not have all the key skills or connections due to their limited size and financial resources, a cost-effective option may be to form an advisory board to which leaders from various fields are invited to contribute their experience and expertise.
- **Corporate venture supervisory board**: As with any ventures, the owners usually claim a seat on the supervisory board. In the case of corporate ventures, these are representatives of the parent company. When other owners are involved, such as corporate officers or outside investors, they often participate to fulfil their fiduciary duties. In many cases,

however, supervisory board members have forgotten that legally speaking (for most jurisdictions other than the USA) they have to represent the interests of the organization they oversee, not the interests of the owners.

- **Corporate venture builder advisory board**: Established companies that operate and oversee a portfolio of corporate ventures are well advised to establish a professional governance structure to ensure proper oversight, but also to leverage needed knowledge. An advisory board for the venture builder can prove very effective, as it can engage key internal stakeholders as well as external experts. Especially when it comes to helping the parent company make decisions and determine the owner benefit, these insights can prove to be very valuable.
- **Corporate venture builder supervisory board**: At the same time, the management of the venture builder should ensure that formal decision-making procedures are clearly defined and followed and are well embedded in the overall corporate governance framework. A corporate venture builder should therefore be managed like any other corporate subsidiary: It should be closely aligned with corporate strategy while fulfilling all fiduciary duties required by the relevant law.

Figure 24.3 Different types of venture boards

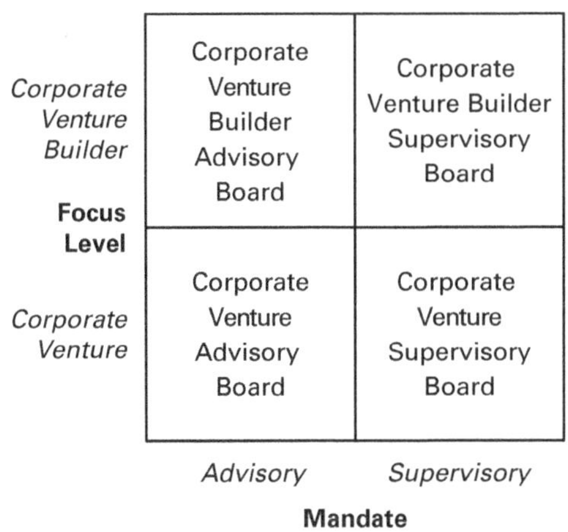

Harnessing the learning advantage

Aside from constantly assessing the venturing and owner advantages to determine the right time and path for harvesting, the parent company should also use each and every harvesting decision to learn from it and integrate the lessons learnt into its modus operandi to strengthen its corporate venturing capabilities.

In this context, it is important to learn from both successes and failures. Very often, failures are hushed up in a business environment instead of being perceived as a source of insights and learning experiences. In this context, it is important to always remember and openly communicate the proven truth of entrepreneurship: failures are the rule, successes the exception. Nevertheless, this rule should not be used as a justification for failure. A genuine and honest post-mortem can be very revealing and even healing for those who are pilloried.

At the same time, it is key not to limit the learning process to the individual case, but also to discuss the implications for building corporate ventures and the parent company. Since the cause of success or failure is rarely one-dimensional, it is crucial to openly assess the role of each party in the process and draw lessons for improving the approach, processes, structures and sometimes even people. In addition, individual cases can also help to reveal a company's true risk appetite, which can be a helpful guide for future corporate venture activities.

In the following sections, the harvesting pathways outlined above are described in detail by addressing their conditions and success factors.

References

ChatGTP4 (2023) Response to 'What are common decision biases in venture decisions?'

Hilb, M (2020a) Cracking the collaboration codes – How to succeed in ecosystems. In Governance of Ventures, 97–106, Haupt, Bern

Hilb, M (2020b) Venture governance – The hidden value driver of entrepreneurial value creation. In Governance of Ventures, 11–23, Haupt, Bern

Portfolio optimization 25

Portfolio optimization strategy

Besides screening and pre-selection, portfolio management is, arguably, the second most important discipline in the value chain of a venture capital organization. This is especially true for corporate venture capital teams. And, to a lesser extent, for private venture capital. Portfolio management is about supporting (and not hindering!) the target company in such a way that it can pursue/implement its own growth agenda – and is prevented from making avoidable mistakes.

As part of the Harvesting assessment (see Chapter 24), the investment corporation has examined and discussed the startup's growth agenda as part of the due diligence. Consequently, the growth agenda is known and can be supported by the corporation.

Corporate venture capitalists with a strategic investment focus will put even more emphasis on portfolio management, as this is about working together with the startup on the *common strategic agenda*, i.e., jointly tackling and implementing the hypotheses from the 'strategic assessment'. After all, the strategically acting and thinking corporate VC has invested to gain a strategic advantage from the investment and collaboration, which in the best-case scenario should be crowned by an additional financial success of the investment (ROI).

In portfolio management, we can assume two simplified time horizons:

1. **Short-term horizon**, i.e., within three months or 100 days after the initial investment, the startup should be connected with the relevant teams within the investing corporation, the 'Business Sponsors'. In addition, the CV team sets up systems to monitor the startup, i.e., continuous monitoring of the startup's performance (in order to identify dramatic deviations and, if necessary, further strategic/operational action or investment requirements at an early stage) and any deadlines resulting from the investment contracts (e.g., maturity dates of convertible loans, milestones, ratchets, minimum liquidity safety limits).

2 **Medium to long-term horizon.** After the 100 days have elapsed, the startup and the respective business sponsors have hopefully found a 'modus operandi' and the CV team transfers the coordination of the operational collaboration to subject matter experts. However, as already mentioned under (1), the investment team remains in touch with the startup via its 'Portfolio Manager' and, if applicable, the 'Transactional Manager' to continuously monitor its economic/financial development and act, where necessary, for example when the preparation of the next round of funding becomes an item.

Portfolio optimization team

As a rule, four essential roles in portfolio management are distinguished, but depending on the size of the investing teams or groups, the same teams or groups sometimes perform multiple roles:

1 **Operational manager** – responsible for operational/technical issues. These are usually project managers or technicians from the corporation's subject matter expert department who work with the startup, for example R&D project managers focusing on innovative materials will manage the relation with a startup from the portfolio that focuses on innovative materials. The startup can consult the operational manager – and vice versa – to address technical and operational questions or challenges.

2 **Investment manager** – responsible for all investment related aspects and usually the person who had managed the transaction so far. The investment manager serves as the point of contact for financial or strategic issues, e.g., next round of funding, or changes in the business model of the startup.

3 **Board member** – if the corporation has successfully negotiated for a board seat, the respective board member is usually a high-ranking officer from the respective department of the corporation (e.g., again, R&D or business development), not necessarily a member of the CV team. The CV team often finds itself in a position where they must negotiate with the startup in the context of follow-up financing rounds, but board members cannot negotiate against the interests of the startup due to potential conflicts of interest.

4 **Controller** – larger CV teams have a dedicated or assigned a controller or even COO who prepares internal portfolio reports on an ongoing basis,

but ideally also works with the investment manager to keep track of deadlines, including expiring loans or convertible loans, milestones to be achieved, defined floors on the startup's minimum remaining liquidity, etc.

Importantly, the roles are sometimes performed by the same person, especially the roles (i) and (iii), and (ii) and (iv).

Portfolio optimization challenges

Both on the corporate side and on the startup side, the 'playing dumb' phenomenon sometimes emerges. Playing dumb is also known as 'I couldn't care less about the stuff I said yesterday'.

On the corporate side, the previously upheld principles of investing in startups are often put into perspective, i.e., yes, we do not want to stifle the creativity and innovation of the startup (because we have seen the negative consequences of this already 1–2 times). And we want to give the entrepreneurs the freedom they require. However, we do want monthly reports from the startup – even in the absence of groundbreaking news or significant KPI changes (e.g., for biotech startups, spectacular developments do not necessarily happen on a monthly or quarterly basis). And we want to stop any activity that we have not yet discussed to the last detail. 'Pivots', i.e., changes to the business model, which are often necessary in startups, do not fare particularly well with corporate managers.

On the startup side, the previously invoked principles of partnership are often put into perspective, too. The founders were happy to accept the investment of €10 million. But the monthly reporting that the investor wants and that is reflected in the contracts feels as if 'they are asking for too much from us'. And honestly, who would have thought that a listed large corporation would want to know how the startup spends the invested monies and what achievements they have made? And how can an investor disapprove our pivot from Artificial Intelligence Fintech to Cryptocurrency?

Similar to a marriage or long-term partnership, the two parties undergoing this 'reality check' can only succeed together in the long term if they learn to consider, anticipate and discuss, with honesty and empathy, each other's constraints, needs and goals. Friction between the parties is not necessarily a bad thing. It generates heat and helps to get to know each other better. However, under no circumstances should mutual respect and professional behaviour be allowed to go overboard.

It is usually helpful if the startup and the corporation continuously encourage and challenge, praise and criticize each other. Here are some examples:

- The investing corporation may become a (paying!) customer of the startup and thereby not only increase the credibility of the startup, but also build trust and liquidity for the startup.
- The corporation should consider simplifying internal processes, for example, to make monthly reporting more manageable.
- The startup may support the partnership with the corporation on a macro and micro level by explaining and praising this partnership to third parties. For example, on LinkedIn and other channels. This applies to both personal partnerships between employees and the partnership between the corporate entities. What could be better than a member of the corporation's top management team sitting in the audience of a conference or reading an article on a startup and learning that the startup comments favourably and gratefully on the CV team and the collaboration with the corporation?
- The founder team may come up with suggestions on how the corporation can support the startup more actively and effectively. Doing so does not require the startup to know all internal processes on the corporate side. Even without such knowledge, the startup can develop ideas in the form of hypotheses and suggest them to board members or bring them up in discussions with their subject matter expert counterparts from the corporation.

Follow-on investments

Follow-on investments are tricky, as we will see. On the one hand, the startup as well as other existing shareholders and the startup community (e.g., other investors not yet invested in the startup) expect a follow-on investment from you, i.e., a corporation that has made a first investment in a startup. On the other hand, your CV team may have good reasons not to agree to a follow-on investment. Let's examine this a bit more closely.

In 99 per cent of all cases, the expectation of your portfolio company is that the CV team who has committed to an initial investment will also do follow-on investments in the next rounds of funding, mostly because a strong pre-commitment (prior to kicking off the startup's fundraising efforts) from existing shareholders sends a very strong and positive signal to other potential investors and often facilitates the fundraising efforts of the startup. In a way, such a pre-commitment confirms positive business prospects of the startup, suggests a satisfying or even strong performance, indicates good reliability of the founders and the company's processes, and reflects a good report between founders and investors. If a commitment from existing investors is missing, on the other hand, this is usually interpreted as the exact opposite, e.g., either a lack of professionality on the part of the investors, or, more importantly, a lack of confidence of existing investors in the startup and its future performance.

As a rule of thumb, startup investors who invest in early-stage startups should always earmark the identical amount of their initial investment for potential follow-up investments. In other words, if you have invested €500,000 in a startup, you should be prepared to invest another €500,000 during follow-on rounds of funding, or even more if your overall investment strategy is focused on steady increases of your stake in prospering ventures.

The main reasons to invest in a follow-on round (or a combination thereof):

- Based on the performance of the startup, the CV team is confident that the company will be successful in the future, and therefore the team wants to invest more in order to limit the dilution of the CV's shareholding or even increase the CV's shareholding to get to a higher return on investment.
- The CV team may want to maintain or even increase their shareholding in the startup in the light of a potential future acquisition of the company.
- The CV team wants to build itself a reputation as a good and reliable investor in the market, which is important to attract top quality startups and investors to share opportunities with them.
- And/or the CV team wants to support the startup's fundraising activities indirectly, based on positive signalling to the market.

Main reasons not to invest (or a combination thereof):

- Based on the performance of the startup, the CV team is anything but convinced that the company will survive. Therefore, the team decides to refrain from an investment. By doing so, the CV team may be risking that the lingering crisis of the startup could be accelerated just because of the CV team's decision not to invest.

- The startup is doing ok, but the CV team has learnt that the startup's technology is not strategic to the corporation's business, and so the size of the shareholding is not important because mergers and acquisitions is becoming less and less likely. This decision implies that the CV shareholding is diluted further, and that the decision not to invest may have repercussions for the reputation of the CV team.
- The startup may inform the CV team that they prefer to have other investors take most if not all of the current round of funding, e.g., because the incoming investor is of strategic importance for the startup or even a potential acquirer. And then the CV team could decide to accept the startup's request.
- A participation of the CV team may not be advisable because the next round is too small (and another investor volunteers to step up to the plate) or too big (another investor plans to invest a lot of money on a much higher valuation, but the company is also more strategic to that investor than it is to the CV team).

Decision-making on follow-on investments

In a corporate context, once the initial investment in a startup was approved, the Investment Committee of the corporation should transfer the decision-making power for follow-up investments to the corporate venture capital team, especially if the follow-on investments are not larger than the pre-viewed 'reserve for follow-up investments', i.e., 1× the initial investment.

Within the CV team itself, the senior managers working with the startup on a regular basis are asked to share their feedback on the performance and the prospects of the underlying startup with the internal group of decision makers. But the same senior managers are often prevented from voting in favour or against the follow-on investment, because they may be positively or negatively biased due to their close collaboration with the startup and its team.

Additional investor support

Follow-on investments are often 'advertised' through existing investors at startup conferences or other investor meetings, or as part of public campaigns of the startup itself dedicated to increase the visibility of the company and its intention to raise more funds. In other words, an investor may recommend a startup from its portfolio to attend startup conferences A, B, and C, and the investor also agrees to attend these conferences as well, to actively support the startup in conversations with potential investors.

Moreover, since the investors have experienced in most cases many more rounds of funding with startups and have built themselves a network of investor contacts, they are also supposed to support the startup regarding the development of a pitch deck for the fundraising process, the setup of a data room, inputs on the draft term sheet that the startup should be preparing, and also provide advice and support on identifying and approaching investors.

Investor selection and approach

The investor selection process follows an analytical process:

1. Long list

In a first step, a 'long list' of potential investors is generated, taking into account how much capital is sought, maturity stage of the company, geography, technology focus and industry of the startup, sometimes special types of investors (e.g., venture debt). Ideally, a long list of investors would contain 50–200 potential investors. Such lists are often generated with online databases.

2. Short list

This 'long list' is then reviewed carefully and in detail to derive a short list of 'likely' investors. Investors are selected from the 'long list' and added to the 'short list' based on how well they fit the case of the fundraising startup, e.g., pace and sequence of the investor's recent investments, previous investments in somewhat similar companies, strong subject matter expertise and/or network contacts of the investor's management team, track record of the investor for successful investments etc. Ideally, such a 'short list' of 'likely' investors would contain 10–20 companies.

3. Talking to investors in reverse order of 'how well they fit'

The short-listed investors are then approached in the reverse order of their suitability and attractiveness and desirability, i.e., the team would start with the least likely (of the likely) and least suitable and least fitting of the short-listed investors. And then, over time, it will work through the short list and up until the most desired investor. This allows the team to practice the pitch as well as subsequent Q&A sessions with investors, and it allows the founders to use feedbacks from investor conversations to further optimize the pitch deck. For instance, if the team has two conversations with investors and in both conversations, investors did not understand the punchline of the innovation or another element of the pitch, then the pitch needs to address these elements better.

4. How to approach investors

The startup's founders (sometimes directly supported by existing investors) should use 'warm introductions' wherever possible, i.e., a person or entity inclined to support the startup will introduce the founders personally to a senior representative of the potential investor. No need to be naïve, the approached investors will not consider (let alone invest) in the startup because of a warm introduction. But the warm introduction ensures that the startup is not ignored by the investor, i.e., it avoids an accidental rejection of the startup by the investor.

5. What to bring to the first conversation with investors

Going into the first investor conversation around an upcoming round of funding, the founders will have equipped themselves with a short, (3–10 slides) non-confidential pitch deck introducing the company and, where possible, taking into account possible fits and links with characteristic aspects of the investor. This short pitch should get a lot of attention from all stakeholders in the process, and will often go through 50 different versions before it is deemed crisp and sound. The other aspect of the fundraising effort is to seduce the investor to spend more time with this case, and then to keep that interest level high. Not every single aspect that suggests a fit between investor and startup needs to be spelled out on the slides. On certain occasions, you may want to be a little bit more subtle. For instance, if the investor's website mentions that they prefer to invest in diverse teams, then the diversity of the startup's team (as far as it is diverse, of course) could be emphasized at some point of the presentation. Or, if a corporate venture capitalist is approached, let's assume from Coca-Cola, the startup could somehow suggest and almost simulate a collaboration of the startup and the corporation, e.g., with a picture that shows how a technology would be featured on a can of Coke. That being said, the first conversations are in many cases still relatively high level, and the chemistry between the investors and the founders is also an important thing.

6. What else to have in the backhand

The startup as well as supporting investors will also make preparations for the steps in the fundraising process, i.e., after the initial conversation. Few things are more awkward than an investor coming back to you and giving you positive feedback, only to find that the startup has not yet prepared a long deck for a more in-depth examination of the company, a file dedicated to financial and non-financial achievements so far and plans looking 3–5 years into the future, and a virtual data room to provide more information corresponding with commercial, technical, financial, legal and sustainability-related questions from investors. So, the basic list of documents required to have before you engage in investor conversations includes but is not limited to:

a. Short pitch deck (non-confidential)

b. Long pitch deck (non-confidential or confidential – if confidential, you also need a standard Non-Disclosure-Agreement)

c. Draft term sheet, especially if you have firm commitments from existing investors

d. Virtual data room populated with additional information around legal, commercial, financial, technical, and sustainability-related aspects of the startup.

Integration 26

Integration rationales

Integration is the approach most often intended, but rarely achieved. Most corporate venture proposals express a desire to build a new business that can one day be integrated, if not the new core business. While the aspiration highlights the unique synergies and comparative advantages that startups offer, the business reality often tests the underlying assumptions, which can frequently fall short.

How do you recognize a venture suitable for integration? First, the venture must be demonstrably successful and viable on its own. If a corporate venture has not been able to realize synergies between the venture and the core company, it is unlikely that this will be the case after integration. Individual excellence is an important prerequisite.

Second, there must be a strong and reconfirmed owner benefit that clearly demonstrates that the value of the venture will be maximized if the parent company remains its owner and solidifies its ownership by fully integrating the venture. In this context, alternative ownership scenarios should be tested, even if only virtually. The parent company should ask itself two simple questions: Could I sell the venture at a higher price than the value the company will generate in the future? Could I buy a comparable asset on the market at a lower price? Only if both questions are answered in the negative should integration be considered.

Third, the business must be mature enough to leave the sheltered protection of the corporate venture builder and face the harsh reality of other companies, i.e., other business units or product groups, where performance is clearly measured in terms of contribution margins rather than future growth potential. This has reduced the risk advantage.

Fourth, this also requires organizational and cultural maturity on both the corporate and business sides to recognize that they need to adapt their behaviour in order to make a success of the integration process, where different types of cultures and values will eventually meet. In this context, it is essential not to completely replace one culture with the other, but rather to combine the best of both.

Integration approaches

There are two main ways of combining a venture with the core business. The most common method of integrating the venture into the core business, and the less frequently carried out method of integrating the old organization into the new one. Theoretically, one could also imagine a merger of equals, but in reality, this is almost impossible, not least from a legal and business management perspective; one side always takes the lead, be it only through the choice of legal form or management personnel. What are the key success factors of the two integration approaches?

- **Integrate the venture into the core business:** If you conclude that the venture is ready to be integrated into the existing organization as a business unit or product group, it is obvious that the corporate structure and processes will be the new modus operandi. There is no point in mourning the good old days and sticking to the old rules that have proven effective in building the business. The established rules will prevail and most likely prove useful for the next stage of a venture's development as it matures. It will be up to the entrepreneurs to decide whether they will stick with it or prefer to find another field of activity within the corporate portfolio or even outside the company. At the same time, further development of the key products and services transferred must be ensured. This may also mean that some entrepreneurial cells remain within the new entity to ensure sustainability.
- **Integrate the core business into the venture:** In the unlikely event that the decision is made to integrate the old organization into the new one, the challenges are usually far greater (which is also the main reason why this approach is rarely chosen in many cases, despite its clear strategic rationale). Such an integration is largely driven by risk considerations. The risk of a failed integration must be avoided at all costs, as the damage could be significant if the core business is affected. A failed integration process is not an option. Therefore, detailed planning and the development of contingency plans are crucial. The question here is who can do this, the team of the new venture or the old core business? Ideally, both teams work together, as they are likely to have complementary knowledge. The corporate venture team knows its systems and processes inside and out, while the core business team usually has more experience in managing transition processes and planning.

Apart from these concept-specific success factors, it is crucial to treat such an integration with the same care that the parent company would apply to any other integration. This means developing and executing a solid pre- and post-integration plan (see the next Deep Dive). This should include virtual commercial and cultural due diligence, i.e., carefully assessing the differences and determining a way to bridge them. In addition, the focus of these activities should not be limited to formal structures but should also consider the impact on the informal organization. This requires a solid approach to stakeholder management and a willingness to foster strong alliances and linkages between the two organizations.

Deep Dive: The key success factors of pre and post venture merger integration

Pre-merger and post-merger integration are critical stages in the process of merging two companies. The most important success factors for pre- and post-merger integration include the following:

1. Strategic alignment: The merging companies should be clear about their strategic goals, culture, values, and vision. They should align their business objectives to ensure they are moving in the same direction.
2. Communication: Effective communication is key to a successful merger. Companies should establish clear communication channels, keep employees informed about the merger and regularly update them on the integration process.
3. Leadership: Strong leadership is necessary to drive the integration process. Companies should identify capable leaders to guide the integration team, communicate the vision and goals, and motivate employees.
4. Cultural integration: Companies should take steps to integrate their cultures to ensure a smooth transition. This may include identifying shared values, developing a common vision, and providing cross-cultural training.
5. Talent management: Companies should identify key talent and retain them. This can include developing a retention strategy, providing professional development opportunities, and offering a competitive salary.

6 Process integration: The merging companies should identify and integrate their critical business processes to ensure smooth post-merger operations. This may include the integration of IT systems, financial systems, and supply chain management.

7 Risk management: Companies should identify potential risks and develop strategies to mitigate them. This may include conducting due diligence, identifying potential legal and regulatory issues, and developing contingency plans.

8 Customer integration: Companies should focus on integrating their customer base to ensure a smooth transition. This can include developing a customer communication strategy, identifying customer needs, and developing a customer retention plan.

Reference

ChatGTP4 (2023) Response to 'What are key success factors of pre and post venture merger integration?'

Exits 27

Exit rationales and approaches

The decision to kick-off an exit process is a joint decision, taken by founders and investors of the startup. By and large, one cannot sell a company successfully without the support from founders and/or the management. And one will struggle to sell a company successfully without the support from its shareholders either. At least, it is not advisable to launch an exit without the support of the previously involved and invested parties.

For certain startups, the founders may not own the majority of shares anymore when the decision is taken. Or the existing investors decide to pull a drag-along clause and 'force' an exit upon the founders, even though they do not own the majority of shares. But one of the main questions is: Are you starting an exit process because you want to? Or are you kicking-off an exit process because you have to?

Must-do exits

The following exit channels are mostly must-do exit channels.

- Bankruptcy – the startup has to file for bankruptcy because it is no longer able to meet the financial requirements to continue the business, i.e., pay debts and liabilities, pay employees, social contributions, etc. In fact, there is a legal obligation to file for bankruptcy if it becomes apparent for Board and Management that they cannot meet the financial obligations of their business.
- Liquidation – the startup has to be liquidated based on an event or development that does not allow the business to continue otherwise, e.g., the company's business is stopped by a regulator, or due to other legal reasons, or because of a tragic accident of sorts.
- Fire sale – with a lingering bankruptcy or, at least, more significant challenges on the horizon, founders and investors may decide that it is better to get out (for a low payment) than not to get out at all (and get no

payment at all). Sometimes, certain shareholders with drag-along preference rights and force other shareholders to sell their shares as part of a fire sale.

Can-do exits

The following exit channels are mostly can-do exit channels.

- Trade sale – the startup is approached by a strategic buyer, often a company from the same industry or an adjacent industry that wants to get their hands on the startup's IP or experts from the startup team or customers or infrastructure or certain existing customers etc. or a combination thereof, and because they see strong synergies with their own business.
- Financial exit – startup is approached by a financial investor, often a private equity house that plans to take the company to the next level (or bring it back from a period of stagnation to a growth path) and then sell it again, completely or in pieces, to another financial investor, or a strategic investor, or list it on the stock exchange.
- Initial public offering (IPO) – the startup itself starts to engage in a process to list the company at the stock exchange, so that it becomes a publicly traded company. This facilitates fundraising on a larger scale with new external investors, and the listing also provides existing shareholders with an opportunity to sell their shares via the stock market.
- Secondary – one or several of the existing investors are approached by other existing shareholders or external shareholders to see if they would be interested in selling their shares in the startup. Often, fresh capital is injected into the startup by the investor who comes in through a secondary.
- Merger – the startup and another company, often from the same or an adjacent industry, develop a joint business concept and decide to join forces systematically. They exchange shares and form a new company, pooling both companies' assets. The new company often carries a new name and brand, and, similar to strategic acquisitions, the underlying logic behind a merger is 1 + 1 = 3 (or more), i.e., we are stronger together than we are on a standalone basis.
- Management buy-out – the founders or managers of the startup make an offer to buy-out the other existing shareholders, because they believe they can run the company better (more effectively and efficiently) than the

current owners / shareholders. Often, such buyouts are leveraged, i.e., banks or other financial investors give loans to the managers, who also invest some of their own money, to buy-out the other shareholders.

Must-do exits are stressful, often happen under a lot of time pressure, often go along with frustrations and anger of all parties involved, and generate, on average, somewhat disappointing returns on investments. The challenge with must-do-exits is that you should want to ensure that the process is run properly – that there is no delay in starting the process, there is a professional structure for the process, assignment of clear responsibilities and accountabilities.

Can-do exits tend to become as stressful as must-do exits at some point, as they also develop a certain momentum and a certain time pressure, but if your portfolio company is in such a strong position that it can steer the process, then it will feel much better than a must-do exit. And, obviously, the returns on investments are much more pleasant for can-do exits than for must-do exits. In some sense, even can-do exits can sometimes be managed poorly, particularly if, for instance, the selling team's diligence decreases over time, because they start to get bored answering the same or similar questions over and over again, or because they do not listen enough to the potential buyers and miss certain signals that could be a reflection of certain concerns or lingering questions. Think about it: the selling team embarks on this process, and at some point, they feel that this could lead to them becoming millionaires in a few weeks – this could cloud your vision a bit, couldn't it?

Exit timing

The deciding parties (founders and existing shareholders) will consider the timing from a *seller's perspective* – is the startup 'mature' enough and economically attractive enough? Sometimes, it makes sense to wait another 2–4 months – for example, until the startup has on-boarded another major new customer – and then kick-off the exit if and when that has happened. Investment bankers sometimes refer to the sellers' activities as 'dressing the bride (or 'dressing the groom')', i.e., trying to make a company look as attractive as possible in the eyes of the buyer. The logic is simple: attractive startups can trigger a competition amongst numerous potential buyers and that will drive exit proceeds to new levels. Moreover, the deciding parties (founders, existing shareholders) will also consider the timing from a *buyer's perspective*, i.e., what is the current momentum of the global economy.

Think of the impact of inflationary periods or supply chain uncertainty, and how this could prevent potential buyers from engaging in the exit process.

Additionally, what is the momentum within the specific industry of the startup (and the buyers), how are the most attractive potential acquirers doing? Maybe, there was a recent increase in interest rates, and loans are more expensive, which leads to a decline in appetite to do leverage acquisitions. Or maybe one of the main players in the industry has just acquired a big target and the others feel inclined to also acquire something? Or maybe the founders and existing shareholders have decided to IPO the company, then the momentum on global stock markets becomes an issue, too.

Both buyers and sellers will think more about an exit transaction *before* the underlying startup begins to work on level of their development. In other words, you would consider selling your B2C business *before* you expand to another country. Or *before* you go from FDA phase 1 to FDA phase 2. The logic is that the next step often requires the full attention of the startup (and potentially more financial and other resources), and it will likely take another 2–3 years until the startup is able to show good performance with that new business activity and engage in an exit process. This then means a longer holding period for existing investors. And it means that the business is likely to be much more expensive to acquire after that next growth step, in other words, the acquirers may get a cheaper deal if they made an offer now, which is also an element for them to consider.

Exit from a seller's point of view

Buyers may want to understand better *why* the startup is selling its business. So, one thing that sellers may want to discuss and prepare before jumping into an exit process is to explain the reasoning for the exit to potential buyers. Maybe the exit is mostly due to entrepreneurial reasons, for example the company has exhausted its growth potential in a certain country, region, or based on existing funds, and in order to go to the next level, international expansion or growing significantly in its current market needs significantly more capital and/or strategic partners. Perhaps the exit is mostly due to private reasons, such as the seller's private agenda has changed and the founders want to focus more on their families or other activities, and decide that it is best to find a new home for the company.

In general, sellers in a can-do exit will often try to convey the impression that *they do not have to sell now*. In other words, if your offer is not good enough, then we will just continue to grow the company. At the same time, they should have a convincing narrative as to why an exit makes sense for all parties.

Exit from a buyer's point of view

The buyer of a company usually wants to explain to its own organization, and to the sellers and other stakeholders, why it is acquiring the startup – what are the synergies, how does the acquisition make the buyer's own business stronger and better and larger, and why is the target company the right company that will find a great new home in the group of the buyers?

The buyers will also think about how desperate the startup needs the exit. They will try to gauge how many other parties are potentially interested in buying, or how fast the startup is running out of money (if the startup's business is not self-sustaining), because with few other buyers in the process or the startup running out of cash quickly, they will have an easier life negotiating for more favourable terms for the acquisition.

Exit management

The deciding parties (founders, existing shareholders) will consider how to manage the exit process. One aspect of this is the internal view. The preparation and execution of an exit strategy is likely going to require significant time and attention from the top management of the startup, so it should be discussed how to manage the workload, so that the underlying business does not suffer too much from the fact that the management is working on the exit. Just imagine, the management has to prepare for and then hold meetings with representatives of the potential buyer(s) where they explain the business, respond to questions, take notes on additional information to be provided after the meetings, etc. Moreover, managing an exit is stressful and can also lead to somewhat unpleasant internal developments on the seller's side, such as irritation and confusion among employees, negligence of the startup's own business because the exit process fuels wishful thinking and greed and gets more attention than the actual core business, etc.

Another aspect is the external view: the founders and shareholders will often decide to hire an external supporter of the exit process, e.g., a mergers and acquisitions boutique or investment bank. One of the main reasons for this is to be able to tap into the experience and know-how and networks of people of have worked on numerous exit transactions before and can advise the selling founders and shareholders. Moreover, even the choice of the external exit supporter may have an influence on the exit price. While most investment bank offer similar services to companies around exits, it is a known phenomenon that certain top tier investment banks with famous brand names may be able increase the exit price because of their own reputation, even though this is not related to the underlying business. More pragmatically, experienced exit professionals can help the startup in terms of the price discovery process and negotiation strategy, as well as in terms of 'building a book' of potential acquires (or investors, in case of an IPO). As a selling party, it will be in your interest to have as many interested acquirers around the table as possible, so that they may eventually engage in an auction process and fight among themselves as to who gets to buy the startup. Last but not least, emotionally, many investors who have gone through exit processes will confirm that it can be helpful and emotionally safer not to have direct discussions (and potentially fights) between buyers and sellers, but to have one or two intermediaries (e.g., investment banks or M&A (mergers and acquisitions) boutiques) who will run back and forth between the parties and broker the deal, suggesting and agreeing upon compromises related to controversial topics.

Exit preparation

In previous chapters, we have talked about individual investment decisions and how startup investors structure their due diligence of a business before they invest. In a way, an exit process is another investment process. Except that this time, the goal is not to prepare for a minority investment or attract another minority investor, but to acquire (or sell) a business. Buyers will follow a process that is somewhat similar to the investment process that we have laid out in front of you in this chapter:

- Origination of several acquisition targets (i.e., companies willing to sell *and* fitting the search profile of the acquirer)
- Screening (from the far, i.e., without talking to the companies directly) of individual shortlisted acquisition targets
- Due diligence and deal negotiations with individual acquisition targets (sometimes as part of an M&A process that may involve more than one other bidder)
- Lastly, the final decision to acquire.

Unsurprisingly, the exit preparations of the selling party follow, to a certain degree, similar ideas and concepts. Similar to the preparation of a follow-on round of funding, the startup will set up a virtual data room (VDR) that it will make available to one or several external parties (i.e., buyers). And in parallel to the due diligence, seller and buyer will negotiate around the deal.

The VDR contains confidential information about the startup – legal, commercial, financial, technical sustainability, and often systems/IT aspects of the business. Therefore, VDRs have to meet the highest standards in terms of cybersecurity – preventing unauthorized access by third parties, following the activities of authorized parties in the data room, preventing the download of certain pieces of information – because at this moment, the selling startup discloses all relevant information to its potential acquirers.

The following elements of the VDR are often to be populated by the startup. The list of documents mentioned is not comprehensive, your portfolio company may feel inclined to add to the information contained in Table 27.1.

Table 27.1 Virtual data room elements

Legal	**Commercial**
Documents relating to the company's shareholder structure (including subsidiaries etc.), rights of existing investors, articles of association, excerpts from legal registers, board structure and board meeting protocols, audited annual reports, tax filings, information around pending litigation, and all sorts of legal contracts linked to running the business, e.g. related to lease contracts, internet domains, key employee work contracts, key supplier contracts, key customer contracts, intellectual property documentation, non-disclosure agreements between the company and other business partners, business licenses or certificates, correspondence with regulators, etc.	Business documents related running the business, e.g. list of top customers and the business with them over the past 1–3 years, list of top suppliers and the business with them over the past 1–3 years, list of top channels or subsidiaries and partners and the business with them over the past 1–3 years. Moreover, overview of market and competition, e.g. market growth rates, market structure, main competitors and competitive advantages, barriers to entry and relevant regulation, aspects around scalability (e.g. how much would it take to expand more).

(continued)

Table 27.1 (Continued)

Financial Audited and unaudited financial statements such as balance sheets, profit & loss accounts, cash flow statements, but also monthly and quarterly performance reports, business plans going forward, as well as current bank account statements and other correspondence regarding loan arrangements with banks, list of current accounts payable and accounts receivable, etc.	**Technical** Information related to the performance and other data around products, processes, and services developed by, used by, sold buy, and purchased by the company. Information related to internal systems and software used by the company to run its business. Detailed overview of manufacturing, machinery in use, etc.
Sustainability Documentation around machines or infrastructure used by the company with positive sustainability implications, e.g. lower carbon footprint, activities to save resources and materials, etc. Documentation around legal investigations and litigation around activities of the company that may or may not have environmental effects.	**IT** Aspects around IT systems currently and previously in use by the company, data protection and compliance with GDPR standards, cybersecurity.

Exit psychology

Looking at an exit from different psychological angles is also helpful, both for sellers and for buyers. From a *seller's perspective*, it is advantageous to be in a position where buyers approach your portfolio company or your CV team. It is less advantageous for the startup or you as investor to approach other parties and sell the company. People in the market say that 'startups are not sold, they are bought'. Or, like one VC put it '*(...) you want to be asked to dance, you do not want to be the one to ask others to dance (...)*'. Having said this, it means that you may want to kick-off your exit process with as little pressure as possible. Ideally, your startup is self-sustaining and under no time pressure. It also means that you may want to approach a somewhat subtle strategy, i.e., make a bit of noise in the market talking about your annual results, or creating a bit of a buzz around your most recent product launch or the achievement of a certain milestone. Guess why biotech startups make a lot of noise around the completion of their phase I or phase II process? It's not only to talk about the scientific achievements, but it's also to make sure that the completion of that phase does not go by unnoticed by potential buyers such as pharma companies. Keep in mind, though, that you are just pretending to be surprised that another party would even entertain the idea of buying your startup. In reality, your virtual data room is already populated with comprehensive information that can be updated quickly

If you are planning to do an IPO, your goal is to create as much positive buzz around your company as possible; you are supporting your IPO process with an elaborate communication strategy. If you are planning to do a trade sale (for example to a financial investor or strategic investor), you still want to have as many potential buyers around the table as possible, so that you can trigger an auction process, which tends to maximize proceeds on your side.

We will not elaborate a lot on the buyer's perspective in this book, because your CV team is unlikely to engage in active M&A discussions to buy a company. But the main challenge for the buyers is the asymmetric distribution of information between seller and buyer. In other words, the buyer constantly fears that the seller is not sharing everything there is to be said about the business.

Rejuvenation and incubation 28

Incubation rationales

In the context of rejuvenation and incubation, the process of 'reusing' and adapting a proven approach from venturing within the parent company for other purposes becomes essential. This approach relies on the assumption that the enterprise has acquired specific capabilities that serve as its core competencies and can be applied throughout the organization. However, for this venturing advantage to be considered stronger than a more administrative approach, the parent company must be convinced that entrepreneurial activity will bring more benefits. To achieve this, a thorough assessment of the conditions and context of the new scope is necessary, including identifying similarities and differences from the current corporate venture environment and understanding their implications. These assessments should involve all key stakeholders and address important questions.

For successful rejuvenation and incubation, the parts of the venture that are to be replicated, such as processes, products, technologies, business models, or the venture as a whole, must be scalable and transferable. Scalability refers to the venture's growth momentum and its ability to achieve economies of scale and scope as it evolves, which are key characteristics of successful companies. Transferability, on the other hand, describes the ability to apply proven approaches in different contexts. This may require a certain degree of codification of procedures and processes, which is not commonly associated with traditional companies.

Furthermore, the venture being replicated must clearly benefit the owner, who sees advantages in retaining the asset. The expected synergies from replicating parts or all of the venture often play a significant role in valuing ownership benefits. However, it is crucial to conduct an honest assessment of the expected benefits, as synergies are frequently overestimated, and the cost and complexity of replication may be underestimated. Comparing alternative outcomes through a benchmark scenario can be helpful, even if those options are hypothetical.

Incubation approaches

To implement rejuvenation and incubation, different forms and scales must be adapted to specific needs. Two high-level approaches can be distinguished: project replication or the venturing approach.

Incubate the venture in another market: This approach involves using the corporate setup to expand the venture business by creating twin ventures in different geographic or industrial markets. The parent company views the original corporate venture as a successful pilot worth expanding. This approach leverages the strengths of both the company and the venture. While the parent company provides its infrastructure, the venture brings its growth mindset and agility. The main challenge lies in turning the different approaches into a mutual advantage through mutual awareness of differences, understanding of structures, and clearly defined roles and responsibilities.

Incubate the venturing approach in another business: In this approach, incubation focuses on mimicking venturing behaviour by transferring certain capabilities to another business unit within the parent company. This can involve exchanging best practices, developing training and development programmes where internal venture leaders share their experiences, seconding corporate venture leaders to other parts of the company, or establishing fully fledged venture skills transfer programmes. Regardless of the specific form, it is essential to not only focus on learnt behaviours but also on the structural changes required to enable entrepreneurial action. This includes fostering a culture of failure, incentivizing innovation, and promoting agility. Without a strong commitment from the parent company to adapt its structures, attempts to transfer the entrepreneurial mindset to other parts of the organization may remain superficial.

In both approaches, the common success factor is viewing incubation as a deliberate step toward developing venturing as a new strategic capability. Only when capabilities are recognized as strategic will they receive the necessary investment and attention to create value for the business, leading to rejuvenation. It is important for all owners, board members, and executives to fully commit to walking the talk when it comes to embracing entrepreneurship with all its consequences (see this chapter's Deep Dive).

Deep Dive: Walk the talk of corporate entrepreneurship

Corporate entrepreneurship, also known as intrapreneurship, is the process of developing new ideas, products, services, or processes within an existing organization. Here are some important success factors that can promote entrepreneurship in companies:

1. Clear strategic objectives: Entrepreneurship in companies requires clear strategic objectives that are consistent with the company's overall mission and vision. Companies should identify areas for growth and innovation and create a culture that encourages risk-taking and experimentation.
2. Committed resources: Companies need to allocate dedicated resources such as money, time, and personnel to support entrepreneurial initiatives. This enables the development of new products, services, and processes without impacting the company's core business.
3. Entrepreneurial leadership: Entrepreneurial action in companies requires leaders who are willing to take risks and support innovative ideas. Leaders must create a culture that encourages experimentation and supports failure as an opportunity to learn and grow.
4. Agile processes: Entrepreneurship requires agile processes that enable rapid experimentation and iteration. Companies must be ready to respond quickly to market feedback and changing customer needs.
5. Strong communication: Effective communication is critical to the success of entrepreneurship. Companies must clearly communicate their goals and objectives to all stakeholders, including employees, customers, and investors.
6. Metrics for success: Entrepreneurial initiatives should be measured against specific metrics to ensure their success. Companies should track key performance indicators (KPIs) such as revenue growth, market share and customer satisfaction to evaluate the success of their initiatives.

Incubation strategy

Incubation should not stop at a single replication but rather lay the foundation for an integrated incubation system supported by a strong incubation culture. Incubation should not be the exception but should become the rule. This requires the development of capabilities and an organization that manages a portfolio of ventures throughout the incubation period. Beyond formal structures, the company must create a culture that not only tolerates incubation but encourages it as a strategic imperative. What are the key formal and informal factors for business incubation success?

Establishing a sustainable incubation system

An effective and value-creating incubation system requires, first and foremost, a long-term commitment by the company to ongoing incubation support and flexibility in dealing with unexpected outcomes, of which there will certainly be many. In addition, companies should try to combine the best of both worlds, corporate and venture, when designing their incubation system.

On the corporate side, they need to bring their proven approaches and practices in business development, risk management, governance infrastructure and resource management, and legal and regulatory management. In this way, the incubation approach can gain acceptance in a corporate environment and facilitate its functioning.

From the world of the venture capital industry, the enterprise should adopt the proven approaches to capital allocation, collaboration, innovation, and portfolio monitoring. These proven approaches, as described earlier, are also relevant to successful corporate incubation. Ultimately, the success of a sustainable and value-creating incubation system depends on a company's ability to effectively balance and combine management approaches from both the corporate and venture worlds.

Establishing an embedded incubation culture

This balancing act can only succeed if it is supported by an appropriate culture – a culture that accepts tensions but also provides a clear orientation toward shared values. Five values are of particular importance in this context:

1 **Collaboration:** An incubation culture should encourage entrepreneurs to share knowledge, experience and resources with each other and with

other business units. Facilitating networking events, peer-to-peer learning and cross-fertilization of ideas help build a strong community and foster collaboration.

2 **Psychological safety:** An incubation culture should foster an environment where participants feel comfortable seeking help, advice, and feedback from mentors, advisors and other entrepreneurs. Fostering mutual support, trust and inclusivity within the community strengthens the ecosystem.

3 **Learning:** An incubation culture should encourage entrepreneurs to expand their knowledge, acquire new skills, and keep abreast of industry trends. Access to educational resources, workshops, training programmes, and mentoring opportunities helps startups develop and adapt to a changing environment.

4 **Diversity:** A diverse community brings a wide range of perspectives, experiences and ideas that can drive innovation and problem solving. Promoting diversity in gender, ethnicity, background, and expertise creates a more vibrant and inclusive ecosystem.

5 **Integrity:** Promoting ethical behaviour and transparency builds trust within the incubation community. Adherence to high ethical standards and transparent practices in decision-making, resource allocation, and governance helps maintain integrity and credibility and strengthens the overall incubation culture.

Incubating the Unicorn inside

Once the incubation structure and culture are established, the journey can begin, with the company applying everything it has learnt along the way. This requires both emulating successful practices observed in the companies invested in and maintaining the company's distinct advantage as a portfolio manager.

Four behaviours that characterize successful businesses and should always be considered when incubating a venture:

- **Reach for the stars:** Ambition and aspiration, easily dismissed as unrealistic, are prerequisites for any successful venture. Without far-reaching goals, the growth path needed to get survive and thrive can hardly be achieved. Therefore, corporate leaders who are used to developing and communicating realistic forecasts must be open to a change of perspective and embrace a growth mindset.

- **Stay lean and agile:** Lean processes, often fuelled by limited resources, are a key success factor for companies, enabling them to remain agile and adapt quickly and effectively to changing requirements. A company must maintain this spirit and should never be constrained by company rules, processes, and procedures.
- **Learn as you go:** The core strength of a challenger is usually the need and ability to listen to and better understand the customer. Without a total customer focus, a company will often not survive. This eagerness to learn and the ability to quickly adapt to the needs of the customer should be maintained at all costs. The insights gained in this process can even inspire other parts of the company.
- **Pivot as needed:** Ultimately, successful companies are characterized by their ability to quickly shift their strategy as needed and constantly examine all options. This can include dramatic moves such as a sale, merger, or ceasing operations. A corporate venture should be guided by the same standards and have the courage to change its business strategy if necessary without having to accept restrictions that limit its room for manoeuvre too much.

Companies setting up their own ventures are therefore well advised to consciously preserve their clear ownership advantage. Here are four rules to follow:

- **Separate the roles of owner and operator:** Although the company is both owner and operator of the business, the roles should remain strictly separated to ensure proper governance. Both sides perform very different tasks and contribute together but in different ways to the success of a business. The main role of a company's management team is to develop a promising business strategy and ensure its smooth implementation, while the owner's representatives, who often sit on the board of directors, need to co-determine and approve the strategy and oversee its implementation, always keeping long-term value creation in mind.
- **Pursue a portfolio approach:** As with external ventures, corporate investments need to be managed as a portfolio. Given the risk profile of an individual company, only a portfolio approach can ensure long-term performance. As mentioned above, this requires management to clearly define performance expectations and rules and to ensure strict adherence to these criteria. As a result, the performance and strategic fit of each individual company to the overall portfolio must be constantly reviewed and appropriate action taken, however disappointing this may be for an

individual company. This includes allowing businesses to fail and creating new businesses to replace them. In the successful management of risk portfolios, creative destruction is not just a buzzword, but the underlying principle.

- **Foster linkages with corporate entities:** As mentioned earlier, as venture owners, companies can bring in the assets of their existing business units as leverage for the venture. While such partnerships between companies and corporate entities have often proved difficult in reality, they can be more promising and easier to implement in the case of corporate ventures, since the often-difficult questions of who owns what, be it the customer, the intellectual property or the route to markets, can be resolved more convincingly since both entities belong to the same group. Nonetheless, turf wars and corporate politics require targeted promotion and incentivisation of such collaborations.
- **Let go when necessary:** Companies should never forget that ventures are by definition only a temporary state of a business. They will hopefully mature and, at least that is the aspiration, become established players that will hopefully one day eclipse the parent company. This requires the parent company to release the company from its care and supervision when the time comes and help it develop into a successful business entity by becoming the partner of choice for new corporate ventures that will fertilize the future venture portfolio.

The incubation of the Unicorn inside embeds itself in a growth process from idea generation, actual incubation, subsequent acceleration and scaling (cf. Yates 2022). The goal is to build your pipeline and a portfolio of own and external ventures for meaningful growth of the parent organization. In ideation, good venture ideas are generated and prioritized for the group strategy. Robert Bosch AG (2023) distinguishes the 'Innovation Zoo', in which a lot of money is burned on making bets on several ventures without selection, from the 'Corporate Validation Engine', in which bets are systematically tested.

In Incubation, you follow the classic start-up method of identifying customer pain points, testing minimum viable products and developing scalable business models. With a launchpad, ventures can be launched in three months. The result of this process is a fundable business, a start-up team, a venture board and a pilot customer in B2B. Once these points have been reached, the next phase begins, or alternatively, the company breaks off.

Figure 28.1 Innovation Zoo and Innovation Funnel [based on Bosch Validation Program (2023)]

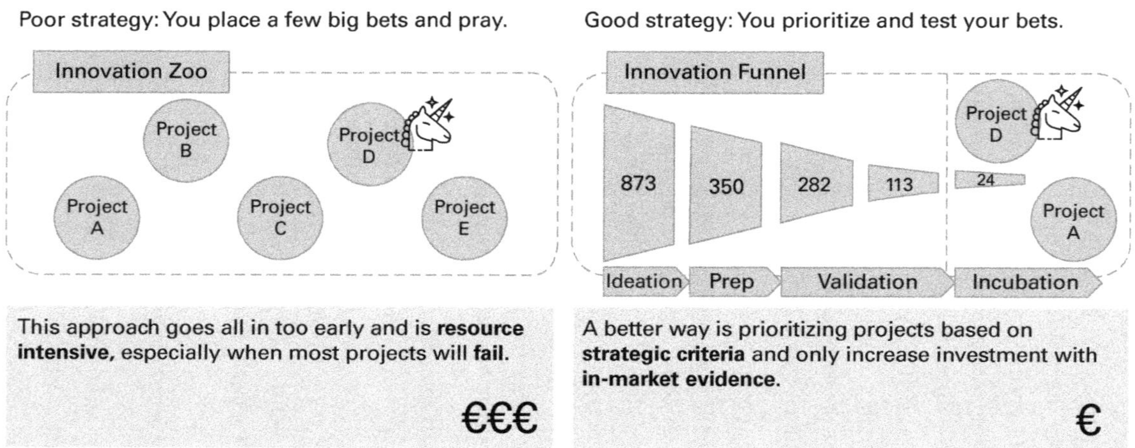

Figure 28.2 Incubation pipeline [based on Bosch Validation Program (2023)]

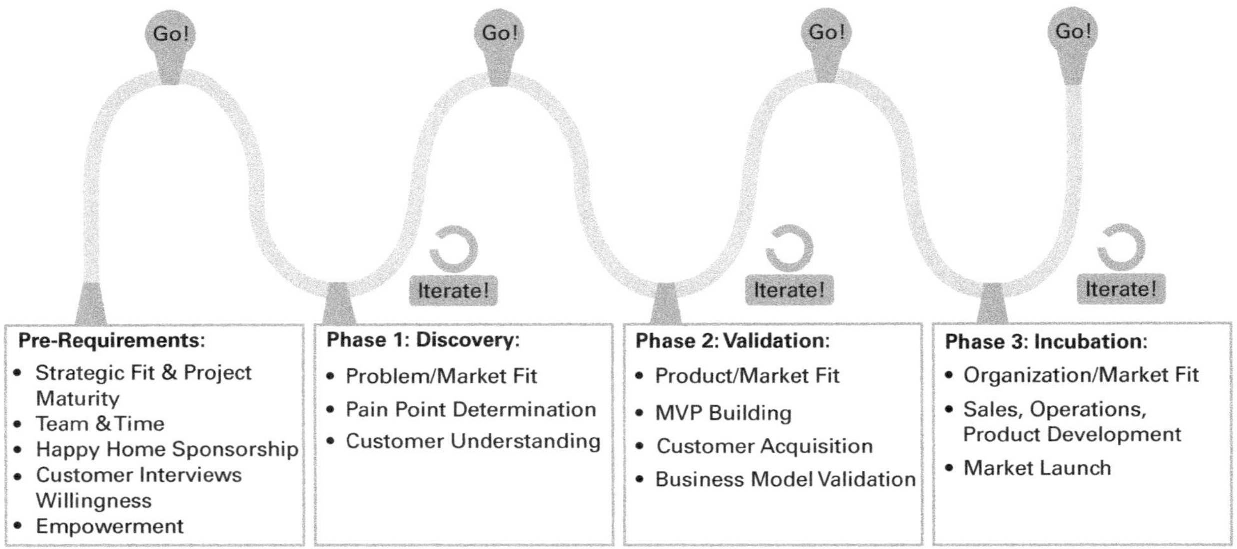

The incubated and corporate-funded venture then enters the acceleration phase, which Yates (2022) describes as a classic Silicon Valley startup approach. Critical risks are eliminated during MVP testing, first sales are achieved, the product-market fit is realized with a go-to-market and automated to enable repeated sales with attractive unit economics. Funding accompanies these phases with seed, Series A+ funding. The business is ready to scale in or outside the parent company (spin-in or spin-out), can transform the parent company and is innovative to disruptive in the market. The team and the board are fully functional for growth, the business model and pricing are proven, reference customers legitimize the product and further verticals. The final phase of scaling has thus been initiated and the door to innovation with a new business line in the group has been opened. Scaling aims at efficiency through reduced costs without reduced quality (for more see our Scale-up Navigator, Grichnik, Hess, Greger, Goeldi, Schweitzer 2023).

References

Bosch Validation Program (2023) https://www.bosch-innovation-consulting.com/de/unsere-services/validation-program/ (archived at https://perma.cc/P2VA-S6ST)

ChatGTP4 (2023) Response to 'What are key success factors of corporate entrepreneurship?'

Grichnik, D, Hess, M, Greger, M, Goeldi, A, Schweitzer, F (2023) *Scale-up Navigator*, Wiley-VCH, Weinheim

Yates, L (2022) *The Unicorn Within: How Companies Can Create Game-Changing Ventures at Startup Speed*, Harvard Business Press, Boston, Massachusetts

CV Cockpit IV 29

A final reminder of what the Cockpit is all about: in the dashboard you will find the so-called specs, which summarize important information about the different elements of the CV Navigator. You will find an interface that shows you the choices you need to make by bringing together all the necessary information at once and giving you a good overview of the key details required to harvest a CV programme.

Cockpit IV covers the dimensions you set out with in the beginning: Strategic Renewal, Innovation, Financial Returns, and Culture. It provides indicators for performance measurements to these corresponding dimensions to aid your harvesting quantification.

Figure 29.1 CV Cockpit IV Collaboration monitoring

CV Cockpit VI

Profile | Design | Investing | **Harvest**

Evaluation CV Harvest

- [ ] Termination
- [ ] Continuation (Follow-on CV program)
- [ ] Venture integration in corporate mother

Performance

Measurement of objectives

Strategic renewal	Measurement conditional (Yes/No)	Measurement non-monitary (number)		Measurement monitary (in EUR)
	us	Planned	Achieved	As a consequence of objectives in general
Validation of existing corporate strategies	Yes	Number corporate strategies to validate	Yes	Revenue from new introduced or old elevated products / services
Insights to new trends	Yes	Number new trends to cover	Yes	Revenue from customers dealing with startup product / services
Access to new trends	Yes	Number new trends to access	Yes	Cost savings through collaboration
Insights to new markets	Yes	Number new markets to cover	Yes	Employee Turnover Rate (ETR)
Access to new markets	Yes	Number new markets to access	Yes	Employee Net Promoter Scores (ENPs)
Inspirations and start of new corporate businesses	Yes	Number new businesses to start	Yes	Employee and Manager Satisfaction Score
Option building / Avoidance of taking wrong decisions	Yes	Number wrong decisions to avoid	Yes	
Involvement in corporate strategic	Yes	Number meetings; number involvement themes	Yes	
Involvement in M&A	Yes	Number meetings; number cross-themes	Yes	
Involvement in R&D dialogue	Yes	Number meetings	Yes	
Collaboration: BU involvement	Yes	Number meetings; number investments	Yes	
Value-add for key customer	Yes	Customer satisfaction rate of XXXX	Yes	
Financial returns				
Financial gains	Yes	XX (EUR) return to achieve	Yes	Profit gained (EUR) (new business generated; savings, time efficiency)
IRR	Yes	IRR in % to achieve	Yes	Share price
Multiples	Yes	Multiple of XX to achieve	Yes	
Innovation				
Strengthening innovation capabilities overall; observe / learn	Yes	Number new innovations; innovation cycle time; enablement of new business for the corporate	Yes	Innovation rate = revenue share of innovations / total turnover * 100; revenue/profit growth from new products; revenue from new introduced products / services; revenue from old elevated products / services; number of new products launched in XX amount of time; ROI of innovation activities
Business model innovation	Yes	Number business model renewals	Yes	Innovation portfolio = ABC analysis
Technology innovation (white spots) / IP transfer	Yes	White spots to cover; enhancement of existing product developed by the corporation; new innovation applications / patents	Yes	Patent income
Abbreviation of R&D / M&A	Yes	Number R&D / M&A actions originating from a CVC investment	Yes	R&D saving; annual R&D budget as a % of annual sale; total R&D headcount or budget as a percentage of sales
Internal organizational innovation	Yes	Number innovation meetings / active projects	Yes	
Market sensing	Yes	Number markets to screen (selected focus areas); insights to share with BUs	Yes	
Culture				
Talent search	Yes	Number interviews; new staff	Yes	
Entrepreneurial teaching	Yes	Number teaching units and participants; knowhow and skills gapc overed; award; number culture conflicts	Yes	Educational budget used
Decision making speed	Yes	Number meetings per project planned; errors made; number culture conflicts; Agility (lean time scales, reduced customer complaints, better quality;scores; operational support needed	Yes	ROI; project budget saved
Brand awareness / reputation	Yes	Customer satisfaction; Net promoter score	Yes	
Marketing	Yes	Number of startup events hosted / participated; number of nations (social listening for reputation); Number of 'likes' / 'followers' / 'mentions' on social media	Yes	Marketing budget
Environmental responsibility	Yes	Number environmental projects; % of innovations that include sustainability goals; % sustainability awareness training penetration; score energy / emission / emission footprin	Yes	Environmental costs or budget; percentage of environmental targets achieved; CSR index
Measurement of enablers				
Budget		Planned	Achieved	
Budget used	Yes	XX amount to use	Yes	XX EUR
Capabilities / Skills				
Top mgmt. support (companywide acceptance of CV)	Yes	Planned mgmt. representation of CV (events; announcements; etc.)	Yes	Income through new IP generated
Expansion of network	Yes	Number network parties; specific relationship secured through investment	Yes	Employee Turnover Rate; Employee Net Promoter Score; Employee and Manager Satisfaction Score
Scouting, startups under review	Yes	Number startups screened	Yes	-
Targets evaluated in detail	Yes	Number DDs	Yes	-
Investments negociated and signed	Yes	Number new startups	Yes	-
Startup used / knowhow or skills incorporated	Yes	Startups knowhow / capabilities incorporated	Yes	-
Milestones met on time	Yes	Number milestones met	Yes	-
First mover advantage	Yes	Number one on the market; press	Yes	-
Risk acceptance	Yes	Number risk taking; number project failures	Yes	-
Talent available	Yes	Number of hires with venture background	Yes	-
Collaboration with ventures				
Observer seats	Yes	Number meeting participation	Yes	Cost savings through collaboration; revenues generated; (time saved)
Access to partnerships and networks	Yes	Number usage; number new customers / contacts through collaboration	Yes	
Access to R&D or technical expertise	Yes	Number usage; Usage of startup technologies/ infrastructure	Yes	
Marketing and public relation	Yes	Good press	Yes	
Board seats	Yes	Startup involvement	Yes	
Co-investor search	Yes	Number co-investor search	Yes	
Other types of financial transactions	Yes	Number transactions	Yes	
Collaboration with Business Units				
Information exchange on business needs / development	Yes	Number of meetings/ roundtables	Yes	BU savings through collaboration; revenues generated; (time saved)
Regular update of venture development / integration into the business	Yes	Number of updates / briefings	Yes	
Joint investment theme developed	Yes	Number of themes developed		
Financial involvement	Yes	Number involvement	Yes	
Involvement of mgmt.				
Information exchange on business needs / development	Yes	Number meetings; announcement of support	Yes	Revenues, savings, risk reduction, customer satisfaction, etc.
Regular update of CV development	Yes	Number updates; frequency of engagement	Yes	Anecdotal parent business impact success stories
Regular involvement in CV progress	Yes	Number invovlements	Yes	Mutual benefit metrics such as startup contract value /valuation)
Collaboration other parties				
Other parties	Yes	Number of partnerships or co-development effort; partnership engagement	Yes	

Summary – Corporate Venturing performance 30

At the beginning of this journey, you established your corporate venturing profile with key focal areas like financial returns, strategic renewal, innovation and culture. Now, it's time to reap the benefits of these carefully chosen focal points based on the objectives you initially set. Let's be frank, from the perspective of the parent corporation, many will still argue that the ultimate objectives are to answer these critical questions: what was the contribution to revenue? How much were costs reduced? Did our EBIT margin improve? Essentially, your primary focus areas and CV programme approach serve as methods to inch closer to the Holy Grail of positively influencing the quantifiable financial performance of the parent corporation in one way or the other.

The way you harvest your CV performance is dependent on the initial setup you have chosen. The different paths described here in Harvesting relate to these setups. View these harvesting opportunities as options you may choose to apply to individual cases. By that we mean if your motivation was primarily strategic renewal but it turns out that one of your CV investments goes wrong, use the exit channel (instead of rejuvenation and incubation). Remember, we set out by telling you that a financial versus strategic focus is an oversimplification of things. These dimensions are not mutually exclusive.

Concerning the 'cultural' aspects of investing in startups, we have established that big corporates are, and will, always be unable to move as quickly as startups. We have told you to think about this as an opportunity, rather than a challenge. In fact, this inability provides a super strong argument to justify startup engagements and investments. If you achieved this change of mindset, you have actually changed the culture of your corporation already.

Figure 30.1 Exemplified setup with examples of corresponding objectives and measurements for performance

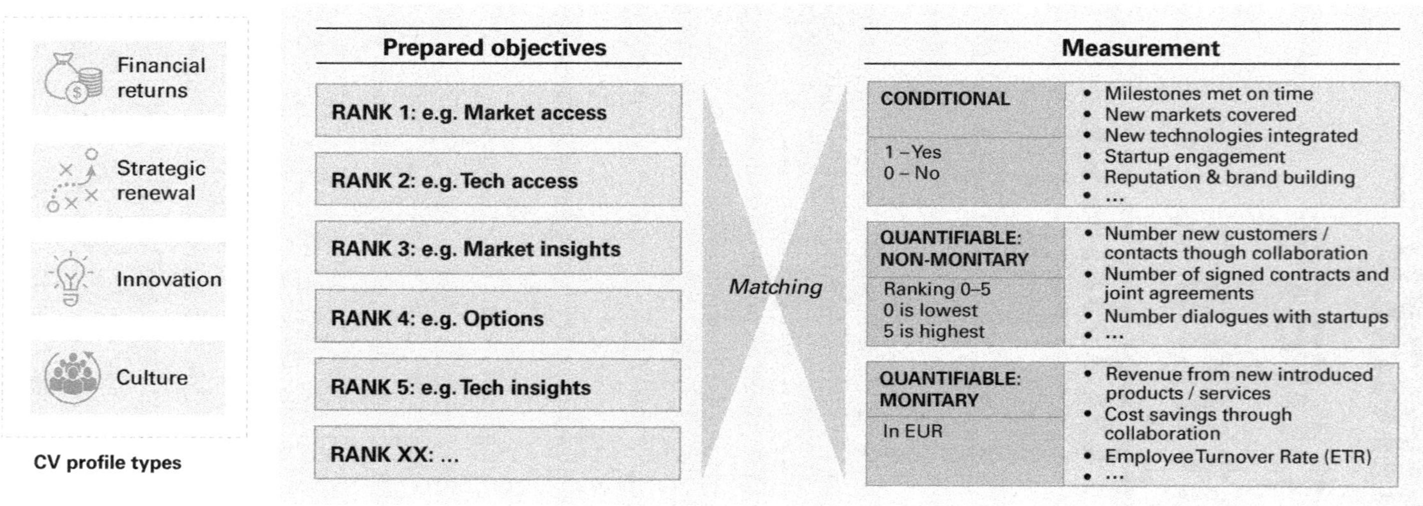

You have somehow managed to empower the company to run certain processes differently, to adjust certain minimum requirements, to cut some corners, and simply to broaden horizons. Congratulations!

Case Insights: Bertelsmann Investments

Bertelsmann Investments pursues a multi-fund approach on a global level as a fund of funds (FOF) with a total of four funds and FoF activities. To date, investments have been made in more than 360 innovative companies. This is quite impressive, especially since the funds focus on fast-developing markets such as Asia, India and Brazil. The total volume of Bertelsmann Investments (BI) is around $1.6 billion as a long-term balance sheet commitment/evergreen. This means that the budget can be drawn down as needed, but although it is an evergreen structure, the compensation is settled before the end of the programme. BI started with investments focused on Bertelsmann's core business, but now also makes investments that diverge from the core business. The CV mandate is aimed at innovation and expansion effects for the parent company Bertelsmann. This means that decisions are made on the basis of the global strategy, with BI serving as a supporting tool.

Since BI seems to be a very rigorous model with its own unique structure and way of working, we spoke with Shobhna Mohn, Chief Strategy Officer at Bertelsmann Investments, to gain further insight and experience, particularly about the harvesting phase of a CV programme. Five key features were highlighted:

- **Global approach:** BI sees great potential to strengthen Bertelsmann's activities through CV investments in the strategic growth regions of China, India and Brazil. But you have to be on the ground, show presence and identify innovation opportunities quickly.
- **Modi operandi:** Your way of working with ventures is critical. You should have a VC-like way of working and definitely an entrepreneurial one (in comparison with Sequoia and co.); fast processes and lean systems are critical for success. BI aims for an investment proposal of maximum five pages and our due diligence process at corporate level can be completed in a few days and investment decisions are made quickly by the respective Investment Committee.

Figure 30.2 Case insights: Bertelsmann Investments

CASE INSIGHTS: BERTELSMANN INVESTMENTS

WIP

Shobhna Mohn
Chief Strategy Officer
Bertelsmann Investments

Established: 2012 (Bertelsmann Investments); first fund in 2006 (BDMI); 2012 (BII + BBI)

Parent: Bertelsmann

HQ: Germany

Industry: Media, services, and education

(1) Profiling

General: 4 funds and FoF
- Bertelsmann Asia Investments (BAI),
- Bertelsmann India Investments (BII),
- Bertelsmann Brazil Investments (BBI)
- Bertelsmann Digital Media Investments
- Fund of Funds (FoF)

CVC mandate
- Innovation / Expansion impact to Bertelsmann

Funding size
- Long-term balance sheet commitment (evergreen)
- ~1.4Mrd EUR

Business advancements
- Started with the core focus, today investments are more distant from core

(2) Designing

(3) Investing

Structure & Governance
- Organizational: Independent unit
- Reporting: CEO corporate parent
- Legal: LP parent

Team
- ~50 employees

Portfolio size
- ~300 ventures globally

Ticket size:
- Average ~1 to 30Mio EUR
- Seed to Series CID (focus Series B)

(4) Harvesting

Collaboration
- Active support
- Board / observer seat

M&A
- Exits: 2

<<To share Bertelsmann'score values and the ambition to drive growth, value creation, and financial returns>>

- **Recruitment and retention:** Funds simply recruit for themselves, and that's how it should be handled, because CV teams know best who is needed. If you want a professional, highly skilled CV team, compensation and incentives need to be aligned with the VC world, such as carry or the volume of investment a team is allowed to work with.
- **Corporate governance:** Have an independent CV unit that is legally optimized and independent to make lean decisions. If there is more than one fund, there should be separate management that reports to an umbrella organization. At BI, the IC is composed of four people: the CEO, the CFO and the CSO of Bertelsmann Investments (Shobha), as well as someone from Controlling, Finance, Legal, etc.
- **Training:** Training is closely related to employee retention. You need to ensure that your employees understand the organization, not just the CV programme, but also the dynamics and mechanics of the parent company. In the case of the China/Indian fund, the CV leaders were previously part of an 18-month programme at the parent company, going through different departments and thus having a good understanding of the company – a unique training method.

Take away any recommendations and let's talk about how you can reap the rewards of your CV programme. When an investment reaches the end of its life, the question is whether there should be follow-on investments or an exit in terms of simply ending the collaboration or eventual acquisition.

With BI, there are usually many follow-on investments, but there is also a limit before an investment is diluted. Follow-on investments are planned within the available budget. Regarding exits, BI has no intention to buy companies, as only two of the 360+ companies have gone through an M&A process so far. Integrating companies had been an expectation early on for few selected cases in the past, but BI recognizes that mergers and acquisitions are not always feasible, for example due to management capacity, regional complexity, local regulations or CV target. However, the overarching goal is value creation. BI looks at two perspectives of value creation:

- Finance with a focus on EBIT generation
- Strategic with focus on which markets were covered by venturing and how much investment to allocate.

Unlike many other CV programmes, BI does not have problems justifying the value of a CV programme because there is strong corporate acceptance. However, this was not the case in the past where the benefits of CV had to be proven and claimed over and over again. Expectation management and communication are key, as value creation is often delayed and companies are generally impatient to wait for the rewards of their investments to be realized. Active communication about what BI does and who it is has proven to be a successful strategy to keep all stakeholders engaged.

Reference

Bertelsmann Investments (2023) https://www.bertelsmann-investments.com/ (archived at https://perma.cc/X4PQ-8WYM)

31 Your CV navigator toolbox

Keep in mind that your CV Navigator Tools constitute the cornerstone of this handbook, serving as the pivotal tools for translating concepts into actions. They hold dual significance: firstly, as the arena where you roll up your sleeves and delve into the practical intricacies and secondly, as the platform for monitoring, charting, and advancing your personal journey and achievements. Essentially, these tools not only empower you within your organization but also help you to gain authenticity and credibility beyond your organization! We have summarized the main ingredients here for your usage.

Digital templates of these tools can be accessed by scanning the QR code provided here:

The main tools underlying the Profiling pillar of the Navigator framework are:

- The Corporate Venturing Cockpit specifications for knowing your profile mix: financial returns, strategic renewal, innovation, and culture.
- The Onion Approach: the distance of innovation to your parent company versus the innovation's origin.

The main tools underlying the Designing pillar of the Navigator framework are:

- Structure and governance, whether the CV programme is integrated and dependent, integrated but independent or completely independent.

Figure 31.1 Your Corporate Venturing profile

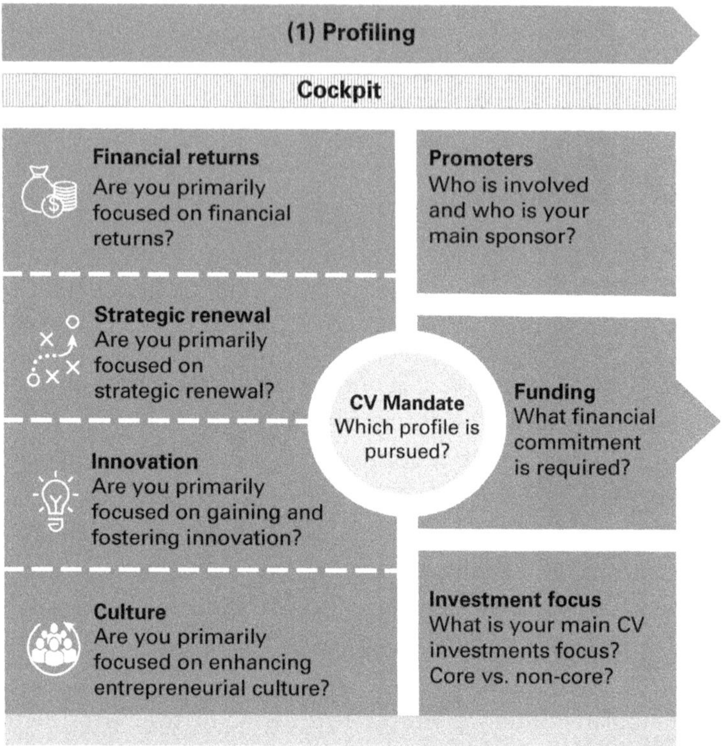

- Your rollout plan.
- Your RACI matrix. Remember: these four letters reflect the roles that stakeholders can play in a given project and governance model. **R** stands for Responsible; **A** stands for Accountable; **C** stands for Consultative; and **I** stands for Informative. This means that RACI aligns the appropriate roles for a given project by indicating who is responsible and accountable, and who needs to be consulted and informed.

Figure 31.2 Designing your Corporate Venturing programme

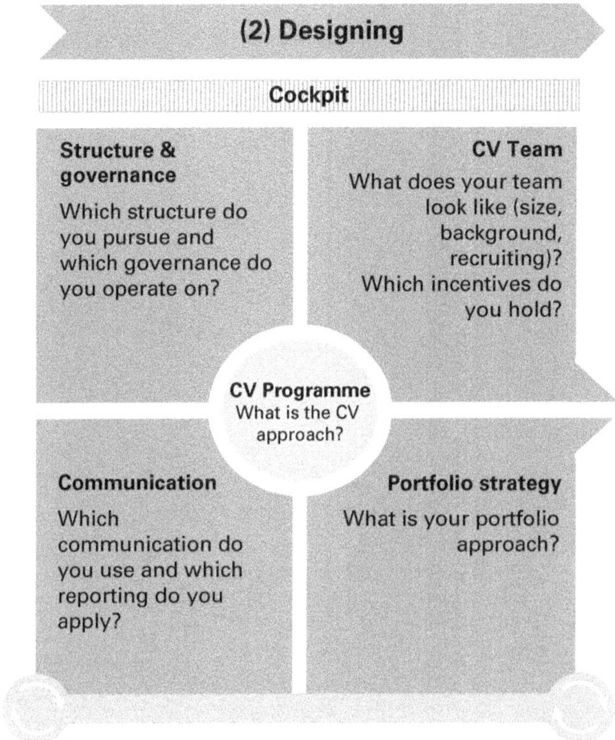

The main tools underlying the Investing pillar of the Navigator framework are:

- The screening questions.
- The Term Sheet Templates from the Swiss Private Equity & Corporate Finance Association (SECA) https://www.seca.ch/Templates/Templates.aspx
- The collaboration and value add monitoring.

The main tools underlying the Harvesting pillar of the Navigator framework are:

- Delivering on your CV objectives by measuring the performance of your CV programme.

Figure 31.3 Investing phase of your Corporate Venturing programme

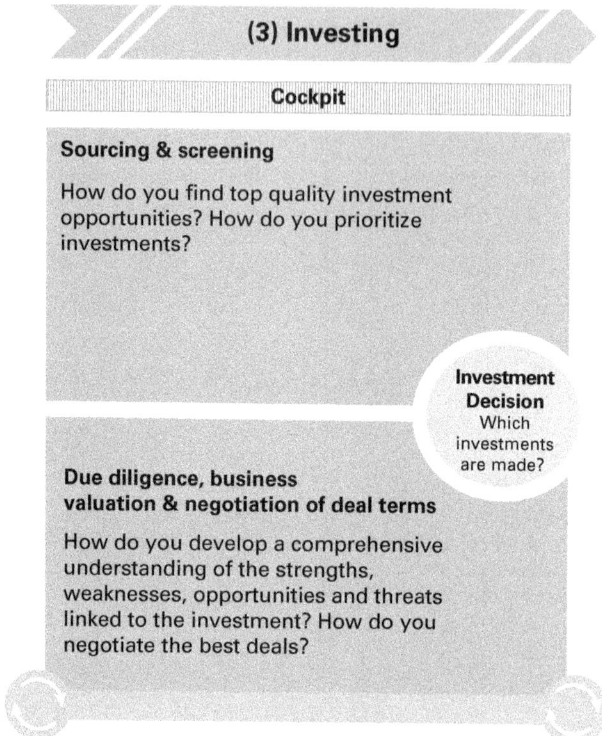

Figure 31.4 Harvesting your Corporate Venturing programme

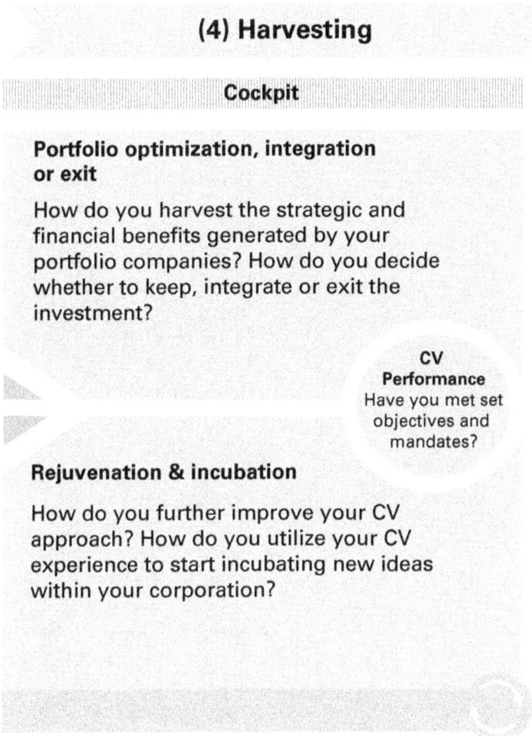

INDEX

Note: Page numbers in *italics* refer to tables or figures.